Joseph Mersand, Ph.D., has devoted himself throughout his long career as a teacher to the theatre and its literature. He has written and edited books about the drama over a period of twenty years. Among these are *The American Drama, 1930–1940; The Play's the Thing* and *The American Drama Since 1930*. Dr. Mersand was chairman of the Editorial Committee of the National Council of Teachers of English, which authorized the publication of *Guide to Play Selection*, a standard work.

For ten years Dr. Mersand served as chairman of the English and Speech departments at Long Island City High School, in New York City. Highly regarded in his field, he has been an instructor at Cornell University, Queens College, Teachers College, Columbia University, Syracuse University and New York University. He is past president of the National Council of Teachers of English and is presently chairman of the English department at Jamaica High School, in New York City.

THE SERIES OF DISTINGUISHED PLAYS

 THE ANTA SERIES OF DISTINGUISHED PLAYS

THREE DRAMAS OF
AMERICAN INDIVIDUALISM

GOLDEN BOY
by Clifford Odets

HIGH TOR
by Maxwell Anderson

THE MAGNIFICENT
YANKEE
by Emmet Lavery

Edited and with Introductions
by Joseph Mersand

WSP

WASHINGTON SQUARE PRESS,   NEW YORK

THREE DRAMAS OF AMERICAN
INDIVIDUALISM

Washington Square Press edition published April, 1961
4th printing........................April, 1971

L

Published by Washington Square Press,
a division of Simon & Schuster, Inc., 630 Fifth Avenue, New York, N.Y.

WASHINGTON SQUARE PRESS editions are distributed in the
U.S. by Simon & Schuster, Inc., 630 Fifth Avenue, New
York, N.Y. 10020 and in Canada by Simon & Schuster
of Canada, Ltd., Richmond Hill, Ontario, Canada.

CONTENTS

Any group that wishes to
produce any of these plays
will find production information
for each play on page 266.

GOLDEN BOY

Introduction

Writing in his *Contemporary American Playwrights,* in 1938, Burns Mantle stated:

> The most promising playwriting talent that has come into the theatre in the last ten years is the possession of a young man named Clifford Odets.[1]

By that time Odets had written *Awake and Sing!, Waiting for Lefty, Till the Day I Die, Paradise Lost* and *Golden Boy.* To many critics and playgoers, *Golden Boy* was his best play to date.

The story of a young Italian-American boy who has been trained to become a violinist but who decides to become a prize fighter was commercially the most successful play the Group Theatre had produced and was eventually sold to Hollywood for $75,000.

In some respects *Golden Boy* marked a considerable departure for Odets. It contains less of the anticapitalistic propaganda that is so characteristic of *Waiting for Lefty.* In other respects *Golden Boy* reinforces the theme of frustrated efforts to live a decent life, which had been so prominent in *Awake and Sing!* The hero, Joe Bonaparte, is an interesting portrait of a sensitive man endeavoring to overcome his feelings of failure by adopting a materialistic philosophy repugnant to his inner self. This is by no means a new theme in American drama, but it is told by Odets in his distinctive idiom and style.

---

[1] P. 115. *See also* John Gassner, (ed.), *A Treasury of the Theatre,* p. 950.

Some critics contended that Bonaparte's sacrifice of his love for music for the more material gains of prize fighting may have been symbolic of Odets' own withdrawal from Broadway in response to the lure of Hollywood. Others, like Harold Clurman, who directed the Broadway production, generalized even further:

> The story of the play is not so much the story of a prize fighter as the picture of a great fight—a fight in which we are all involved. . . . What the golden boy of this allegory is fighting for is a place in the world as an individual.[2]

Regardless of the various interpretations that the reader may care to give to the play today, its virtues remain as vivid now as they were in 1937, when it opened to almost unanimous critical acclaim. Thus, the opening-night review by John Mason Brown summarized some of Odets' excellence as a dramatist:

> Certainly it is not new to report that Mr. Odets' dramaturgy can be possessed of uncommon vitality. Or that he has an astonishing ear for dialogue. When he is writing at his best, none of our younger dramatists can equal him in giving the essence of a scene or an individual with almost telegraphic brevity. He is a shrewd observer. He has a fierce humor and a relentless vigor. Among his high talents he can count a gift of revealing everything by the uncanny use he makes of humanizing details.[3]

All of these aspects of Odets' skill as a dramatist have been praised repeatedly. Eleanor Flexner described his power of constructing a play as the best up to 1938. To John Gassner,

---

[2] Introduction to *Golden Boy* in *The Plays of Clifford Odets* (New York: Random House, 1939), pp. 429–430.
[3] *Two on the Aisle*, p. 220.

Introduction

writing in 1939, it was "his best constructed and least rampant play." [4] The dialogue was praised by Joseph Wood Krutch: "His dialogue is brilliantly suggestive, especially when he puts it into the mouths of ignorant or uncultivated people."[5]

Odets' power of characterization has also won praise from many critics. Montrose J. Moses and Oscar J. Campbell in their anthology *Dramas of Modernism* state:

> But all the characters live and breathe with an almost painful intensity, and their encounters create moments of poignant emotion. Their speech is pungent and subtly accommodated to the lips of the actors.[6]

To Eleanor Flexner, his talent had never been seen to better advantage than in "its long and rich gallery of characterization in *Golden Boy*."[7]

Perhaps the fact that the first New York production was in the capable hands of Harold Clurman and the actors of the Group Theatre helped to give the play the intensity and moving power felt by so many playgoers. One of the most fascinating accounts of an acting group's development of a philosophy of acting consonant with its philosophy of life is in Harold Clurman's *The Fervent Years,* which includes some of the trials and tribulations, frustrations and triumphs of *Golden Boy.*

THE PLAYWRIGHT

Clifford Odets was born in Philadelphia on July 18, 1906, but spent his childhood and adolescence in the Bronx. He attended Morris High School but left before graduation to go into radio as actor, announcer and author. He had considerable acting experience in stock and on Broadway. Odets

---

[4] *Twenty Best Plays of the Modern American Theatre* (New York: Crown, 1939), p. xxi.
[5] *The American Drama Since 1918,* p. 272.
[6] P. 853.
[7] *American Playwrights, 1918–1938,* p. 300.

first came into prominence with his prize-winning one-act play, *Waiting for Lefty* (1935), which was based on the New York taxi strike of 1934. The novelty of construction and power of characterization revealed an exciting new talent. The success of *Waiting for Lefty* encouraged the Group Theatre to produce his *Awake and Sing!* (1935), a study of middle-class life in the Bronx, a life Odets knew very well. That same year saw two other productions, *Till the Day I Die* and *Paradise Lost.*

Odets' other plays include: *Rocket to the Moon* (1938), *Night Music* (1940), *Clash by Night* (1941), *The Big Knife* (1949) and *The Country Girl* (1950). Odets has served in Hollywood as both writer and producer (*None But the Lonely Heart*). His later plays have not been charged with the social propaganda that was blatant in *Waiting for Lefty.* His ability to reveal character quickly and brilliantly, his memorable dialogue and his deep interest in the frustrations of lonely individuals in their struggles toward self-realization are present in almost all of his plays. While the encomiums of the thirties, when he was looked upon as the American Chekhov and the greatest new talent since O'Neill, may not be apropos today, Odets maintains his position as the leading social dramatist of the Depression. Odets, the propagandist for a better social order, may have lost his followers; but Odets, the dramatist, the creator of vivid characters and unforgettable dialogue, remains a part of our literary heritage of the thirties and forties.

FURTHER READING

Brown, John Mason. *Two on the Aisle.* New York: W. W. Norton, 1938, pp. 220-222.

Clurman, Harold. *The Fervent Years.* New York: Knopf, 1945.

Flexner, Eleanor. *American Playwrights, 1918–1938.* New York: Simon and Schuster, 1938, pp. 299-302, 313-314.

Gagey, Edmond M. *Revolution in American Drama*. New York: Columbia, 1947, pp. 171-172.

Gassner, John. *Masters of the Drama*. 3rd ed., New York: Dover, 1954, pp. 687-694.

——. (ed.). *A Treasury of the Theatre*. New York: Simon and Schuster, 1955, pp. 950-951.

Krutch, Joseph Wood. *The American Drama Since 1918*. New York: Random House, 1938, pp. 271-273.

Kunitz, Stanley J. *Twentieth Century Authors: First Supplement*. New York: H. W. Wilson, 1955, pp. 731-732.

——, and Haycraft, Howard. *Twentieth Century Authors*. New York: H. W. Wilson, 1942, pp. 1040-1041.

Mantle, Burns. (ed.). *The Best Plays of 1937–1938*. New York: Dodd, Mead, 1938.

——. *Contemporary American Playwrights*. New York: Dodd, Mead, 1938, pp. 115-121.

Moses, Montrose J., and Campbell, Oscar J. (eds.). *Dramas of Modernism*. Boston: Little, Brown, 1941, pp. 851-853.

Rowe, Kenneth Thorpe. *A Theatre in Your Head*. New York: Funk & Wagnalls, 1960.

GOLDEN BOY

CLIFFORD ODETS

ACT I

SCENE 1

SCENE: *The small Broadway office of* TOM MOODY, *the fight manager.*

The office is scantily furnished, contains desk, chairs, telephone (on phone) and couch. With MOODY *at present is his girl,* LORNA MOON. *There is a certain quiet glitter about this girl, and if she is sometimes hard, it is more from necessity than choice. Her eyes often hold a soft, sad glance. Likewise,* MOODY'S *explosiveness covers a soft, boyish quality, and at the same time he possesses a certain vulnerable quality which women find very attractive.*

The time is eighteen months ago. As the lights fade in, we catch these two at the height of one of their frequent fights.

9

CLIFFORD ODETS

MOODY: Pack up your clothes and go! Go! Who the hell's stopping you?

LORNA: You mean it?

MOODY: You brought up the point yourself.

LORNA: No, I didn't!

MOODY: Didn't you say you had a good mind to leave me?

LORNA: No, I said—

MOODY: You said you were going to pack!

LORNA: I said I feel like a tramp and I don't like it. I want to get married, I want—

MOODY: Go home, Lorna, go home! I ain't got time to discuss it. Gimme some air. It's enough I got my wife on my neck.

LORNA: What does she say?

MOODY: Who?

LORNA: Your wife—your sweet God damn Monica!

MOODY: She wants five thousand dollars to give me the divorce. (LORNA *laughs.*) I don't see that it's funny.

LORNA: Look, Tom, this means as much to me as it does to you. If she's out of the way, we can get married. Otherwise I'm a tramp from Newark. I don't like the feeling.

MOODY: Lorna, for pete's sake, use your noodle! When I get rid of Monica, we'll marry. Now, do I have to bang you on the nose to make you understand?

LORNA: Go to hell! . . . But come back tonight. (MOODY's *answer is to look at her, smile, walk to her. They kiss.*)

MOODY: If I had the money, I'd buy you something—I don't know what—a big ostrich feather! If Kaplan wins tonight, I'll take you dancing at the park.

LORNA: He won't win.

MOODY: How do you know? *I* don't know—how do *you* know?

LORNA: Are you crazy? Do you think your Mr. Kaplan can go ten rounds with the Baltimore Chocolate Drop?

MOODY: How do I know?

LORNA: It's the twentieth century, Tom—no more miracles. (MOODY's *face turns worried.* LORNA *smiles.*) You know what I like about you—you take everything so serious.

10

MOODY: Who will if I don't? I've been off the gold standard for eight years. This used to be a gorgeous town. New York was hot with money. Kaplan gets four hundred bucks tonight. In the old days, that was nothing. Those were the days when I had Marty Welch, the heavyweight contender—Cy Webster, who got himself killed in a big, red Stutz. In '27 and 8 you couldn't go to sleep—the town was crawling with attractions. . . .

LORNA: My mother died in '28.

MOODY: I haven't had a break in years. "Carry me back to old Virginny"—that's how I feel. There isn't much of a future. (*Suddenly despondent,* MOODY *goes to his desk.*)

LORNA: I was fooling.

MOODY: What about?

LORNA: Do you think I'd leave you?

MOODY: Why not? I'm an old man. What can I give you?

LORNA: A bang on the nose for a start. But what can I give you?

MOODY: A boy who can fight. Find me a good black boy and I'll show you a mint.

LORNA: Are good boys so hard to find?

MOODY: Honest to God, you make me sick to my stomach! What do you think I took a trip to Philadelphia? What do you think I went to Chicago? Wasn't I up in Boston for a week? You think good boys are laying around like pop-corn? I'd even take a bantamweight, if I found one.

LORNA: How about a nice lady fighter with a beard— (*Preparing to leave.*) Well, I'll see you tonight, Moody.

MOODY (*thoughtfully*): I'd give me right eye for a good black boy.

LORNA: Let me have your right eye for a minute. (*She kisses his eye.* MOODY *begins to embrace her—she eludes his grasp.*) That's to keep you hot. But if the truth were known—"yours till hell freezes over."

MOODY: I need you, I need you, Lorna—I need you all the time. I'd like to give you everything you want. Push your mouth over. . . . (LORNA *holds her face to his, he kisses*

11

her. Suddenly a Boy *is standing at office door.* Lorna *sees him and breaks away.*)

Boy (*entering, breathing quickly*): Mr. Moody . . .

Moody (*spinning around*): Don't you knock when you come in an office?

Boy: Sometimes I knock, sometimes I don't.

Moody: Say your piece and get the hell out!

Boy: I just ran over from the gym. . . .

Moody: What gym?

Boy: Where Kaplan trains. He just broke his hand. . . . (Moody *stiffens to attention.*) It's a fact.

Moody (*grasping phone*): Is Tokio over there? My trainer?

Boy: He's looking after Kaplan. (Moody *begins to dial phone but abruptly changes his mind and replaces phone.*)

Moody: You can put me in the bughouse right now. Moody is the name, folks—step right up and wipe your shoes! Ah, that Kaplan! That phonus bolonus! (*He sits at his desk in despair.*) Now I have to call up Roxy Gottlieb and cancel the match. His club's in the red as it is.

Boy: I don't think it's necessary to cancel, Tom.

Moody: Oh, you don't? Who the hell are you? And who the hell are you to call me Tom? Are we acquainted?

Boy: I wrote you a couple of letters. I can do that stretch.

Moody: What stretch?

Boy: Why don't you let me take Kaplan's place tonight?

Moody (*sarcastically*): Go slow and tell me again. . . . What?

Boy (*coolly*): I can take Kaplan's place. . . .

Moody: You mean you want to fight the Baltimore Chocolate Drop? *You.* (*The* Boy *remains silent.* Moody *comes out from behind his desk and stands face to face with the* Boy. *With sudden discovery.*) You're cockeyed too.

Boy (*quietly*): Can't you fix it up with Roxy Gottlieb?

Moody (*suddenly*): Looka, kid, go home, kid, before I blame Kaplan's glass mitts on *you.* Then you won't like it, and I won't like it, and Miss Moon here, she won't like it.

Boy (*turning to* Lorna): How do you do, Miss Moon. (Lorna *smiles at the* Boy's *quiet confidence.*) I need a

12

good manager, Mr. Moody. You used to be tops around town—everyone says so. I think you can develop me. I can fight. You don't know it, but I can fight. Kaplan's been through for years. He may be the best fighter in your stable, but he's a stumble-bum for the younger boys growing up. Why don't you give me this chance, Tom?

MOODY: I don't want you calling me Tom! (*He glares at the* BOY *and then returns to desk and telephone.*)

BOY: I'm waiting for your answer. (MOODY's *answer is an exasperated glance as he begins to dial phone. The* BOY *half approaches desk.*) There are forty-three thousand minutes in a month—can't you give me five?

MOODY: I'll give you this phone in the head in a minute! Who are you? What the hell do you want? Where do you fight?

BOY (*with cool persistence*): We ought to get together, Tom.

MOODY: I don't want you calling me Tom. You're brash, you're fresh, you're callow—and you're cockeyed! In fact, you're an insult to my whole nature! Now get out! (MOODY *turns back to phone and begins dialing again. The* BOY *stands there, poised on his toes, not sure of his next move. He turns and looks at* LORNA. *She nods her head and gives him a faint smile of encouragement. On phone.*) This is Tom Moody. . . . Is Tokio there? . . . (*He hangs up phone and holds it thoughtfully.*) Tokio's on his way over.

BOY: The Baltimore Chocolate Drop is not as good as you think he is. (MOODY *suddenly whirls around and holds phone high over his head in a threatening gesture. The* BOY *steps back lightly and continues.*) I've studied his style for months; I've perfected the exact punch to quench his thirst. Did you ever watch closely? (*Acting it out.*) He likes to pull your lead—he hesitates for a second—he pulls your lead—he slips his face away and then he's in. Suppose you catch that second when he hesitates—he's open for the punch!

MOODY (*sarcastically*): And what do you do with his left hook?

13

BOY (*simply*): Avoid it.

MOODY (*lowering phone*): Looka, you idiot, did you ever hear of Phil Mateo?

BOY: I heard of him.

MOODY: The Chocolate Drop marked him lousy in twelve minutes and ten seconds. Was Kid Peters within your ken? And did you ever hear of Eddie Newton? The Chocolate gave him the blues in two rounds. And Frisco Samuels and Mike Mason . . .

BOY: Did you ever hear of me?

MOODY (*sarcastically*): No, who are you? I would honestly like to know—who are you?

BOY (*quietly*): My name is Bonaparte. (MOODY *howls with laughter, and even* LORNA, *sympathetic to the* BOY, *laughs. The* BOY *continues.*) I don't think it's funny. . . .

MOODY: Didn't that name used to get you a little giggle in school? Tell the truth, Bonaparte. Didn't it?

BOY: Call me Joe.

MOODY (*laughing*): And your eyes . . . didn't they used to get a little giggle too?

JOE: You don't seem as intelligent as I thought you were.

LORNA (*to the laughing* MOODY, *seeing the* BOY's *pain*): Stop it, Tom.

MOODY (*laughing*): You can't blame me, Bonaparte. . . . I haven't laughed for years.

JOE: I don't like it. . . . I don't want you to do it. (*Suddenly* JOE *grabs* MOODY *by the coat lapels.* MOODY, *surprised, shakes him off. At the same time a small, quiet man enters office. He is* TOKIO, MOODY's *trainer.*) I'm sorry I did that, Tom. We ought to be together, Tom—not apart.

MOODY: Tokio, did you send this kid here?

TOKIO: No.

MOODY: Take him out before I brain him! (*He storms back to his desk.*)

TOKIO (*after looking at the* BOY): You hear about Kaplan?

MOODY: This idiot told me. It's the end of everything! I'm off my top with the whole thing! Kaplan was our meal ticket. I'm up to the throat in scandal, blackmail, perjury, alimony and all points west!

TOKIO (*turning to* JOE): You oughta be ashamed to show your face in this office.

JOE: If Kaplan's mother fed him milk, he wouldn't have those brittle bones.

MOODY: ? ? ? ?

TOKIO (*to* MOODY): This is the boy who did it to Kaplan.

MOODY: ? ? ?

TOKIO: I went down for an apple and I came back and Kaplan's sparring with this kid—picked him up in the gym. The next thing I know, Kaplan's down on the floor with a busted mitt.

JOE (*modestly*): I took it on the elbow.

MOODY: ! ! (*Silence finally.*)

LORNA: Where do you come from, Bonaparte?

JOE: Here.

LORNA: How old are you?

JOE: Twenty-one—tomorrow.

MOODY (*after a look at* LORNA): Fight much?

JOE: Enough.

MOODY: Where?

JOE (*fabricating*): Albany, Syracuse . . .

LORNA: Does Roxy Gottlieb know you?

JOE: I never fought at his club.

MOODY (*harshly*): Does he know you?

JOE: No. (TOKIO *and* MOODY *look at each other. Phone rings.*)

MOODY (*on the phone*): Hello . . . "What's this you hear?" . . . You hear the truth, Roxy. . . . He bust his mitt again. . . . I can't help it if you got *fifty* judgments on your club. . . . The same to you . . . your mother too! (*Keeping his eyes on* BONAPARTE.) If you tie up your big flabby mouth for a minute, I'll give you some news. I'm in a position to do you a big favor. I got a replacement—*better* than Kaplan . . . Bonaparte. . . . No, Bon-a-parte. (*Holds hand over mouthpiece and asks* BOY.) Is that crap?

JOE: No, that's my name.

MOODY (*back at phone*): That's right, like in Napoleon. . . .
(*Looks the* BOY *over appraisingly.*) One hundred and
thirty . . .

JOE: Three.

MOODY: Hundred and thirty-three. Your customers'll eat him
up. I'll bring him right over . . . you can take my word—
the kid's a cockeyed wonder . . . *your* mother too! (*He
hangs up and turns around.* JOE *is the focus of all eyes.*)
It's revenge on somebody—maybe God.

JOE (*quietly*): I think you'll be surprised.

MOODY (*sadly*): Do your worst, kid. I've been surprised by
experts.

JOE: Don't worry, Tom.

MOODY: Call me Tom again and I'll break your neck! !

ACT I

SCENE 2

SCENE: *Later that night.*

*The combination dining and front room of the Bonaparte
home. A round dining-room table, littered with newspapers, is lighted from directly above like a billiard table.
Plaster busts of Mozart and Beethoven are on the sideboard. A cage of lovebirds at the other side of the room.
Sitting at the table are two men:* MR. BONAPARTE, *the father
of* JOE, *and a Jewish friend, a* MR. CARP, *who owns the
local candy and stationery store.*

As the lights fade in, MR. BONAPARTE *turns his newspaper.*
MR. CARP *is slowly pouring beer from a bottle. He begins
to sip it as* SIGGIE, MR. BONAPARTE'S *son-in-law, enters
from kitchen. He is barefooted, dressed in an undershirt,
trousers and hung-down suspenders. He brings his own
beer and glass, which he begins to fill with an expert's eye.*

In the silence, MR. CARP *takes a long, cool sip of beer combined with a murmur of relish.*

CARP (*finally*): I don't take it easy. That's my trouble—if I could only learn to take it easy . . .

SIGGIE: What do you call it now, what you're doing?

CARP: Say, it's after business hours.

SIGGIE: That's a business? A man who runs a candy store is an outcast of the world. Don't even sell *nickel* candies—*penny* candies!

CARP: And your taxicab business makes you higher in the social scale?

SIGGIE: So I'm an outcast too. Don't change the subject. Like my father-in-law here—he's always changing the subject when I get a little practical on him. (*Putting his beer on table and scratching himself under the arms like a monkey.*) You—I'm talking about you, Mr. Bonaparte.

BONAPARTE (*suddenly shooting out two words*): Ha, ha! (*He then resumes his reading.*)

SIGGIE: Every time I talk money, he gives me that horse laugh. Suppose you bought me a cab—I could pay it off by the week.

BONAPARTE (*who talks with an Italian accent*): I don't go in taxicab business.

SIGGIE: I am married to your daughter and when you do this little thing, you do it for her and me together. A cab in two shifts is a big source of profit. Joe takes the night shift. I'm a married man so you don't expect me to take the night shift. (ANNA, SIGGIE's *wife, in a nightgown, pokes her head in at door.*)

ANNA: Come to bed, Siggie. You'll wake up the whole neighborhood. (ANNA *disappears.*)

SIGGIE: See? I'm a married man! You don't expect me to take the night shift.

BONAPARTE (*having heard his talk for months*): No, Siggie . . . no.

SIGGIE: No, what?

BONAPARTE: No taxicab.

SIGGIE: Don't you wanna help your own family, foolish? After all, Joe's your own son—he's a man, no kid no more—

BONAPARTE: Tomorrow's twenty-one.

SIGGIE: If he don't work he'll turn into a real bum. Look how late he's staying out at night.

BONAPARTE: I don't expects for Joe to drive taxi.

SIGGIE: He's got to do something. He can drive like a fire engine. Why not?

BONAPARTE: He gonna do something.

SIGGIE: What? Play his violinsky in the back yards?

ANNA (*looking in at door again*): Come to bed, Siggie! Poppa, don't talk to him so he'll come to bed! (ANNA *disappears again.*)

SIGGIE (*annoyed*): Women! Always buzzing around. (BONA-PARTE'S *only answer is to turn over newspaper on table before him.*)

CARP (*reflectively*): Women . . . the less we have to do with women the better. As Schopenhauer says, "Much ado about nothing . . . the comedy of reproduction." (*He wags his head bitterly.*) Women . . . !

SIGGIE: I'm hungry, but I ain't got the heart to go in the kitchen again. It reminds me of how my wife slaves for this family of crazy wops! A fine future for an intelligent woman!

BONAPARTE: She'sa your wife, but also my daughter. She'sa not so intelligent as you say. Also, *you* are not so intelligent!

SIGGIE: You can't insult me, I'm too ignorant! (ANNA *now comes fully into the room. She is buxom, energetic, good-natured and adenoidal.*)

ANNA: Poppa, why don't you let Siggie come to bed? Looka him, walking around barefooted!

BONAPARTE: I don't stop him. . . .

SIGGIE: Sure he stops me—he stops me every night. I'm worried. I don't sleep. It's my Jewish disposition. He don't wanna help me out, your old man. He wants me to drive a company cab and submit to the brutalities of the foremen all my life. I could be in a healthy little enterprise for myself, but your old man don't wanna help me out.

ANNA: Why don't you buy Siggie a cab, Poppa? You got the cash.

SIGGIE: Buy it for Siggie and Joe.

ANNA: For Siggie and Joe—it don't have to be a new one.

SIGGIE (*after giving his wife a stabbing glance*): Sure, even an old one—the way they recondition them nowadays—

BONAPARTE: Children, gone to bed.

SIGGIE: Don't tell a lie—how much you got in the bank?

BONAPARTE (*with a smile*): Millions.

SIGGIE: Four thousand?

BONAPARTE: No.

SIGGIE: Three? (BONAPARTE *shakes his head.*) Three? . . .

ANNA: What's your business how much he's got?

SIGGIE: Shut up, Duchess! Am I asking for my health? If I wanna take you out of the kitchen, is that the gratitude I get? You and your father, you get my goat! I'm sore!

ANNA: Come to bed, Siggie.

SIGGIE: "Come to bed, come to bed!" What the hell's so special in bed? (ANNA's *answer is a warm prolonged giggle.*) It's a conspiracy around here to put me to bed. I'm warning one thing: if matters go from worse to worse, don't ever expect me to support this family, I'm warning!

BONAPARTE (*smiling kindly*): We have-a receive the warning. We are in a conspiracy against you—go to bed. (*He turns back to his newspaper.* SIGGIE *sees he has lost again and now turns on his wife.*)

SIGGIE: Who asked you to stick in your two cents about secondhand cabs? As long as I'm not gonna get it, I'll tell you what I want—a first-class job, fresh from the factory. (*He suddenly swats her on the head with a rolled-up newspaper. She hits him back. He returns her blow.*)

ANNA: Don't be so free with your hands! (*He hits her again. She hits him back.*) You got some nerve, Siggie!

SIGGIE (*hitting her again*): The next time I'll break your neck—I'm super-disgusted with you!

BONAPARTE (*standing up*): Stop this. . . .

SIGGIE (*turning to him*): And with you, I'm super-finished! (*Turning back to his wife.*) Sit out here with this unholy alliance—I'll sleep alone tonight. (*He starts for door.* BONAPARTE *puts his arm around* ANNA *who begins to sob.*)

BONAPARTE: Hit your wife in private, not in public!

CARP: A man hits his wife and it is the first step to Fascism!

SIGGIE (*to* CARP): What are you talking about, my little prince! I love my wife. You don't stop talking how you hate yours. (*Now to* BONAPARTE.) And as for you, don't make believe you care! Do I have to fall on my knees to you otherwise? We wanna raise a family—it's a normal instinct. Take your arm off her.

ANNA (*suddenly moving over to* SIGGIE.) That's right, Poppa. He can hit me any time he likes.

SIGGIE (*his arm around her*): And we don't want you interfering in our affairs unless you do it the right way!

ANNA: That's right, Poppa—you mind your g.d. business! (BONAPARTE, *repressing a smile, slowly sits.*)

SIGGIE: In the bed, Duchess.

ANNA (*with a giggle*): Good night.

BONAPARTE and CARP: Good night. (*She exits. After a belligerent look at the pair at table,* SIGGIE *follows her.*)

BONAPARTE (*bursting into hushed laughter*): There'sa olda remark—never interfere in the laws of nature and you gonna be happy. Love! Ha, ha!

CARP (*gloomily*): Happy? A famous man remarked in the last century, "Pleasure is negative."

BONAPARTE: I feela good. Like-a to have some music! Hey, where'sa my boy, Joe? (*Looks at his watch, is surprised.*) One o'clock . . . don't come home yet. Hey, he make'a me worry!

CARP: You think you got worries? Wait, you're a young man yet. You got a son, Joe. He practised on his fiddle for ten years? He won a gold medal, the best in the city? They gave him a scholarship in the Erickson Institute? Tomorrow he's twenty-one, yeah?

BONAPARTE (*emphatically*): Yeah!

CARP (*leaning forward and dramatically making his point*):
Suppose a war comes? Before you know it, he's in the army!

BONAPARTE: Naw, naw, Whata you say! Naw!

CARP (*wagging his head in imitation*): Look in the papers!
On every side the clouds of war—

BONAPARTE: My Joe gotta biga talent. Yesterday I buy-a him
present! (*With a dramatic flourish he brings a violin case
out of the bottom part of sideboard.*)

CARP (*as the case is opened*): It looks like a coffin for a baby.

BONAPARTE (*looking down at violin in its case*): His teacher
help me to picka him.

CARP (*the connoisseur*): Fine, fine—beautiful, fine! A cultural
thing!

BONAPARTE (*touching it fondly*): The mosta golden present
for his birthday which I give him tonight.

CARP: How much, if I'm not getting too personal, did such a
violin cost you?

BONAPARTE: Twelve hundred dollars.

CARP (*shocked*): What?

BONAPARTE: You're surprised of me? Well, I waita for this
moment many years.

CARP (*sitting*): Ask yourself a pertinent remark: could a boy
make a living playing this instrument in our competitive
civilization today?

BONAPARTE: Why? Don't expect for Joe to be a millionaire.
He don't need it, to be millionaire. A good life'sa possible—

CARP: For men like us, yes. But nowadays is it possible for a
young man to give himself to the Muses? Could the Muses
put bread and butter on the table?

BONAPARTE: No millionaire is necessary. Joe love music.
Music is the great cheer-up in the language of all countries.
I learn that from Joe. (CARP *sighs as* BONAPARTE *replaces
violin in buffet.*)

CARP: But in the end, as Schopenhauer says, what's the use
to try something? For every wish we get, ten remains un-
satisfied. Death is playing with us as a cat and her mouse!

BONAPARTE: You make-a me laugh, Mr. Carp. You say life'sa bad. No, life'sa good. Siggie and Anna fight—good! They love-good! You say life'sa bad. . . . Well, is pleasure for you to say so. No? The streets, winter a' summer—trees, cats —I love-a them all. The gooda boys and girls, they who sing and whistle—(*bursts into a moment of gay whistling*)— very good! The eating and sleeping, drinking wine—very good! I gone around on my wagon and talk to many people —nice! Howa you like the big buildings of the city?

CARP: Buildings? And suppose it falls? A house fell down last week on Staten Island!

BONAPARTE: Ha, ha, you make me laugh, ha, ha! (*Now enters FRANK BONAPARTE, oldest son of the family, simple, intelligent, observant.*) Hello, Frank.

FRANK: Hello, Poppa . . . Mr. Carp . . .

CARP (*nodding*): What's new in the world?

FRANK (*dropping newspapers to table, but keeping one for himself*): Read 'em and weep. March first tomorrow—spring on the way. Flowers soon budding, birds twittering—south wind . . . cannons, bombs and airplane raids! Where's Joe? Did you give him the fiddle yet?

BONAPARTE: No, not in yet. Siggie and Anna sleep. Hungry?

FRANK (*beginning to undress—putting his coat on the back of a chair*): No, I'm tired. I'll see you in the morning, before I leave.

CARP: Going away again?

FRANK: South Textiles. There's hell down there in textiles. (*He sits in chair on the other side of the room and looks at a paper.*)

CARP: I don't begin to understand it—textiles! What's it his business if the workers in textiles don't make good wages!

BONAPARTE: Frank, he fighta for eat, for good life. Why not!

CARP: Foolish!

BONAPARTE: What ever you got ina your nature to do isa not foolish!

CARP (*flipping over newspaper*): For instance—look: playing baseball isn't foolish?

BONAPARTE: No, if you like-a to do.

CARP: Look! Four or five pages—baseball—tennisball—it gives you an idea what a civilization! You ever seen a baseball game?

BONAPARTE: No.

CARP (*wagging his head*): Hit a ball, catch a ball . . . believe me, my friend—nonsense!

FRANK: Poppa, where did you say Joe was?

BONAPARTE: Don't know—

FRANK: Poppa, you better brace yourself in your chair!

BONAPARTE: What? (FRANK *places paper before* BONAPARTE. *He reads aloud.*)

FRANK: Looka this, Joe's had a fight. "Flash: Chocolate Drop fails to K.O. new cockeyed wonder." Take a look at the picture.

CARP: What?

BONAPARTE: What?

FRANK: It's my little brother Joey, or I don't know a scab from a picket!

BONAPARTE: Had a fight? That is foolish—not possible.

FRANK (*pointing with his finger*): There's his name—Bonaparte.

BONAPARTE (*puzzled*): Musta be some other boy. (FRANK *suddenly flips over newspaper. The others immediately see the reason:* JOE *stands in the door, in the shadows.*)

JOE (*in the shadows*): Gee, you're up late. . . .

BONAPARTE: We waita for you. (JOE *slowly moves into the light. His face is bruised and over one eye is a piece of adhesive tape.*)

JOE (*seeing their looks*): I had a fight—a boy in the park—

BONAPARTE: He hit you?

JOE: I hit him.

BONAPARTE: You hurt?

JOE: No. (BONAPARTE *casts a furtive look in the direction of the other men.*)

BONAPARTE: Whata you fight him for?

JOE: Didn't like what he said to me.

BONAPARTE: What he said?

JOE (*evasively*): It's a long story and I'm tired.

BONAPARTE (*trying to break a pause of embarrassment*): I was say to Mr. Carp tomorrow is your birthday. How you like to be so old?

JOE: I forgot about that! I mean I forgot for the last few hours. Where do you think I was? Do you want the truth?

FRANK: Truth is cheap. We bought it for two cents. (*He turns over paper and shows* JOE *his own face.* JOE *looks at picture, likes it. General silence.*)

JOE (*finally, belligerently*): Well, what are you going to do about it?

BONAPARTE (*still puzzled*): Abouta what?

JOE (*challengingly*): Tomorrow's my birthday!

FRANK: What's that got to do with being a gladiator?

JOE (*turning to* FRANK, *with sudden vehemence*): Mind your business! You don't know me—I see you once a year; what do you know about me?

FRANK (*smiling*): You're a dumb kid!

BONAPARTE (*starting to his feet*): Hey, waita one-a minute. What'sa for this excite-a-ment?

JOE (*hotly*): I don't want to be criticized! Nobody takes me serious here! I want to do what I want. I proved it tonight I'm good—I went out to earn some money and I earned! I had a professional fight tonight—maybe I'll have some more.

CARP: You honest to God had a fight?

JOE (*glaring at* CARP): Why not?

FRANK (*to* JOE): No one's criticizin'.

BONAPARTE: That's right.

JOE (*half sheepishly*): I don't know why I got so sore. . . .

FRANK: You're expecting opposition all the time—

BONAPARTE: Sit down, Joe—resta you'self.

JOE: Don't want to sit. Every birthday I ever had I sat around. Now'sa time for standing. Poppa, I have to tell you—I don't like myself, past, present and future. Do you know there are men who have wonderful things from life? Do you think they're better than me? Do you think I like this feel-

ing of no possessions? Of learning about the world from
Carp's encyclopedia? Frank don't know what it means—he
travels around, sees the world! (*Turning to* FRANK.) You
don't know what it means to sit around here and watch the
months go ticking by! Do you think that's a life for a boy
my age? Tomorrow's my birthday! I change my life!

BONAPARTE: Justa like that?

JOE: Just like that!

FRANK: And what do you do with music?

JOE: Who says I'm married to music? I take a vacation—the
notes won't run away!

FRANK: You're a mysterious kid. Where did you learn the
fighting game?

JOE: These past two years, all over the city—in the gyms—

BONAPARTE: Hey, Joe, you sounda like crazy! You no gotta
nature for fight. You're musician. Whata you say, heh?
Whata you do?

JOE: Let's call it a day.

BONAPARTE: Isa no true whata I say—?

JOE: That's all for tonight. (*His lips tightened, he abruptly
exits.*)

BONAPARTE (*calling after him*): Take a gooda sleep, Joe.

FRANK (*smiling*): It looks like the gold bug has visited our
house.

CARP (*sadly*): Fortunes! I used to hear it in my youth—the
streets of America are paved with gold. Say, you forgot to
give him the present.

BONAPARTE (*slowly, puzzled*): I don'ta know . . . he say he
gonna fight. . . .

Act I

Scene 3

SCENE: *Two months later;* MOODY's *office as in Act I, Scene 1.*
MOODY *is pacing back and forth in one of his fuming moods.*
Those present include LORNA, *stretched out on the couch,*
blowing cigarette smoke into the air; TOKIO *sitting quietly*
on a chair, and ROXY GOTTLIEB, *comfortably spread out in*
the desk chair, wearing a big white panama hat which he
seldom removes.

ROXY: They don't like him. They seen him in five fights already. He's a clever boy, that Bonaparte, and speedy—but
he's first-class lousy in the shipping department! I bought
a piece of him, so I got a right to say it: a mosquito gives
out better! Did you read what he wrote in his column, that
Drake? He writes he's a regular "brain trust."

LORNA: What's wrong with that?

ROXY: I'll tell you in a capsule: the people who'll pay to watch
a "brain trust" you could fit in a telephone booth! Roxy
Gottlieb is telling you!

MOODY: Roxy's right. Joe pulls his punches. Two months already and he don't throw his hands right and he don't throw
them enough.

LORNA: Tom, what do you want the boy to do? You surely
know by now he's not a slugger. His main asset is his
science—he's a student.

ROXY (*loftily*): Excuse me, Miss Moon. In the prize-fight ring
the cash customer don't look for stoodents. Einstein lives in
a college—a wonderful man in *his* line! Also, while I think of
it, a woman's place is in the hay, not in the office!

MOODY (*indignantly*): Where do you come off to make a remark like that?

LORNA (*standing up*): At the moment a woman's place is in the bar—see you later. (*She looks at others with a peculiar smile and exits.* MOODY *stares at* ROXY *who realizes he has said the wrong thing.*)

MOODY: I'm worried about that boy!

TOKIO: I'd trust him, Tom. Joe knows his own needs, as he says. Don't ask him to change his style. A style is best when it's individual, when it comes out of the inner personality and the lay of the muscles and the set of the bones. That boy stands a chance to make the best lightweight since Benny Simon.

ROXY: On *your* nose!

TOKIO: He's got one of the best defenses I ever seen. And speedy as the wind.

MOODY: But he won't fight!

ROXY: A momma doll gives out better!

TOKIO: He's a peculiar duck—I want him thinking he's the best thing in shoe leather.

MOODY: He thinks so now.

TOKIO: I don't like to contradict you, Tom, but he don't. It's seventy-five percent front. If you want the goods delivered you have to treat him delicate, gentle—like a girl.

ROXY: Like a girl? Why didn't you say so before?

MOODY: No, Roxy, not you—you just treat him like a human being.

TOKIO: I think we can begin the build-up now.

MOODY: A road tour?

TOKIO: I'd like to take him around the Middle West, about fifteen bouts.

ROXY (*answering a look from* MOODY): I didn't say no. But will he co-operate?

TOKIO: As soon as I find the password.

MOODY: What's the password to make this kid go in and slug —that's the problem. (*There is a knock at the door.* MOODY

27

calls.) Yes? (*Door opens and* BONAPARTE *stands there hesitantly.*)

BONAPARTE (*timidly*): My name is Joe Bonaparte's father. I come-a to see my son's new friends.

MOODY (*expansively*): Come in, sit down, Mr. Bonaparte.

ROXY (*sitting comfortably*): Take a seat.

BONAPARTE: Am I interrupt?

MOODY: Not at all.

ROXY: What's the matter with your boy?

TOKIO (*to* BONAPARTE): This is Mr. Moody and Mr. Gottlieb.

BONAPARTE (*sitting*): Good afternoon.

MOODY: We were just discussing your son.

BONAPARTE: I please to hear. I like find out froma you how's this boxer business for Joe. Whata good in it for him.

MOODY: Your Joe's a very clever fighter.

ROXY: Can you take it? We want to make your boy famous— a millionaire, but he won't let us—won't co-operate. How do you like it?

BONAPARTE: Why? Whatta he do?

ROXY (*going over and facing the old man in a lecturing position*): I'll ask *you*. What does he do? What does he do that's right? *Nothing!* We offer him on a gold platter! Wine, women and song, to make a figure of speech. We offer him *magnitudes!*

BONAPARTE (*waiting*): Yes—?

MOODY: But he won't fight.

BONAPARTE (*puzzled*): He'sa fighta for you, no?

ROXY: You're right—no! Your boy's got unexplored possibilities—*unexplored!* But you can't make a purse out of somebody's ear.

MOODY (*trying to counteract* ROXY's *volubility*): My colleague is trying to say that Joe keeps holding back in the ring.

BONAPARTE: Holda back?

TOKIO: He nurses his self—

MOODY: He keeps holding back—

TOKIO: His defense is brilliant—

MOODY: Gorgeous—!

Golden Boy

ROXY: But where's the offense? You take but you can't give. Figure it out—where would you be in a traffic jam? You know how to reverse—but to shift in second or high?—nothing!

BONAPARTE (*quietly to* ROXY): Hey, you talka too much—nobody's contradicta you.

ROXY (*after a momentary setback*): "Everybody'sa contradicta me!" Even you, and I never met you before. (*With a reproachful glance he retires to desk where he sits and sulks.*)

BONAPARTE (*singling out* TOKIO *as a man to whom he can speak*): Who are you?

TOKIO: Your son's trainer . . .

BONAPARTE: You interest to helpa my boy?

TOKIO (*respectfully*): Very much . . .

BONAPARTE: Me too. Maybe not so as plan by these-a gentleman here. I don't say price fight'sa no good for Joe. Joe like-a to be fame, not feel ashame. . . .

TOKIO: Is Joe afraid of his hands?

BONAPARTE: I don't know. You tella me what'sa what . . . I don't know price fight. His hand coulda get hurt?

MOODY: Every fighter hurts his hands. Sometimes they break—

TOKIO: They heal up in no time.

ROXY (*flaring out*): What's so special about hands? I suppose your kid plays piano!

BONAPARTE: Coulda get hurt? Coulda break?!

ROXY: So what?

BONAPARTE (*up on his feet*): Hey, you! I don't like-a you! You no interest in my boy! (*Proudly.*) My boy'sa besta violin' in New York!

MOODY (*suddenly sickened*): What . . . ?

BONAPARTE: Yes, play the violin!

MOODY: That's it!

ROXY (*anguished by this stupidity*): If I had hair I'd tear it out! Five hundred fiddlers stand on Broadway and 48th Street, on the corner, every day, rain or shine, hot or cold. And your boy dares—! (*Turning to* MOODY.) How do you

29

like it? (*He waves his hands in despair and retires to desk, where he sits in fuming disgusted silence.*)

MOODY (*repressing a feeling of triumph*): Your boy's afraid of his hands because he fiddles?

BONAPARTE: Yes, musta be!

TOKIO: Why did you come and tell us this?

BONAPARTE: Because I like-a to help my boy. I like-a for him to try himself out. Maybe thisa better business for him. Maybe not. He mus' try to find out, to see whata he want. . . . I don't know. Don't help Joe to tell him I come here. Don't say it. (*He slowly walks to door.*)

MOODY: That means you won't stand in his way?

BONAPARTE: My boy coulda break his hand? Gentleman, I'ma not so happy as you . . . no! (*He slowly exits.*)

MOODY (*joyously*): I'm beginning to see the light! Joe's mind ain't made up that the fist is mightier than the fiddle.

ROXY (*bouncing up and down*): I'll make up his mind. For the money that's involved I'd make Niagara Falls turn around and go back to Canada.

TOKIO: Don't try to bully him into anything.

ROXY: In Roxy Gottlieb he met his match.

MOODY (*explosively*): What the hell's the matter with you, Roxy! Sit down a minute. (ROXY *sits.*) As I see it, the job is to handle him gently, to make him see how much we prize him—to kill his doubts with goodness.

ROXY: I got it: the password is honey!

MOODY: Right! The Middle West tour is on! Tokio goes along to build up a real offensive. I take care of the newspapers here. Chris', I thought it was something serious! I'm getting to feel like 1928 again. Call it intuition: I feel like the Resurrection. (*He gets up and begins to stroll about.*) Once we're out of the tunnel, with thirty bouts behind us—

ROXY: If you hear a noise, it's my mouth watering— (*The telephone rings.* MOODY *answers.*)

MOODY: Hello? Yeah . . . I think he'll win— (*Hangs up.*) Who do you think that was? (*Imitating.*) "Fuseli is speaking." Eddie Fuseli!

ROXY: Fuseli? What's he want?

MOODY: Will Joe win against Vincenti Tuesday. Tokio, from now on it's your job.

TOKIO: I got faith in the boy.

MOODY (*to Roxy*): I have to ask one thing—when Joe comes over from the gym let me do the talking.

TOKIO: And don't mention music! (LORNA *enters.*)

LORNA: Shh! Here's Joe. (JOE BONAPARTE *enters the office. Immediately* MOODY *and* ROXY *put on their softest kid gloves. Their methods of salesmanship will shortly become so apparent that both* JOE *and* LORNA *become suspicious.*)

MOODY (*slowly circling around*): Glad to see you, Joe. Joe, you remember in reference to what we were speaking about yesterday? Well . . . we had several friends on the long distance phone. We're booking fifteen out of town bouts for you. Tough ones, too.

ROXY: Tonight I'm calling my Chicago connections.

MOODY: We talked it over with Tokio and he says—well, tell him what you said, Tokio—tell him the truth.

TOKIO: I think you got a wonderful future.

MOODY (*to* TOKIO): Name the names, Tokio.

TOKIO: Well, I said Benny Simon—as good as Simon, I said.

MOODY: Tokio's gonna work with you—help you develop a right—

ROXY: And a left! What'sa right without a left?

MOODY: Tokio thinks that when he brings you back you'll be a contender for Number One.

JOE (*a little defensively*): Really?

MOODY: But *you* have to help *us* help *you.*

ROXY: Could Webster say it better?

MOODY (*softly singing a siren song, his arms around* JOE'*s shoulders*): This job needs gorgeous concentration. All your time and thoughts, Joe. No side lines, no side interests—

JOE (*defensively*): I don't go out with girls.

MOODY: You're in the fighting game. It's like being a priest—

your work comes first. What would you rather do than fight?

JOE (*defensively*): I don't know what you mean.

MOODY (*carefully picking his words*): Some boys, for instance, like to save their looks. They'd practically throw the fight to keep their nose intact.

JOE (*smiling wryly*): My looks don't interest me. (LORNA *is listening with rapt attention.*)

MOODY (*still singing the siren song*): Then what's holding you back, Joe? You can tell me, Joe. We've set up housekeeping together, Joe, and I want you to tell me if you can't cook a steak—it don't matter. We're married anyway. . . .

JOE (*uneasily*): Who's being put to bed?

MOODY: What do you mean?

JOE: I don't like this seduction scene. (*To* TOKIO.) What are they after?

TOKIO: They think you're afraid of your hands.

MOODY: Are you?

JOE: Half . . .

TOKIO: Why?

ROXY (*bouncing up*): Tell the truth!

JOE: What truth?

MOODY (*holding back* ROXY *with a look*): Are you afraid your hands'll bust, Joe? (JOE *remains silent.*) What's a busted hand to a *fighter*? You can't go in and do your best if you're scared of your mitts . . . can you? You tell me. . . .

JOE: No. . . .

MOODY: Whyn't you give up outside ideas, Joe?

ROXY (*suddenly, in a loud voice to* TOKIO): You shoulda seen that bunch of musicians on 48th Street before. Fiddlers, drummers, cornetists—not a dime in a carload. Bums in the park! Oh, excuse me, Tom, I was just telling Tokio— (JOE *is now aware that the others know of the violin. Now he is completely closed to them.* MOODY *sees this.*)

MOODY (*wrathfully—to* ROXY): What would you like to say, my fine-feathered friend?

ROXY (*simulating bewilderment*): What's the matter? What

happened? (*Receiving no answer, he looks around several times and adds, with a shrug.*) I think I'll run across the street and pick up an eight-cylinder lunch.

MOODY: Sprinkle it with arsenic. Do that for me, for me, sweetheart!!

ROXY (*hurt*): That's a fine remark from a friend. (*He haughtily exits.*)

JOE: What do you want, Mr. Moody?

MOODY: At the moment, nothing. I'm puffed out. See you to-morrow over the gym.

JOE: Maybe I won't be there. I might give up fighting as a bad job. I'm not overconvinced it's what I want. I can do other things. . . .

TOKIO: I'll see you tomorrow at the gym, Joe. (*JOE looks at both the men, says nothing, exits.*) That Mr. Gottlieb is a case. See you later.

MOODY (*not looking up*): Okay. (*TOKIO exits. LORNA and MOODY are alone. She blows cigarette smoke to the ceiling. MOODY puts his feet up on desk and leans back wearily. Snorting through his nostrils.*) The password is honey!

LORNA: What was that all about? (*Telephone rings.*)

MOODY (*of the ringing bell*): If that's for me, tear it up. I ain't in, not even for God.

LORNA (*answering*): Hello? . . . (*Putting her hand on mouthpiece.*) It's Mrs. God—your wife. (*MOODY makes a grimace of distaste but picks up phone and puts on a sweet voice.*)

MOODY: Yes, Monica darling. . . . Yeah . . . you and your support . . . You're gonna fifty-buck me to death! . . . Monica, if I had fifty bucks I'd buy myself a big juicy coffin. What? So throw me in jail. (*He hangs up phone.*) Bitch! That'll be time number three. She means it too.

LORNA: What was that scene with Bonaparte?

MOODY: Sweetheart, the jig is up! Believe it or not, Bonaparte's a violinist. Maybe he was on the radio. I don't know what the hell he was. His old man came here and told us. His mitts are on his mind. You can't do a thing with a nut like that.

LORNA: Won't he give up the violin?

MOODY: You heard him stalling. This is the end, Lorna. It's our last chance for a decent life, for getting married—we have to make that kid fight! He's *more* than a meal ticket— he's everything we want and need from life! (LORNA *goes over and slaps him on the back.*)

LORNA: Put up your chin, little man.

MOODY: Don't Brisbane me, Lorna. I'm licked. I'm tired. Find me a mouse hole to crawl in. . . .

LORNA: Why don't you ask me when you want something? You got the brains of a flea. Do you want Bonaparte to fight?

MOODY: Do I wanna see tomorrow?

LORNA: I'll make him fight.

MOODY: How?

LORNA: How? . . . I'm "a tramp from Newark," Tom . . . I know a dozen ways. . . .

ACT I

SCENE 4

SCENE: *A few nights later.*

JOE *and* LORNA *sit on a bench in the park. It is night. There is carousel music in the distance. Cars ride by the boy and girl in the late spring night. Out of sight a traffic light changes from red to green and back again throughout the scene and casts its colors on the faces of the boy and girl.*

LORNA: Success and fame! Or just a lousy living. You're lucky you won't have to worry about those things. . . .

JOE: Won't I?

LORNA: Unless Tom Moody's a liar.

JOE: You like him, don't you?

LORNA (*after a pause*): I like him.

JOE: I like how you dress. The girls look nice in the summer time. Did you ever stand at the Fifth Avenue Library and watch those girls go by?

LORNA: No, I never did. (*Switching the subject.*) That's the carousel, that music. Did you ever ride on one of those?

JOE: That's for kids.

LORNA: Weren't you ever a kid, for God's sake?

JOE: Not a happy kid.

LORNA: Why?

JOE: Well, I always felt different. Even my name was special —Bonaparte—and my eyes . . .

LORNA: I wouldn't have taken that too serious. . . . (*There is a silent pause. JOE looks straight ahead.*)

JOE: Gee, all those cars . . .

LORNA: Lots of horses trot around here. The rich know how to live. You'll be rich. . . .

JOE: My brother Frank is an organizer for the C.I.O.

LORNA: What's that?

JOE: If you worked in a factory you'd know. Did you ever work?

LORNA (*with a smile*): No, when I came out of the cocoon I was a butterfly and butterflies don't work.

JOE: All those cars . . . whizz, whizz. (*Now turning less casual.*) Where's Mr. Moody tonight?

LORNA: He goes up to see his kid on Tuesday nights. It's a sick kid, a girl. His wife leaves it at her mother's house.

JOE: That leaves you free, don't it?

LORNA: What are you hinting at?

JOE: I'm thinking about you and Mr. Moody.

LORNA: Why think about it? I don't. Why should you?

JOE: If you belonged to me I wouldn't think about it.

LORNA: Haven't you got a girl?

JOE: No.

LORNA: Why not?

JOE (*evasively*): Oh . . .

LORNA: Tokio says you're going far in the fighting game.

JOE: Music means more to me. May I tell you something?

35

LORNA: Of course.

JOE: If you laugh I'll never speak to you again.

LORNA: I'm not the laughing type.

JOE: With music I'm never alone when I'm alone— Playing music . . . that's like saying, "I am man. I belong here. How do you do, World—good evening!" When I play music nothing is closed to me. I'm not afraid of people and what they say. There's no war in music. It's not like the streets. Does this sound funny?

LORNA: No.

JOE: But when you leave your room . . . down in the street . . . it's war! Music can't help me there. Understand?

LORNA: Yes.

JOE: People have hurt my feelings for years. I never forget. You can't get even with people by playing the fiddle. If music shot bullets I'd like it better—artists and people like that are freaks today. The world moves fast and they sit around like forgotten dopes.

LORNA: You're loaded with fireworks. Why don't you fight?

JOE: You have to be what you are—!

LORNA: Fight! See what happens—

JOE: Or end up in the bughouse!

LORNA: God's teeth! Who says you have to be one thing?

JOE: My nature isn't fighting!

LORNA: Don't Tokio know what he's talking about? Don't Tom? Joe, listen: be a fighter! Show the world! If you made your fame and fortune—and you can—you'd be anything you want. Do it! Bang your way to the lightweight crown. Get a bank account. Hire a great doctor with a beard—get your eyes fixed—

JOE: What's the matter with my eyes?

LORNA: Excuse me, I stand corrected. (*After a pause.*) You get mad all the time.

JOE: That's from thinking about myself.

LORNA: How old are you, Joe?

JOE: Twenty-one and a half, and the months are going fast.

LORNA: You're very smart for twenty-one and a half "and the months are going fast."

JOE: Why not? I read every page of the Encyclopædia Britannica. My father's friend, Mr. Carp, has it. A shrimp with glasses had to do something.

LORNA: I'd like to meet your father. Your mother dead?

JOE: Yes.

LORNA: So is mine.

JOE: Where do you come from? The city is full of girls who look as if they never had parents.

LORNA: I'm a girl from over the river. My father is still alive—shucking oysters and bumming drinks somewhere in the wilds of Jersey. I'll tell you a secret: I don't like you.

JOE (*surprised*): Why?

LORNA: You're too sufficient by yourself . . . too inside yourself.

JOE: You like it or you don't.

LORNA: You're on an island—

JOE: Robinson Crusoe . . .

LORNA: That's right—"me, myself, and I." Why not come out and see the world?

JOE: Does it seem that way?

LORNA: Can't you see yourself?

JOE: No. . . .

LORNA: Take a bird's-eye view; you don't know what's right or wrong. You don't know what to pick, but you won't admit it.

JOE: Do you?

LORNA: Leave me out. This is the anatomy of Joe Bonaparte.

JOE: You're dancing on my nose, huh?

LORNA: Shall I stop?

JOE: No.

LORNA: You're a miserable creature. You want your arm in *gelt* up to the elbow. You'll take fame so people won't laugh or scorn your face. You'd give your soul for those things. But every time you turn your back your little soul kicks you in the teeth. It don't give in so easy.

JOE: And what does your soul do in its perfumed vanity case?

LORNA: Forget about me.

JOE: Don't you want—?

LORNA (*suddenly nasty*): I told you forget it!

JOE (*quietly*): Moody sent you after me—a decoy! You made a mistake, Lorna, for two reasons. I made up my own mind to fight. Point two, he doesn't know you don't love him—

LORNA: You're a fresh kid.

JOE: In fact he doesn't know anything about you at all.

LORNA (*challengingly*): But you do?

JOE: This is the anatomy of Lorna Moon: she's a lost baby. She doesn't know what's right or wrong. She's a miserable creature who never knew what to pick. But she'd never admit it. And I'll tell you why you picked Moody!

LORNA: You don't know what you're talking about.

JOE: Go home, Lorna. If you stay, I'll know something about you. . . .

LORNA: You don't know anything.

JOE: Now's your chance—go home!

LORNA: Tom loves me.

JOE (*after a long silence, looking ahead*): I'm going to buy a car.

LORNA: They make wonderful cars today. Even the lizzies—

JOE: Gary Cooper's got the kind I want. I saw it in the paper, but it costs too much—fourteen thousand. If I found one second hand—

LORNA: And if you had the cash—

JOE: I'll get it—

LORNA: Sure, if you'd go in and really fight!

JOE (*in a sudden burst*): Tell your Mr. Moody I'll dazzle the eyes out of his head!

LORNA: You mean it?

JOE (*looking out ahead*): Those cars are poison in my blood. When you sit in a car and speed you're looking down at the world. Speed, speed, everything is speed—nobody gets me!

LORNA: You mean in the ring?

JOE: In or out, nobody gets me! Gee, I like to stroke that gas!

Golden Boy

LORNA: You sound like Jack the Ripper.
JOE (*standing up suddenly*): I'll walk you back to your house—your hotel, I mean. (LORNA *stands.* JOE *continues.*) Do you have the same room?
LORNA (*with sneaking admiration*): You're a fresh kid!
JOE: When you're lying in his arms tonight, tell him, for me, that the next world's champ is feeding in his stable.
LORNA: Did you really read those Britannica books?
JOE: From A to Z.
LORNA: And you're only twenty-one?
JOE: And a half.
LORNA: Something's wrong somewhere.
JOE: I know. . . . (*They slowly walk out.*)

ACT I

SCENE 5

SCENE: *The next week.*
It is near midnight in the dining room of the Bonaparte home. Same as Act I, Scene 2. An open suitcase rests on table. SIGGIE is pouring samples of wine for LORNA MOON. He himself drinks appreciatively. To one side sits BONAPARTE silently, thoughtfully, watchfully—pretending to read the newspaper.

SIGGIE: I was fit to be knocked down with a feather when I heard it. I couldn't believe it until I seen him fight over at the Keystone last week. You never know what somebody's got in him—like the man with germs—suddenly he's down in bed with a crisis! (JOE *enters with an armful of clothes which he begins to pack in suitcase.*)
LORNA: Joe's road tour will do him lots of good. (ANNA *enters and takes off an apron. Silence, in which* SIGGIE *and* LORNA *sip their wine.*)

39

ANNA: How do you like that wine, Miss Moon? My father
makes better wine than any Eyetalian in New York. My
father knows everything—don't you, Poppa? (*With a faint
smile,* BONAPARTE *shrugs his shoulders.*)

SIGGIE: We're thinking of sending the old man to a leper
colony. . . .

ANNA: Don't my husband say funny things? Tell her what you
told the janitor Tuesday, Siggie.

SIGGIE: Never mind, never mind.

ANNA: You know how I met Siggie? He was a United Cigar
Store clerk and I walked in for a pack of Camels and the
first thing you know he said something funny. It was raw,
so I can't say it. He had me laughing from the first. Seven
years and I haven't stopped laughing yet. (*She laughs
loudly, pleasurably.*) This will be the first time Joe ever
went traveling. Was you ever out of New York, Miss Moon?

LORNA: Oh, many times.

ANNA: That's nice. Far?

LORNA: California, Detroit, Chicago. I was an airplane hostess
for two months.

ANNA: That's nice—it's a real adventure. I'd like to fly.

SIGGIE: Stay on the ground! Fly! What for? Who do you know
up there? Eagles?

ANNA: It must be a wonderful way to see life.

LORNA (*drinking*): I've seen life in all its aspects. (BONA-
PARTE *stands up with a smile.* LORNA's *eyes follow him as
he exits. To* JOE.) I think your father left because he don't
like me.

JOE: He likes you.

ANNA: My father likes everybody. He's a very deep man. My
father has more friends than any man alive. But best of all
he likes his horse, Dolly, who drives the fruit wagon. My
father can't sit still on Sunday afternoon—he has to go see
what that horse is doing. (*Her eyes catch sight of suitcase.*)
Joe, you don't know how to pack. (*She starts over to assist
him.*)

SIGGIE (*querulously*): Rest the feet awhile, Duchess.

40

ANNA (*explaining her move*): He don't know how to pack. (*Beginning to rearrange suitcase.* BONAPARTE *returns and hands* JOE *a sweater.*)

BONAPARTE: You forget your good sweater.

JOE: Thanks. (BONAPARTE *sits.* JOE *looks at him sideways.*)

ANNA: When you get out to Chicago, buy yourself some new underwear, Joe. I hear everything's cheaper in Chicago. Is that right, Miss Moon?

LORNA (*after taking another drink*): Chicago? I don't know. I was there only one night—I got news that night my mother died. As a matter of fact, she killed herself.

ANNA: That's very sad.

LORNA: No, my father's an old drunk son-of-a-bitch. Did you ask me about my father?

BONAPARTE (*who has been listening intently*): Yes. . . .

LORNA: Twice a week he kicked my mother's face in. If I let myself go I'd be a drunkard in a year.

ANNA: My father never said one bad word to my mother in her whole lifetime. And she was a big nuisance right up till the day she died. She was more like me, more on the stout side. Take care of your health, Joe, when you're out there. What's better than health?

LORNA (*turning to* BONAPARTE, *with whom she is self-conscious*): The question is, do you like me or do you not?

BONAPARTE (*with a faint smile*): Yes. . . .

LORNA: Your family is very cute— Now do you like me?

BONAPARTE: Yes. . . .

LORNA: Why do you look at me that way?

BONAPARTE: I don't look special. You gonna travel on those train with my son?

LORNA: God's teeth, no! I'm a friend of his manager's, that's all. And a friend of Joe's too.

BONAPARTE: You are in favor for my son to prize-fight? (JOE *looks at his father sideways and exits.*)

LORNA: Certainly. Aren't you?

BONAPARTE: Joe has a dream many year to be superior violin'. Was it boyhood thing? Was it real? Or is this real now?

Those are-a my question, Miss Moon. Maybe you are friend
to my son. Then I aska you, look out for him. Study him.
Help him find what'sa right. Tell me, Miss Moon, when you
find out. Help Joe find truthful success. Will you do it for
me?

LORNA: I'll be glad to keep my eye on him. (JOE *enters with
slippers, which he puts in bag.*)

ANNA (*to* JOE): You could stand some new shirts, too.

SIGGIE: Listen, Pop, I'm a natural man and I don't like wise
guys. Joe went in the boxing game 'cause he's ashamed to
be poor. That's his way to enter a little enterprise. All
other remarks are so much alfalfa! (JOE *locks bag.*)

ANNA (*taking wine glass from* SIGGIE's *hand*): Drunk as a
horsefly!

JOE: It's getting late and the train won't wait.

SIGGIE (*standing up*): My God is success. Need I say more?
I'm prouda you, Joe. Come home a champ. Make enough
dough to buy your sister's boy friend a new cab. Yes, boys
and girls, I'm looking in that old crystal ball and I see
strange and wonderful events! Yazoo!

ANNA (*giggling*): Drunk as a horsefly!

JOE (*to* SIGGIE): You can't drive us down to the station in this
condition.

SIGGIE: What condition?

ANNA: You're drunk, stupid.

SIGGIE: Shut the face, foolish! Just because I don't hold in my
nerves she thinks I'm drunk. If you hold in your nerves you
get ulcers. (*To* JOE.) Get your "chapow" and let's go. Or
don't you want me to drive you down?

JOE: No.

SIGGIE: I should worry—my cab's in the garage anyway!
(*Suddenly he sits.*)

JOE: We'd better start. . . .

LORNA (*to* BONAPARTE): I'd like to have another talk with
you sometime.

BONAPARTE: Come any time in the evening. You are a very

lovely girl. (MR. CARP *stands in the doorway.*) Here is Mr.
Carp to say good-by.

SIGGIE: Come in, my little prince.

CARP (*coming in and shaking hands with* JOE): I wish you
good luck in every undertaking.

JOE (*uneasily, because his father is looking at him*): Thanks.

BONAPARTE (*introducing* CARP): Miss Moon, my neighbor,
Mr. Carp.

CARP: A pleasure to meet you.

LORNA: Hello. (BONAPARTE *brings violin case from its hiding
place in buffet.*)

BONAPARTE: Joe, I buy you this some time ago. Don't give
'cause I don't know whatta you gonna do. Take him with
you now. Play for yourself. It gonna remember you your old
days of musical life. (JOE *puts down suitcase and picks up
violin. He plucks the strings, he tightens one of them. In
spite of the tension his face turns soft and tender.*)

LORNA (*watching intently*): We better not miss the train—
Tokio's waiting.

BONAPARTE (*of violin*): Take him with you, Joe.

JOE: It's beautiful. . . .

BONAPARTE: Practice on the road. (JOE *abruptly turns and
exits with the violin. The others listen, each standing in his
place, as rich violin music comes from the other room.* JOE
*returns. There is silence as he places the violin on the table
in front of his father.*)

JOE (*in a low voice*): Return it, Poppa.

ANNA (*hugging* JOE): Have a good trip, Joey.

CARP: Eat in good restaurants. . . . (*There is silence: the
father and son look at each other. The others in the room
sense the drama between the two. Finally:*)

JOE: I have to do this, Poppa.

BONAPARTE (*to* JOE): Be careful fora your hands.

JOE: Poppa, give me the word—

BONAPARTE: What word?

JOE: Give me the word to go ahead. You're looking at yesterday—I see tomorrow. Maybe you think I ought to spend my whole life here—you and Carp blowing off steam.

BONAPARTE (*holding himself back*): Oh, Joe, shut your mouth!

JOE. Give me the word to go ahead!

BONAPARTE: Be careful fora your hands!

JOE: I want you to give me the word!

BONAPARTE (*crying out*): No! No word! You gonna fight? All right! Okay! But I don't gonna give no word! No!

JOE: That's how you feel?

BONAPARTE: That'sa how I feel! (BONAPARTE'S *voice breaks and there is nothing for father and son to do but to clutch each other in a hasty embrace. Finally* BONAPARTE *disentangles himself and turns away.* JOE *abruptly grabs up his suitcase and exits.* LORNA *follows, stopping at the door to look back at* BONAPARTE. *In the ensuing silence* ANNA *looks at her father and shakes her head.* SIGGIE *suddenly lumbers to his feet and sounds off like a chime.*)

SIGGIE: Gong gong gong gong!

ANNA: Gee, Poppa . . .

SIGGIE: Come to bed, Anna. . . . Anna-banana . . . (SIGGIE *exits.*)

ANNA: Gee, Poppa . . . (*She touches her father sympathetically.*)

BONAPARTE (*without turning*): Gone to bed, Anna. . . . (ANNA *slowly exits.* BONAPARTE *now slowly comes back to the table and looks down at violin.*)

CARP (*seating himself slowly*): Come, my friend . . . we will have a nice talk on a cultural topic. (*Looking at the violin.*) You'll work around a number of years before you make it up, the price of that fiddle. (BONAPARTE *stands looking down at violin. Sadly.*) Yes, my friend, what is man? As Schopenhauer says, and in the last analysis . . .

ACT II

SCENE 1

SCENE: *Six months later. Present in the corner of a gymnasium are* ROXY, MOODY, LORNA *and* TOKIO. *They are looking offstage, watching* JOE BONAPARTE *work out with a partner. From off right come the sounds of typical gym activities: the thud of boxing gloves, the rat-a-tat of the punching bag, and from time to time the general bell which is a signal for rest periods. Tacked on the tin walls are an ad for Everlast boxing equipment, boxing "card" placards, a soiled American flag, some faded exit signs.*

The group watches silently for several seconds after the lights fade in. A BOXER, *wiping his perspiring body with a towel, passes from left to right and looks back at* LORNA'S *legs. As* ROXY *watches, his head moves to and fro in the rhythm of* JOE'S *sparring offstage.* ROXY *nods his head in admiration.*

ROXY: Tokio. I gotta give the devil his dues: in the past six months you done a noble job!

TOKIO (*calling offstage*): With the left! A long left, Joe! . . .

LORNA (*looking offstage*): Joe's a very good-looking boy. I never quite noticed it before. (*General bell sounds; the boxing din offstage stops.*)

MOODY (*rubbing his hands enthusiastically*): "Let it rain, let it pour! It ain't gonna rain where we're headed for!"

ROXY: I'm tickled to death to see the canary bird's left his gloves.

TOKIO: He's the king of all he surveys.

MOODY: Boy, oh, boy, how he surprised them in the Bronx last

45

night! . . . But one thing I can't explain—that knockout he took in Philly five weeks ago.

TOKIO: That night he was off his feed, Tom. Where do you see speed like that? That's style, real style—you can't tag him. And he's giving it with both hands.

MOODY: You don't have to sell me his virtues—I'm sold. Nevertheless, he got tagged in Philly.

TOKIO: Here's what happened there: we run into some man when we're leaving the hotel. Joe goes pale. I ask him what it is. "Nothing," he says. But I see for myself—a man with long hair and a violin case. When we turn the corner, he says, "He's after me," he says. As if it's cops and robbers! (*The general bell sounds; the fighting din begins again.*)

ROXY: A kidnaper?

LORNA: Don't be a fool. He was reminded . . .

ROXY: Speak when spoken to, Miss Moon!

MOODY (*moodily*): And when he got in the ring that night, he kept his hands in his pockets?

TOKIO: Yeah. I didn't mention this before—it's not important.

MOODY: But it's still a danger—

TOKIO: No. No.

MOODY: But anyway, we better get him away from his home. We can't afford no more possible bad showings at this stage of the game. No more apparitions, like suddenly a fiddle flies across the room on wings! (*The group again intently watches* JOE *offstage.*) Ooh! Did you see that? He's packing a real Sunday punch in that right. (*Calling offstage.*) Hit 'im, Joe, hit 'im! (*As an indistinct answer comes back.*) Ha, ha, looka that, hahaha . . . (*Now turning to* TOKIO.) What's your idea of a match with Lombardo?

TOKIO: Can you get it?

MOODY: Maybe.

TOKIO: Get it.

MOODY: Sure?

TOKIO: It's an easy win, on points at least. (*During the last few lines a thin dark man has entered. His dark hair is*

grayed at the temples, an inarticulate look in his face. He is
EDDIE FUSELI, *a renowned gambler and gunman.*)

EDDIE FUSELI (*approaching the group*): Hello.

ROXY (*nervously*): Hello, Eddie.

MOODY (*turning*): I haven't seen you for a dog's age, Fuseli.

EDDIE (*pointing offstage*): You got this certain boy—Bonaparte. I like his looks. American born?

ROXY: Right from here.

EDDIE (*watching* JOE *offstage*): Like a cat, never off his position. He appeals to me. (*To* MOODY.) They call you the Brown Fox. What's your opinion of this boy?

MOODY (*coolly, on guard*): Possibilities . . .

EDDIE (*to* TOKIO): What's your idea?

TOKIO: Tom said it.

EDDIE: Could he get on top?

MOODY (*still on guard*): I can't see that far ahead. I don't read palms.

EDDIE: Could I buy a piece?

MOODY: No.

EDDIE (*coolly*): Could I?

MOODY: No!

EDDIE (*with a certain tenderness*): I like a good fighter. I like to see you after, Tom. (*Of* LORNA.) This your girl?

LORNA (*pertly*): I'm my mother's girl.

EDDIE (*with a small mirthless laugh*): Ha, ha—that's a hot one. (*He coolly drifts out of the scene on his cat's feet. General bell sounds. The din ceases.*)

LORNA: What exhaust pipe did he crawl out of?

ROXY: I remember this Eddie Fuseli when he came back from the war with a gun. He's still got the gun and he still gives me goose pimples!

MOODY: That Fuseli's a black mark in my book. Every once in a while he shoots across my quiet existence like a roman candle!

LORNA: Sell or don't sell. But better be careful, that guy's tough! (*A* FIGHTER, *robed, hooded with towel, passes across:* A GAMBLING TYPE *passes in the opposite direction. Both look at* LORNA'S *legs.*)

MOODY: Give a rat like that a finger and you lose a hand before you know it!

TOKIO: Did you know Joe bought a car this morning?

ROXY: What kinda car?

TOKIO: A Deusenberg.

MOODY: One of those fancy speed wagons?

TOKIO (*agreeing*): It cost him five grand, second hand.

MOODY (*flaring up:*) Am I a stepchild around here? I'm glad you tell me now, if only outa courtesy!

ROXY (*indignantly*): Whatta you keep a thing like that incognito for?

MOODY: He drives like a maniac! That time we drove to Long Beach? I almost lost my scalp! We can't let him drive around like that! Boy, he's getting a bushel of bad habits! We gotta be careful. (*The general bell sounds again; the fighting din stops.*) Here's the truth: our boy can be the champ in three easy lessons—Lombardo, Fulton, the Chocolate Drop. But we gotta be careful!

LORNA: Here he comes. (JOE *enters in bathrobe, taking off his headgear, which* TOKIO *takes from him.*)

MOODY (*completely changing his tone*): You looked very good in there, Joe. You're going swell and I like it. I'd work more with that long left if I were you.

JOE: Yes, I was speaking to Tokio about that. I feel my form's improving. I like to work. I'm getting somewhere—I feel it better every day.

LORNA: Happy?

JOE (*looking at her intently*): Every day's Saturday!

ROXY (*officiously*): Say, what's this I hear you bought a Deusenberg?

JOE: What's your objection—I might have some fun?

ROXY: I got my wampum on you. I like to know your habits. Ain't I permitted? (JOE *is about to retort hotly when* MOODY *gently takes his arm in an attempt to soothe him.*)

MOODY: Wait a minute, Joe. After all we have your welfare

at heart. And after all a Deusenberg can go one fifty per— (EDDIE FUSELI *appears, unseen by the others. He listens.*)

JOE: Who'd want to drive that fast?

MOODY: And since we're vitally interested in your future—

JOE (*shaking off* MOODY's *arm and saying what is really on his mind*): If you're vitally interested in my future, prove it! Get me some fights—fights with contenders, not with dumb-bunny club fighters. Get me some main bouts in the metropolitan area—!

MOODY (*losing his temper*): For a kid who got kayoed five weeks ago, your mouth is pretty big! (*The general bell sounds; the din begins.*)

JOE: That won't happen again! And how about some mention in the press? Twenty-six bouts—no one knows I'm alive. This isn't a vacation for me—it's a profession! I'm staying more than a week. Match me up against real talent. You can't go too fast for me. Don't worry about autos!

MOODY: We can go too fast! You're not so good!

JOE (*with a boyish grin*): Look at the records! (JOE *abruptly exits.* TOKIO *follows him, first giving the others a glance.*)

MOODY: Boy, oh, boy, that kid's changing!

ROXY: He goes past my head like a cold wind from the river!

LORNA: But you're gettin' what you want—the contender for the crown!

MOODY: I wish I was sure.

ROXY: Frankenstein! (EDDIE FUSELI *saunters down to the others.*)

EDDIE: I thought it over, Tom. I like to get a piece of that boy.

MOODY (*angrily*): I thought it over, too—not for sale. In fact I had a visitation from Jehovah. He came down on the calm waters and he said, "Let there be unity in the ownership."

EDDIE (*with a dead face*): I had a visit, too. He come down in the bar and he ate a pretzel. And he says, "Eddie Fuseli, I like you to buy a piece!"

MOODY (*trying to delay the inevitable*): Why not see me in my office tomorrow?

EDDIE: It's a cheap office. I get depressed in that office.

MOODY (*finally*): I can't make any guarantees about the boy.

EDDIE: How do you mean it, Tom?

MOODY: I don't know what the hell he'll do in the next six months.

ROXY: Eddie, it's like flapjacks—up and down—you don't know which side next!

EDDIE (*with his small mirthless laugh*): Ha, ha, that's a good one. You oughta be on the radio.

MOODY: No, it's a fact—

ROXY: We had enough headaches already. He's got a father, but how!

EDDIE: Don't want him to fight?

ROXY: His father sits on the kid's head like a bird's-nest! (ROXY *puts his hand on* EDDIE's *arm.*)

EDDIE: Take your hand off. (ROXY *hastily withdraws.*) Let the boy decide. . . .

MOODY: If you buy in?

EDDIE: Let the boy decide.

MOODY: Sure! But if he says no— (*Before* MOODY *can finish* JOE *enters.* EDDIE *whirls around and faces* JOE, *getting his cue from the others. Curiously,* EDDIE *is almost embarrassed before* JOE. *The bell sounds, the din stops.*) Joe, this is Eddie Fuseli. He's a man around town—

EDDIE (*facing* JOE, *his back to the others*): With good connections—

MOODY: He wantsa buy a piece of you—

EDDIE (*whirling around*): I will tell him myself.) *Turning back to* JOE; *with quiet intense dignity.*) I'm Eyetalian too—Eyetalian born, but an American citizen. I like to buy a piece of you. I don't care for no profit. I could turn it back to—*you* could take my share. But I like a good fighter; I like a good boy who could win the crown. It's the in-terrest of my life. It would be a proud thing for me when Bonaparte could win the crown like I think he can.

MOODY (*confidently*): It's up to you, Joe, if he buys in.

EDDIE (*wooingly*): Some managers can't give you what you need—

MOODY: Don't say that!

EDDIE: *Some* managers can't! I'll see you get good bouts . . . also press notices . . . I know you. You're a boy who needs that. You decide. . . . (*There is a pause;* JOE's *eyes flit from* LORNA *to the others and back to* EDDIE.)

JOE: Not my half.

EDDIE: Not your half.

JOE: As long as Mr. Fuseli doesn't mix in my private life . . . cut it up any way you like. Excuse me, I got a date with Miss Deusenberg. (*The others silently watch* JOE *exit.*)

EDDIE: A date with who?

MOODY (*snorting*): Miss Deusenberg!

ROXY: An automobile. It gives you an idea what a boy—"Miss Deusenberg"!

EDDIE: How do you like it, Tom? Big bills or little bills?

MOODY: Don't think you're buying in for an apple and an egg.

EDDIE: Take big bills—they're new, they feel good. See you in that office tomorrow. (*The bell clangs offstage.* EDDIE *starts off, but abruptly turns and faces* ROXY, *whom he inwardly terrifies.*) It's a trick you don't know, Roxy: when a bird sits on your head and interferes with the championship, you shoot him off. All kinds of birds. You be surprised how fast they fall on the ground. Which is my intention in this syndicate. (*He smiles thinly and then moves out of the scene like a cat.*)

MOODY: I don't like that!

ROXY: I'm not so happy myself at the present time. How do you like it with our boy for gratitude? He leaves us here standing in our brevities!

LORNA: What makes you think you're worthy of gratitude?

MOODY (*to* LORNA): For pete's sake, pipe down! Are you with us or against us?

ROXY (*haughtily, to* MOODY): Take my advice, Tom. Marry her and the first year give her a baby. Then she'll sit in the corner and get fat and sleepy, and not have such a big mouth! Uncle Roxy's telling you!

LORNA (*to* ROXY): Couldn't you keep quiet about the father

51

to that gunman? Go home and let your wife give *you* a baby!

ROXY: A woman shouldn't interfere—

MOODY: Peace, for chri' sake, peace! Lorna, we're in a bad spot with Joe. He's getting hard to manage and this is the time when everything's gotta be right. I'm seeing Lombardo's manager tomorrow! Now that gunman's on my tail. You have to help me. You and I wanna do it like the story books, "happy ever after"? Then help me.

LORNA: How?

MOODY: Go after the boy. Keep him away from his folks. Get him away from the buggies—

LORNA: How?

MOODY (*impatiently*): You know how.

ROXY: Now you're talking.

LORNA (*pointing to* ROXY): You mean the way I see it on his face?

MOODY: For crying out loud! Where do you come off to make a remark like that?

LORNA: You expect me to sleep with that boy?

MOODY: I could tear your ears off for a remark like that!

ROXY (*discreetly*): I think I'll go grab a corn-beef sandwich. (*He exits.*)

MOODY (*after silence*): Are you mad?

LORNA (*tight-lipped*): No.

MOODY (*seductively*): I'm not a bad guy, Lorna. I don't mean anything bad. . . . All right, I'm crude—sometimes I'm worried and I'm crude. (*The bell clangs, the boxing din stops.*) But what the hell, my heart's in the right place. . . . (*Coming behind her and putting his arms around her as she looks ahead.*) Lorna, don't we both want that sun to come up and shine on us? Don't we? Before you know it the summer'll be here. Then it's the winter again, and it's another year again . . . and we're not married yet. See? . . . See what I mean?

LORNA (*quietly*): Yes. . . .

MOODY (*beaming, but with uncertainty*): That sounds like the girl I used to know.

LORNA: I see what you mean. . . .

MOODY (*worried underneath*): You're not still mad?

LORNA (*briefly*): I'm not mad. (*But she abruptly cuts out of the scene, leaving* MOODY *standing there.*)

MOODY (*shaking his head*): Boy, I still don't know anything about women!

ACT II

SCENE 2

SCENE: *A few nights later. Same scene as Act I, Scene 4.* LORNA *and* JOE *sit on same park bench.*

JOE: Some nights I wake up—my heart's beating a mile a minute! Before I open my eyes I know what it is—the feeling that someone's standing at my bed. Then I open my eyes . . . it's gone—ran away!

LORNA: Maybe it's that old fiddle of yours.

JOE: Lorna, maybe it's you. . . .

LORNA: Don't you ever think of it any more—music?

JOE: What're you trying to remind me of? A kid with a Buster Brown collar and a violin case tucked under his arm? Does that sound appetizing to you?

LORNA: Not when you say it that way. You said it different once. . . .

JOE: What's on your mind, Lorna?

LORNA: What's on yours?

JOE (*simply*): You. . . . You're real for me—the way music was real.

LORNA: You've got your car, your career—what do you want with me?

JOE: I develop the ability to knock down anyone my weight.

But what point have I made? Don't you think I know that? I went off to the wars 'cause someone called me a name—because I wanted to be two other guys. Now it's happening. . . . I'm not sure I like it.

LORNA: Moody's against that car of yours.

JOE: I'm against Moody, so we're even.

LORNA: Why don't you like him?

JOE: He's a manager! He treats me like a possession! I'm just a little silver mine for him—he bangs me around with a shovel!

LORNA: He's helped you—

JOE: No, Tokio's helped me. Why don't you give him up? It's terrible to have just a Tuesday-night girl. Why don't you belong to me every night in the week? Why don't you teach me love? . . . Or am I being a fool?

LORNA: You're not a fool, Joe.

JOE: I want you to be my family, my life— Why don't you do it, Lorna, why?

LORNA: He loves me.

JOE: I love you!

LORNA (*treading delicately*): Well . . . anyway, the early bird got the worm. Anyway, I can't give him anguish. I . . . I know what it's like. You shouldn't kick Moody around. He's poor compared to you. You're alive, you've got yourself— I can't feel sorry for you!

JOE: But you don't love him!

LORNA: I'm not much interested in myself. But the thing I like best about you . . . you still feel like a flop. It's mysterious, Joe. It makes me put my hand out. (*She gives him her hand and he grasps it.*)

JOE: I feel very close to you, Lorna.

LORNA: I know. . . .

JOE: And you feel close to me. But you're afraid—

LORNA: Of what?

JOE: To take a chance! Lorna darling, you won't let me wake you up! I feel it all the time—you're half dead, and you don't know it!

54

LORNA (*half smiling*): Maybe I do. . . .

JOE: Don't smile—don't be hard-boiled!

LORNA (*sincerely*): I'm not.

JOE: Don't you trust me?

LORNA (*evasively*): Why start what we can't finish?

JOE (*fiercely*): Oh, Lorna, deep as my voice will reach—*listen!* Why can't you leave him? Why?

LORNA: Don't pull my dress off—I hear you.

JOE: Why?

LORNA: Because he needs me and you don't—

JOE: That's not true!

LORNA: Because he's a desperate guy who always starts out with two strikes against him. Because he's a kid at forty-two and you're a man at twenty-two.

JOE: You're sorry for him?

LORNA: What's wrong with that?

JOE: But what do *you* get?

LORNA: I told you before I don't care.

JOE: I don't believe it!

LORNA: I can't help that!

JOE: What did he ever do for you?

LORNA (*with sudden verve*): Would you like to know? He loved me in a world of enemies, of stags and bulls! . . . and I loved him for that. He picked me up in Friskin's hotel on 39th Street. I was nine weeks behind in rent. I hadn't hit the gutter yet, but I was near. He washed my face and combed my hair. He stiffened the space between my shoulder blades. Misery reached out to misery—

JOE: And now you're dead.

LORNA (*lashing out*): I don't know what the hell you're talking about!

JOE: Yes, you do. . . .

LORNA (*withdrawing*): Ho hum. . . . (*There is silence. The soft park music plays in the distance. The traffic lights change.* LORNA *is trying to appear impassive.* JOE *begins to whistle softly. Finally* LORNA *picks up his last note and continues, he stops. He picks up her note, and after he whistles*

55

*a few phrases she picks him up again. This whistling duet
continues for almost a minute. Then the traffic lights change
again.* LORNA, *beginning in a low voice.*) You make me feel
too human, Joe. All I want is peace and quiet, not love. I'm
a tired old lady, Joe, and I don't mind being what you
call "half dead." In fact it's what I like. (*Her voice mount-
ing higher.*) The twice I was in love I took an awful beating
and I don't want it again! (*Now half crying.*) I want you to
stop it! Don't devil me, Joe. I beg you, don't devil me . . .
let me alone. . . . (*She cries softly.* JOE *reaches out and takes
her hand; he gives her a handkerchief which she uses.*
LORNA, *finally.*) That's the third time I cried in my life. . . .

JOE: Now I know you love me.

LORNA (*bitterly*): Well . . .

JOE: I'll tell Moody.

LORNA: Not yet. Maybe he'd kill you if he knew.

JOE: Maybe.

LORNA: Then Fuseli'd kill him. . . . I guess I'd be left to kill
myself. I'll tell him. . . .

JOE: When?

LORNA: Not tonight.

JOE: Swiftly, do it swiftly—

LORNA: Not tonight.

JOE: Everything's easy if you do it swiftly.

LORNA: He went up there tonight with six hundred bucks to
bribe her into divorce.

JOE: Oh . . .

LORNA (*sadly*): He's a good guy, neat all over—sweet. I'll tell
him tomorrow. I'd like a drink.

JOE: Let's drive over the Washington Bridge.

LORNA (*standing*): No, I'd like a drink.

JOE (*standing and facing her*): Lorna, when I talk to you . . .
something moves in my heart. Gee, it's the beginning of a
wonderful life! A man and his girl! A warm, living girl who
shares your room . . .

LORNA: Take me home with you.

JOE: Yes.

LORNA: But how do I know you love me?

JOE: Lorna . . .

LORNA: How do I know it's true? You'll get to be the champ. They'll all want you, all the girls! But I don't care! I've been undersea a long time! When they'd put their hands on me I used to say, "This isn't it! This isn't what I mean!" It's been a mysterious world for me! But, Joe, I think you're it! I don't know why, I think you're it! Take me home with you.

JOE: Lorna!

LORNA: Poor Tom . . .

JOE: Poor Lorna! (*The rest is embrace and kiss and clutching each other.*)

ACT II

SCENE 3

SCENE: *The next day. The office as in Act I, Scene 1. LORNA and MOODY are present. She has a hangover and is restless.*

MOODY: Boy, you certainly double-Scotched yourself last night. What's the idea, you making a career of drinking in your old age? Headache?

LORNA: No.

MOODY: I won't let you walk alone in the park any more, if you do that.

LORNA (*nasty in spite of her best intentions*): Well, if you stayed away from your wife for a change . . .

MOODY: It's pretty late to bring that up, isn't it? Tuesday nights—

LORNA: I can't help it—I feel like a tramp. I've felt like a tramp for years.

MOODY: She was pretty friendly last night.

LORNA: Yeah? Did you sleep with her?

57

MOODY: What the hell's the matter with you, Lorna? (*He goes to her. She shrugs away from him.*)

LORNA: Keep off the grass! (MOODY *gives her a quizzical look, goes back to his desk and from there gives her another quizzical look.*)

MOODY: Why do you drink like that?

LORNA (*pointing to her chest*): Right here—there's a hard lump and I drink to dissolve it. Do you mind?

MOODY: I don't mind—as long as you keep your health.

LORNA: Aw, Christ!—you and your health talks!

MOODY: You're looking for a fight, dolly-girl!

LORNA: And you'll give it?

MOODY (*with a grin*): No, I'm feeling too good.

LORNA (*sitting wearily*): Who left you a fortune?

MOODY: Better. Monica's seen the light. The truth is she's begun to run around with a retired brewer and now *she* wants the divorce.

LORNA: Good, now she can begin paying *you*.

MOODY: She goes to Reno in a few months.

LORNA (*moodily*): I feel like a tramp. . . .

MOODY: That's what I'm telling you— In a few months we'll be married! (*He laughs with pleasure.*)

LORNA: You still want to marry me? Don't I feel like an old shoe to you?

MOODY (*coming to her*): Honest, you're so dumb!

LORNA (*touched by his boyishness*): You're so sweet. . . .

MOODY: And flash!—I signed Lombardo today! They meet six weeks from tonight.

LORNA: Goody. . . .

MOODY (*disappointed by her flippant reaction, but continuing*): I'm still not sure what he'll show with Lombardo. But my present worry is this: help me get that kid straight. Did you speak to him about the driving last night?

LORNA: I didn't see him. . . .

MOODY: It's very important. A Lombardo win clinches everything. In the fall we ride up to the Chocolate's door and dump him in the gutter! After that . . . I don't like to exaggerate—but the kid's primed! And you and I—Lorna baby, we're set. (*Happily.*) What do you think of that?

LORNA (*evasively*): You draw beautiful pictures. (*A knock sounds on the door.*)

MOODY: Come in. (SIGGIE *enters, dressed in cab-driver's garb.*)

SIGGIE: Hello, Miss Moon.

LORNA: Hello. You know Mr. Moody.

SIGGIE (*to* MOODY): Hello.

MOODY: What can we do for you?

SIGGIE: For me you can't do nothing. I'm sore. I'm here against my better instinct. (*Taking a roll of money from his pocket and slapping it on desk.*) He don't want it—no part of it! My father-in-law don't want it. Joe sent it up—two hundred bucks—enough to choke a horse—but he don't want it!

MOODY: Why?

LORNA: That's nice he remembers his folks.

SIGGIE: Listen, I got a father-in-law nothing's nice to him but feeding his horse and giving a laugh and slicing philosophical salami across the table! He's sore because Joe don't come home half the time. As a matter of fact, ain't he suppose to come to sleep no more? The old man's worried.

MOODY: That's not my concern.

SIGGIE: I can't see what it's such a worry. A boy gets in the higher brackets—what's the worry? He's got enough clothes now to leave three suits home in the closet. (*Turning to* LORNA.) It won't hurt if he sends me a few passes—tell him I said so.

LORNA: How's the wife?

SIGGIE: The Duchess? Still laughing.

LORNA: When you getting that cab?

SIGGIE: Do me a favor, Miss Moon—tell him I could use this wad for the first instalment.

LORNA: I'll tell him. Tell Mr. Bonaparte I saw Joe last night. He's fine.

MOODY: I'll see you get some passes.

SIGGIE: Thanks, thanks to both of you. Adios. (*He exits.*)

LORNA: He and his wife are crazy for each other. Married . . . they throw each other around, but they're like lovebirds. Marriage is something special. . . . I guess you have to deserve it.

MOODY: I thought you didn't see Joe last night.

LORNA: I didn't, but why worry his father?

MOODY: The hell with his father.

LORNA: The hell with you!

MOODY (*after a brooding pause*): I'll tell you something, Lorna. I'm not overjoyed the way Joe looks at you.

LORNA: How's he look?

MOODY: As if he saw the whole island of Manhattan in your face, and I don't like it.

LORNA: You thought of that too late.

MOODY: Too late for what?

LORNA: To bawl me out.

MOODY: Who's bawling you out?

LORNA: You were about to. Or warn me. I don't need warnings. (*Coasting away from the argument.*) If you saw Joe's father you'd like him.

MOODY: I saw him.

LORNA: If you knew him you'd like him.

MOODY: Who wantsa like him? What do I need him for? I don't like him and I don't like his son! It's a business—Joe does his work, I do mine. Like this telephone—I pay the bill and I use it!

LORNA: He's human. . . .

MOODY: What're we fighting about?

LORNA: We're fighting about love. I'm trying to tell you how cynical I am. Tell the truth, love doesn't last—

MOODY (*suddenly quietly serious*): Everything I said about Joe—the opposite goes for you. Love lasts . . . if you want it to. . . . I want it to last. I need it to last. What the hell's all this struggle to make a living for if not for a woman and a home? I don't kid myself. I know what I need. I need you, Lorna.

LORNA: It has to end. . . .

MOODY: What has to end?

LORNA: Everything.

MOODY: What're you talking about?

LORNA: I oughta burn. I'm leaving you. . . .

MOODY (*with a sick smile*): That's what you think.

LORNA (*not looking at him*): I mean it.

MOODY (*with the same sick smile*): I mean it too.

LORNA (*after looking at him for a moment*): You can't take a joke?

MOODY (*not knowing where he stands*): It all depends. . . . I don't like a joke that pushes the blood down in my feet.

LORNA (*coming to him and putting her arms around his neck*): That's true, you're pale.

MOODY: Who's the man?

LORNA (*heartsick, and unable to tell him the truth*): There's no man, Tom . . . even if there was, I couldn't leave you. (*She looks at him, unable to say more.*)

MOODY (*after a pause*): How about some lunch? I'll buy it. . . .

LORNA (*wearily*): Where would I put it, Tom?

MOODY (*impulsively*): In your hat! (*And suddenly he embraces her roughly and kisses her fully and she allows it. JOE walks into office, EDDIE FUSELI behind him. They break apart.*)

JOE: The first time I walked in here that was going on. It's one long duet around here.

MOODY: Hello.

EDDIE (*sardonically*): Hello, Partner. . . . (*LORNA is silent and avoids JOE's looks.*)

JOE: How about that fight with Lombardo?

MOODY: Six weeks from tonight.

JOE: He's gonna be surprised.

MOODY (*coolly*): No one doubts it.

JOE (*sharply*): I didn't say it was doubted!

MOODY: Boy, everyone's off his feed today. It started with the elevator boy—next it's Lorna—now it's you! What are *you* sore about?

LORNA (*trying to turn the conversation; to* JOE): Siggie was here looking for you. Your father's worried—

JOE: Not as much as my "manager" worries me.

MOODY: I don't need you to tell me how to run my business. I'll book the matches—

JOE: That doesn't worry me.

MOODY: But you and your speeding worries me! First it's music, then it's motors. Christ, next it'll be girls and booze!

JOE: It's girls already.

LORNA: Joe—

JOE (*bitterly*): Certainly! By the dozens!

EDDIE: Haha—that's a hot one. Don't ask me which is worst —women or spiders.

LORNA: Siggie left this money—your father won't take it. Siggie says buy him a cab— (JOE *takes money.*)

EDDIE: Your relative? I'll get him a cab. (*To* MOODY.) How about a flock of bouts for Bonaparte over the summer?

MOODY (*bitterly*): All he wants—practice fights—to make him a better "artiste."

EDDIE: That is what we like. (JOE *is looking at* LORNA.)

MOODY: "We?" Where do *I* come in?

EDDIE: You push the buttons, the *right* buttons. I wanna see Bonaparte with the crown.

MOODY (*sarcastically*): Your concern touches me deep in my heart!

EDDIE: What's the matter, Tom? You getting tired?

MOODY (*coolly*): I get tired, don't you?

EDDIE: Don't get tired, Tom . . . not in a crucial time.

MOODY: Get him to give up that Deusenberg.

EDDIE (*after looking at* JOE): That's his fun. . . .

MOODY: His fun might cost your crown.

JOE (*suddenly, to* LORNA): Why did you kiss him?

MOODY (*to* JOE): It's about time you shut your mouth and minded your own God damn business. Also, that you took some orders.

JOE (*suddenly savage*): Who are you, God?

MOODY: Yes! I'm your maker, you cockeyed gutter rat! Outa sawdust and spit I made you! I own you—without me you're a blank! Your insolence is gorgeous, but this is the end! I'm a son-of-a-gun! What're you so superior about?

EDDIE: Don't talk so quick, Tom. You don't know . . .

MOODY: I wouldn't take the crap of this last six-eight months from the President himself! Cut me up in little pieces, baby —but not me!

EDDIE (*quietly*): You could get cut up in little pieces.

MOODY (*retiring in disgust*): Sisst!

EDDIE: You hear me?

MOODY (*from his desk*): You wanna manage this boy? Help yourself—do it! I'll sell my piece for half of what it's worth. You wanna buy?

EDDIE: You arc a funny man.

MOODY: Gimme twenty thousand and lemme out. Ten, I'll take ten. I got my girl. I don't need crowns or jewels. I take my girl and we go sit by the river and it's everything.

JOE: What girl?

MOODY: I'm not on speaking terms with you! (*To* EDDIE.) Well?

EDDIE: It would be funny if your arms got broke.

JOE: Wait a minute! Lorna loves me and I love her.

MOODY (*after looking from* JOE *to* LORNA *and back*): Crazy as a bat! (*He laughs.*)

JOE (*frigidly*): Is it so impossible?

MOODY: About as possible as hell freezes over. (*He and* JOE *simultaneously turn to* LORNA.)

JOE: Tell him. . . .

LORNA (*looking* JOE *in the face.*) I love Tom. Tell him what? (JOE *looks at her intently. Silence.* JOE *then turns and quietly exits from the office.* MOODY *shakes his head with a grin.*)

MOODY: Eddie, I take everything back. I was a fool to get sore—that boy's a real Nutsy-Fagan! (*He offers his hand.* EDDIE *looks at it and then viciously slaps it down.*)

EDDIE (*repressing a trembling voice*): I don't like no one to laugh at that boy. You call a boy like that a rat? An educated boy? What is your idea to call him cockeyed? When you do it in front of me, I say, "Tom don't like himself" . . . for Bonaparte is a good friend to me . . . you're a clever manager for him. That's the only reason I take your slop. Do your business, Tom. (*To* LORNA.) And that goes for you, too! No tricks, Miss Moon! (*He slowly exits.* MOODY *stands there thoughtfully.* LORNA *moves to couch.*)

MOODY: I'm a son-of-a-gun!

LORNA: I feel like I'm shot from a cannon.

MOODY: Why?

LORNA: I'm sorry for him.

MOODY: Why? Because he's a queer?

LORNA: I'm not talking of Fuseli. (*Suddenly* LORNA'S *eyes flood with tears.* MOODY *takes her hand, half sensing the truth.*)

MOODY: What's wrong, Lorna? You can tell me. . . .

LORNA: I feel like the wrath of God.

MOODY: You like that boy, don't you?

LORNA: I love him, Tom.

ACT II

SCENE 4

SCENE: *Six weeks later.*

A dressing room before the Lombardo fight. There are a couple of rubbing tables in the room. There are some lockers and a few hooks on which hang pieces of clothing. A door to the left leads to the showers; a door to the right leads to the arena.

As the lights fade in, BONAPARTE *and* SIGGIE *are sitting to one side, on a long wooden bench.* TOKIO *is fussing around in a locker. A fighter,* PEPPER WHITE, *hands already*

bandaged, is being rubbed down by his trainer-manager,
MICKEY. *Throughout the scene is heard the distant roar of
the crowd and the clanging of the bell.*

BONAPARTE (*after a silence of intense listening*): What is
that noise?

SIGGIE: That's the roar of the crowd.

BONAPARTE: A thousand people?

SIGGIE: Six thousand.

PEPPER WHITE (*turning his head as he lies on his belly*):
Nine thousand.

SIGGIE: That's right, nine. You're sitting under nine thousand
people. Suppose they fell down on your head? Did you
ever think of that? (*The outside door opens,* EDDIE FUSELI
enters. The distant bell clangs.)

EDDIE (*looks around suspiciously—to* TOKIO): Where's Bonaparte?

TOKIO: Still with the newspapermen.

EDDIE (*unpleasantly surprised*): He's what?

TOKIO: Tom took him upstairs—some sports writers.

EDDIE: A half hour before a fight? What is Moody trying to
do?

TOKIO: Tom's the boss.

EDDIE: Looka, Tokio—in the future you are gonna take your
orders from me! (*Pointing to* SIGGIE *and* BONAPARTE.)
Who is this?

TOKIO: Joe's relatives.

EDDIE (*going over to them*): Is this his father?

BONAPARTE (*somberly*): Yes, thisa his father.

SIGGIE: And this is his brother-in-law. Joe sent passes up the
house. We just got here. I thought it was in Coney Island—
it's lucky I looked at the tickets. Believe it or not, the old
man never seen a fight in his life! Is it human?

EDDIE (*coldly*): Shut your mouth a minute! This is The Arena
—Bonaparte is fighting a good man tonight—

SIGGIE: Ahh, that Lombardo's a bag of oats!

EDDIE: When Bonaparte goes in there I like him to have one

65

thing on his mind—fighting! I hope you understand me. An' I don't like to find you here when I return! I hope you understand that. . . . (*After a full glance at them* EDDIE *gracefully exits.*)

SIGGIE: That's a positive personality!

TOKIO: That's Eddie Fuseli.

SIGGIE: Momma mia! No wonder I smelled gunpowder! (*Turning to* BONAPARTE.) Pop, that's a paradox in human behavior: he shoots you for a nickel—then for fifty bucks he sends you flowers!

TOKIO (*referring to distant bell*): That's the next bout.

SIGGIE (*to* BONAPARTE): Come on, we don't wanna miss the whole show.

BONAPARTE: I waita for Joe.

SIGGIE: You heard what Fuseli said—

BONAPARTE (*with somber stubbornness*): I gonna wait!

SIGGIE: Listen, Pop, you—

BONAPARTE (*with sudden force*): I say I gonna wait!

SIGGIE (*handing* BONAPARTE *a ticket*): Ticket. (*Shrugging.*) Good-by, you're letting flies in! (SIGGIE *exits jauntily.* BONAPARTE *silently watches* TOKIO *work over the fighter's materials. A* SECOND *comes in, puts a pail under table where* TOKIO *hovers, and exits.* PEPPER WHITE, *his head turned, watches* BONAPARTE *as he hums a song.*)

PEPPER:

Oh, Sweet Dardanella, I love your harem eyes,
Oh, Sweet Dardanella, I'm a lucky fellow to get
such a prize. . . .

(*To* BONAPARTE.) So you're Bonaparte's little boy, Buddy? Why didn't you say so before? Come over here and shake my hand. (BONAPARTE *does so.*) Tell Bonaparte I like to fight him.

BONAPARTE: Why?

PEPPER: I like to beat him up.

BONAPARTE (*naïvely, not amused*): Why? You don't like him?

PEPPER: Don't kid me, Buddy! (*A* CALL BOY *looks in at the door.*)

CALL BOY: Pepper White! Ready, Pepper White! (CALL BOY *exits.* PEPPER WHITE *slips off table and begins to change his shoes.*)

PEPPER (*to* BONAPARTE): When I get back I'll explain you all the ins and outs. (*A* SECOND *enters, takes a pail from* MICKEY *and exits.* LORNA *enters.* PEPPER, *indignantly.*) Who told girls to come in here?

LORNA: Modest? Close your eyes. Is Moody . . . ? (*Suddenly seeing* BONAPARTE.) Hello, Mr. Bonaparte!

BONAPARTE (*glad to see a familiar face*): Hello, hello, Missa Moon! Howa you feel?

LORNA: What brings you to this part of the world?

BONAPARTE (*somberly*): I come-a to see Joe. . . .

LORNA: Why, what's wrong?

BONAPARTE (*with a slow shrug*): He don't come-a to see me. . . .

LORNA: Does he know you're here?

BONAPARTE: No. (LORNA *looks at him sympathetically.*)

LORNA (*finally*): It's a three-ring circus, isn't it?

BONAPARTE: How you mean?

LORNA: Oh, I mean you . . . and him . . . and other people. . . .

BONAPARTE: I gonna see how he fight.

LORNA: I owe you a report. I wish I had good news for you, but I haven't.

BONAPARTE: Yes, I know . . . he gotta wild wolf inside—eat him up!

LORNA: You could build a city with his ambition to be somebody.

BONAPARTE (*sadly, shaking his head*): No . . . burn down! (*Now the outside door is thrust open—the distant bell clangs.* JOE *enters, behind him* MOODY *and* ROXY. JOE *stops in his tracks when he sees* LORNA *and his father together —the last two persons in the world he wants to see now. His hands are already bandaged, a bathrobe is thrown around his shoulders.*)

JOE: Hello, Poppa. . . .

BONAPARTE: Hello, Joe. . . .

JOE (*turning to* TOKIO): Throw out the girls—this isn't a hotel bedroom!

MOODY: That's no way to talk!

JOE (*coolly*): I talk as I please!

MOODY (*angrily*): The future Mrs. Moody—

JOE: I don't want her here!

LORNA: He's right, Tom. Why fight about it? (*She exits.*)

JOE (*to* MOODY): Also, I don't want to see writers again before a fight; it makes me nervous!

ROXY (*softly, for a wonder*): They're very important, Joe—

JOE: *I'm* important! My mind must be clear before I fight. I have to think before I go in. Don't you know that yet?

ROXY (*suddenly*): Yeah, we know—you're a stoodent—you gotta look in your notes.

JOE: What's funny about that? I do, *I do!*

ROXY (*retreating*): So I said you do! (PEPPER WHITE *comes forward, about to exit; to* MOODY.)

PEPPER: How 'bout a bout with Napoleon?

MOODY: On your way, louse!

PEPPER (*with a grin*): Pickin' setups? (JOE *suddenly turns and starts for* PEPPER. TOKIO *quickly steps in between the two boys.*)

TOKIO: Save it for the ring! (*The two fighters glare at each other.* JOE *slowly turns and starts back for the table.*)

PEPPER: You think he'll be the champ? Where'd you ever read about a cockeyed champ? (JOE *spins around, speeds across the room—*PEPPER *is on the floor!* MICKEY *now starts for* JOE. TOKIO *starts for* MICKEY. PEPPER *gets up off floor and finds himself occupied with* MOODY. *For a moment the fight is general.* EDDIE FUSELI *enters. All see him. The fighting magically stops on the second.*)

EDDIE: What'sa matter? Cowboys and Indians? (*To* PEPPER.) Out! (MICKEY *and* PEPPER *sullenly exit. To* MOODY.) I'm lookin' for you! You're a manager and a half! You and your fat friend! (*Meaning* ROXY.) You think this boy is a toy?

JOE: Eddie's the only one here who understands me.

Golden Boy

MOODY: Who the hell wantsa understand you! I got one wish—for Lombardo to give you the business! The quicker he taps you off tonight, the better! You gotta be took down a dozen pegs! I'm versus you! Completely versus!

EDDIE (*quietly, to* MOODY): Moody, your brains is in your feet! This is how you handle a coming champ, to give him the jitters before a bout? Go out and take some air! (*Seeing* EDDIE's *quiet deadliness,* MOODY *swallows his wrath and exits;* ROXY *follows with pursed lips.*)

EDDIE: Lay down, Joe—take it easy. (JOE *sits on a table.*) Who hurt you, Joe? Someone hurt your feelings?

JOE: Everything's all right.

EDDIE: Tokio, I put fifty bucks on Bonaparte's nose for you. It's my appreciation to you. . . .

TOKIO: Thanks.

EDDIE (*of* BONAPARTE): Whatta you want me to do with him?

JOE: Leave him here.

EDDIE: Tell me if you want something. . . .

JOE: Nothing.

EDDIE: Forget that Miss Moon. Stop lookin' down her dress. Go out there and kill Lombardo! Send him out to Woodlawn! Tear his skull off! . . . as I know Bonaparte can do it! (EDDIE *gives* BONAPARTE *a sharp look and exits. There is silence intensified by the distant clang of the bell and the muted roar of the crowd.* TOKIO *looks over at* BONAPARTE *who has been silently seated on bench all this time.*)

JOE (*not quite knowing what to say*): How is Anna, Poppa?

BONAPARTE: Fine.

JOE: Siggie watching the fights?

BONAPARTE: Yes. . . .

JOE: You look fine. . . .

BONAPARTE: Yes, feela good. . . .

JOE: Why did you send that money back? (*There is no answer.*) Why did you come here? . . . You sit there like my conscience. . . .

BONAPARTE: Why you say so?

69

Joe: Poppa, I have to fight, no matter what you say or think!
This is my profession! I'm out for fame and fortune, not
to be different or artistic! I don't intend to be ashamed of
my life!

Bonaparte (*standing up*): Yeah, I understanda you. . . .

Joe: Go out and watch the fights.

Bonaparte (*somberly*): Yeah . . . you fight. Now I know
. . . is'a too late for music. The men musta be free an'
happy for music . . . not like-a you. Now I see whatta you
are . . . I give-a you every word to fight . . . I sorry for
you. . . . (*Silence. The distant roar of the crowd climbs up
and falls down; the bell clangs again.*)

Tokio (*gently*): I'll have to ask you to leave, Mr. Bonaparte. . . .

Bonaparte (*holding back his tears*): Joe . . . I hope-a you
win every fight. (Bonaparte *slowly exits. As he opens
and closes the door the roar of the crowd swells up for
an instant.*)

Tokio: Lay down, Joe. There's five minutes left to tune you up.

Joe (*in a low voice*): That's right, tune me up. . . . (Joe
stretches out on his stomach and Tokio's *busy hands start
up the back of his legs.*)

Tokio (*working with steady briskness*): I never worried less
about a boy . . . in my life. You're a real sweetheart. . . .
(*Suddenly* Joe *begins to cry in his arms.* Tokio *looks
down, momentarily hesitates in his work—then slowly goes
ahead with his massaging hands. The* Boy *continues to
shake with silent sobs. Again the bell clangs in the distance. In a soft caressing voice.*) You're getting good, honey.
Maybe I never told you that before. I seen it happen before. (*Continuing the massaging.*) It seems to happen
sudden—a fighter gets good. He gets easy and graceful. He
learns how to save himself—no energy wasted . . . he
slips and slides—he travels with the punch. . . . Oh, sure,
I like the way you're shaping up. (Tokio *continues massaging.* Joe *is silent. His sobbing stops. After a moment*
Tokio *continues.*) What was you saying about Lombardo's

Golden Boy

trick? I understood you to say he's a bull's-eye for a straight shot from the inside. I think you're right, Joe, but that kind of boy is liable to meet you straight-on in a clinch and give you the back of his head under the chin. Watch out for that.

JOE: He needs a straight punch. . . . (JOE *suddenly sits up on table, his legs dangling.*) Now I'm alone. They're all against me—Moody, the girl . . . you're my family now, Tokio—you and Eddie! I'll show them all—nobody stands in my way! My father's had his hand on me for years. No more. No more for her either—she had her chance! When a bullet sings through the air it has no past—only a future— like me! Nobody, nothing stands in my way! (*In a sudden spurt of feeling* JOE *starts sparring around lightly in a shadow-boxing routine.* TOKIO *smiles with satisfaction. Now the roar of the crowd reaches a frenzied shriek and hangs there. The bell clangs rapidly several times. The roar of the crowd settles down again.*)

TOKIO: That sounds like the kill. (JOE *draws his bathrobe around him and prances on his toes.*)

JOE: I'm a new boy tonight! I could take two Lombardos! (*Vigorously shaking out his bandaged hands above his head.*) Hallelujah! We're on the Millionaire Express to-night! Nobody gets me! (*The door is thrust open and a* CALL BOY *shouts.*)

CALL BOY: Bonaparte, ready. Bonaparte, ready. (PEPPER WHITE *and* MICKEY *enter as the* CALL BOY *speeds away.* PEPPER *is flushed with victory.*)

PEPPER (*to* JOE): Tell me when you want it; you can have it the way I just give it to Pulaski! (JOE *looks* PEPPER *in the face, flexes his hands several times and suddenly breaks out in laughter, to* PEPPER's *astonishment.* JOE *and* TOKIO *exit.* PEPPER *throws off his robe and displays his body.*) Look me over—not a mark. How do you like that for class! I'm in a hurry to grab a cab to Flushing.

MICKEY (*impassively*): Keep away from her.

PEPPER: I don't even hear you.

MICKEY: Keep away from her!

PEPPER: I go for her like a bee and the flower.

MICKEY (*in a droning prophetic voice*): The flower is married. Her husband is an excitable Armenian from the Orient. There will be hell to pay! Keep away from her! (*Now in the distance is heard the indistinct high voice of the announcer.*)

PEPPER: You oughta get me a fight with that cockeyed Napoleon—insteada sticking your nose where it don't belong! I could slaughter him in next to nothing.

MICKEY (*impassively*): If you could make his weight and slaughter him, you'd be the next world's champ. But you can't make his weight, you can't slaughter him, and you can't be the champ. Why the hell don't you take a shower? (*The bell clangs—in the arena,* JOE'S *fight is on.*)

PEPPER (*plaintively, beginning to dress at his locker*): If my girl don't like me without a shower, I'll tell her a thing or two.

MICKEY: If her husband don't tell you first. (*The roar of the crowd swells up as the door opens and* BONAPARTE *enters. He is unusually agitated. He looks at* PEPPER *and* MICKEY *and sits on a bench. The roar of the crowd mounts higher than before, then drops.*)

PEPPER (*to* BONAPARTE): What's the matter with you?

BONAPARTE (*shaking his head*): Don't like to see . . .

PEPPER (*delighted*): Why? Your boy gettin' smeared?

BONAPARTE: They fighta for money, no?

MICKEY: No, they're fighting for a noble cause—

BONAPARTE: If they wasa fight for cause or for woman, woulda not be so bad.

PEPPER (*still dressing behind locker door*): I fight for money and I like it. I don't fight for under a thousand bucks. Do I, Mickey?

MICKEY: Nope.

PEPPER (*boasting naïvely*): I didn't fight for under a thousand for five years. Did I, Mickey?

MICKEY (*impassively*): Nope.

72

PEPPER: I get a thousand bucks tonight, don't I?

MICKEY: Nope.

PEPPER (*up like a shot*): How much? How much tonight?

MICKEY: Twelve hundred bucks.

PEPPER: What? Mickey, I oughta bust you in the nose. How many times do I have to say I don't fight for under one thousand bucks! (*To* BONAPARTE.) Now you see what I'm up against with this manager!

MICKEY (*impassively*): Okay, you'll get a thousand.

PEPPER: I better, Buddy! That's all I say—I better! (*To* BONAPARTE.) I tell him I want to fight your kid and he don't lift a finger. (*The roar of the crowd crescendos and drops down again.*)

MICKEY: You don't rate no fight with Bonaparte. (*To* BONAPARTE, *of* PEPPER.) He's an old man, a fossil!

BONAPARTE: Who?

MICKEY: Him—he's twenty-nine.

BONAPARTE: Old?

MICKEY: In this business, twenty-nine is ancient.

PEPPER: My girl don't think so.

MICKEY: Keep away from her. (*The roar of the crowd mounts up to a devilish shriek.*)

PEPPER: Wow, is your boy getting schlocked!

BONAPARTE: My boy isa win.

PEPPER: Yeah, and that's why you ran away?

BONAPARTE: Whatta the difference who's-a win? Is terrible to see!

PEPPER (*grinning*): If I wasn't in a hurry, I'd wait around to help pick up your little Joey's head off the floor. (*He draws on a sport shirt.*)

MICKEY (*to* PEPPER): What are you wearing a polo shirt on a winter night for?

PEPPER: For crying out loud, I just bought it! So long, Mr. Bonaparte.

BONAPARTE: I aska you please—whatta happen to a boy's hands when he fight a longa time?

73

PEPPER (*holding up his fists*): Take a look at mine—I got a good pair. See those knuckles? Flat!

BONAPARTE: Broke?

PEPPER: Not broke, flat—pushed down!

BONAPARTE: Hurt?

PEPPER: You get used to it.

BONAPARTE: Can you use them?

PEPPER: Go down the hall and look at Pulaski.

BONAPARTE: Can you open theesa hands?

PEPPER: What for?

BONAPARTE (*gently touching the fists*): So strong, so hard . . .

PEPPER: You said it, Buddy. So long, Buddy. (*To* MICKEY.) Take my stuff.

MICKEY: Sam'll take it after. Keep away from her. (PEPPER *looks at* MICKEY *with a sardonic grin and exits followed by* MICKEY.)

BONAPARTE (*to himself*): So strong . . . so useless . . . (*The roar of the crowd mounts up and calls for a kill.* BONAPARTE *trembles. For a moment he sits quietly on the bench. Then he goes to the door of the shower room and looks around at the boxing paraphernalia. In the distance the bell begins to clang repeatedly.* BONAPARTE *stares in the direction of the arena. He goes to the exit door. The crowd is cheering and howling.* BONAPARTE *hesitates a moment at the door and then rapidly walks back to the bench, where he sits. Head cocked, he listens for a moment. The roar of the crowd is heated, demanding and hateful. Suddenly* BONAPARTE *jumps to his feet. He is in a murderous mood. He shakes his clenched fist in the direction of the noise— he roars aloud. The roar of the crowd dies down. The door opens,* PEPPER'S *second,* SAM, *enters, softly whistling to himself. Deftly he begins to sling together* PEPPER'S *paraphernalia.*) What'sa happen in the fight?

SAM: Knockout.

BONAPARTE: Who?

SAM: Lombardo's stiff. (BONAPARTE *slowly sits. Softly whis-*

74

tling, SAM *exits with the paraphernalia. The outside door
is flung open. In come* JOE, TOKIO, MOODY *and* ROXY, *who
is elated beyond sanity.* JOE's *eyes glitter, his face is hard
and flushed. He has won by a knockout.*)

ROXY (*almost dancing*): My boy! My darling boy! My dear
darling boy! (*Silently* JOE *sits on the edge of the table,
ignoring his father after a glance. His robe drops from his
shoulders.* ROXY *turns to* MOODY.) How do you like it,
Tom? He knocks him out in two rounds!

MOODY (*stiffly, to* JOE): It's good business to call the sports
writers in—

ROXY: That's right, give a statement! (MOODY *gives* JOE *a
rapid glance and hurriedly exits.*) I'm collecting a bet on
you. All my faith and patience is rewarded. (*As he opens
the door he almost knocks over* EDDIE FUSELI.) Haha! How
do you like it, Eddie? Haha! (*He exits.* EDDIE FUSELI
closes the door and stands with his back to it. TOKIO *moves
to* JOE *and begins to remove a glove.*)

TOKIO (*gently*): You're a real sweetheart. . . . (TOKIO *removes the sweaty glove and begins to fumble with the
lace of the other one.* JOE *carefully moves this glove out
of* TOKIO's *reach, resting it on his opposite arm.*)

JOE (*almost proudly*): Better cut it off. . . . (BONAPARTE *is
watching tensely.* EDDIE *watches from the door.*)

TOKIO: Broke?

JOE (*holding the hand out proudly*): Yes, it's broke. . . .
(TOKIO *slowly reaches for a knife. He begins carefully to
cut the glove.*) Hallelujah!! It's the beginning of the world!
(BONAPARTE, *lips compressed, slowly turns his head away.*
EDDIE *watches with inner excitement and pleasure;* JOE
has become a fighter. TOKIO *continues with his work.* JOE
*begins to laugh loudly, victoriously, exultantly—with a deep
thrill of satisfaction.*)

Act III

Scene 1

SCENE: Moody's *office, same as Act I, Scene 1, six months later.*

Present *are* Moody, *acting the persuasive salesman with two sports writers,* Drake *and* Lewis; Roxy Gottlieb *being helpful in his usual manner;* Tokio, *to one side, characteristically quiet . . . and* Joe Bonaparte. Joe *sits on desk and diffidently swings his legs as he eats a sandwich. His success has added a certain bellicosity to his attitude, it has changed his clothing to silk shirts and custom-made suits.*

Moody: He's got his own style. He won't rush—

Roxy: Nobody claims our boy's Niagara Falls.

Drake (*a newspaperman for twenty years*): Except himself!

Moody: You newspaper boys are right.

Drake: We newspaper boys are always right!

Moody: He won't take chances tomorrow night if he can help it. He'll study his man, pick out flaws—then shoot at them.

Joe (*casually*): It won't matter a helluva lot if I win late in the bout or near the opening. The main thing with Bonaparte is to win.

Drake (*dryly*): Well, what does Bonaparte expect to do tomorrow night?

Joe (*as dryly*): Win.

Moody: Why shouldn't we have a win from the Chocolate Drop? Look at our record!

Lewis (*good-natured and slow*): We just wanna get an impression—

76

MOODY: Seventeen knockouts? Fulton, Lombardo, Guffy Talbot—?

JOE: Phil Weiner . . .

MOODY: Weiner?

ROXY: That's no powder-puff hitter!

LEWIS: In this fight tomorrow night, can you name the round?

JOE: Which round would you like?

DRAKE: You're either a genius or an idiot!

MOODY: Joe don't mean—

DRAKE (*sharply*): Let him talk for himself.

JOE (*getting off the desk*): Listen, Drake, I'm not the boy I used to be—the honeymoon's over. I don't blush and stammer these days. Bonaparte goes in and slugs with the best. In the bargain his brain is *better* than the best. That's the truth; why deny it?

DRAKE: The last time you met Chocolate you never even touched him!

JOE: It's almost two years since I "never even touched him." Now I know how!

MOODY: What Joe means to say—

DRAKE: He's the genuine and only modest cockeyed wonder!

JOE: What good is modesty? I'm a fighter! The whole essence of prize fighting is immodesty! "I'm better than you are— I'll prove it by breaking your face in!" What do you expect? A conscience and a meek smile? I don't believe that bull that the meek'll inherit the earth!

DRAKE: Oh, so it's the earth you want!

JOE: I know what I want—that's my business! But I don't want your guff!

DRAKE: I have two sons of my own—I like boys. But I'm a son-of-a-bitch if I can stomach your conceit!

MOODY (*trying to save the situation*): They serve a helluva rum Collins across the street—

DRAKE: Bonaparte, I'll watch for Waterloo with more than interest.

MOODY: Why don't we run across for a drink? How 'bout some drinks?

77

DRAKE: Tom, you can buy me twenty drinks and I still won't change my mind about him. (*He exits.*)

LEWIS (*smiling*): You're all right, Bonaparte.

JOE: Thanks. . . .

LEWIS (*clinching a cigarette at desk*): How's that big blonde of yours, Tom?

MOODY: Fine.

LEWIS: How does she feel about the wedding bells? Sunday is it? (*This is news to* JOE, *and* MOODY *knows it is.*)

MOODY (*nervously*): Happy, the way I am. Yeah, Sunday.

ROXY: How about the drinks? We'll drink to everybody's health!

LEWIS (*to* JOE): Good luck tomorrow.

JOE: Thanks. . . . (*They exit,* MOODY *throwing a resentful look at* JOE. JOE *and* TOKIO *are left. In the silence* JOE *goes back to the remains of his lunch.*)

TOKIO: That Drake is a case.

JOE (*pushing food away*): They don't make cheesecake the way they used to when I was a boy. Or maybe I don't like it any more. When are they getting married?

TOKIO: Moody? Sunday.

JOE: Those writers hate me.

TOKIO: You give them too much lip.

JOE (*looking down at his clenched fists*): I'd rather give than take it. That's one reason I became a fighter. When did Moody get his divorce?

TOKIO: Few weeks ago . . . (*Cannily.*) Why don't you forget Lorna?

JOE (*as if not understanding*): What?

TOKIO: I'll say it again . . . why not forget her? (*No answer comes.*) Joe, you're loaded with love. Find something to give it to. Your heart ain't in fighting . . . your *hate* is. But a man with hate and nothing else . . . he's half a man . . . and half a man . . . is no man. Find something to love, or someone. Am I stepping on your toes?

JOE (*coldly*): I won't be unhappy if you mind your business.

78

TOKIO: Okay. . . . (TOKIO *goes to door, stops there.*) Watch your dinner tonight. No girls either.

JOE: Excuse me for saying that—

TOKIO (*with a faint smile*): Okay. (TOKIO *opens door and* LORNA MOON *enters.* TOKIO *smiles at her and exits. She carries a pack of newspapers under her arm.* JOE *and she do not know what to say to each other—they wish they had not met here.* LORNA *crosses and puts newspapers on desk. She begins to bang through desk drawers, looking for scissors.*)

JOE: I hear you're making the leap tomorrow. . . .

LORNA: Sunday . . .

JOE: Sunday. (*Intense silence.*)

LORNA (*to say anything*): I'm looking for the scissors. . . .

JOE: Who're you cutting up today?

LORNA (*bringing out shears*): Items on Bonaparte, for the press book. (*She turns and begins to unfold and clip a sheet of newspaper.* JOE *is at a loss for words.*)

JOE (*finally*): Congratulations. . . .

LORNA (*without turning*): Thanks. . . . (*In a sudden irresistible surge* JOE *tears papers out of* LORNA's *hands and hurls them behind desk. The two stand facing each other.*)

JOE: When I speak to you, look at me!

LORNA: What would you like to say? (*They stand face to face, straining.*)

JOE (*finally*): Marry anyone you like!

LORNA: Thanks for permission!

JOE: Queen Lorna, the tramp of Newark!

LORNA: You haven't spoken to me for months. Why break your silence?

JOE: You're a historical character for me—dead and buried!

LORNA: Then everything's simple; go about your business.

JOE: Moody's right for you—perfect—the mating of zero and zero!

LORNA: I'm not sorry to marry Tom—

JOE (*scornfully*): That's from the etiquette book—page twelve: "When you marry a man say you like it!"

LORNA: I know I could do worse when I look at you. When did you look in the mirror last? Getting to be a killer! You're getting to be like Fuseli! You're not the boy I cared about, not you. You murdered that boy with the generous face— God knows where you hid the body! I don't know you.

JOE: I suppose I never kissed your mouth—

LORNA: What do you want from me? Revenge? Sorry—we're all out of revenge today!

JOE: I wouldn't look at you twice if they hung you naked from a Christmas tree! (*At this moment* EDDIE FUSELI *enters with a pair of packages. He looks intently at* LORNA, *then crosses and puts packages on desk. He and* JOE *are dressed almost identically.* LORNA *exits without a word.* EDDIE *is aware of what has happened but begins to talk casually about the packages.*)

EDDIE: This one's your new headgear. This is shirts from Jacobs Brothers. He says the neckbands are gonna shrink, so I had him make sixteens—they'll fit you after one washing. (*Holding up a shirt.*) You like that color?

JOE: Thanks.

EDDIE: Your brother-in-law drove me over. Picked him up on 49th. Don't you ever see them no more?

JOE (*sharply*): What for?

EDDIE: What'sa matter?

JOE: Why? You see a crowd around here, Eddie?

EDDIE: No.

JOE: That's right, you don't! But I do! I see a crowd of Eddies all around me, suffocating me, burying me in good times and silk shirts!

EDDIE (*dialing phone*): You wanna go to the *Scandals* tonight? I got tickets. (*Into telephone.*) Charley? Fuseli is speaking. . . . I'm giving four to five on Bonaparte tomorrow. . . . Four G's worth . . . yes. (*Hanging up phone.*) It's gonna be a good fight tomorrow.

JOE (*belligerently*): How do you know?

EDDIE: I know Bonaparte. I got eighteen thousand spread out on him tomorrow night.

JOE: Suppose Bonaparte loses?

EDDIE: I look at the proposition from all sides—I know he'll win.

JOE: What the hell do you think I am? A machine? Maybe I'm lonely, maybe—

EDDIE: You wanna walk in a parade? Everybody's lonely. Get the money and you're not so lonely.

JOE: I want some personal life.

EDDIE: I give Bonaparte a good personal life. I got loyalty to his cause. . . .

JOE: You use me like a gun! Your loyalty's to keep me oiled and polished!

EDDIE: A year ago Bonaparte was a rookie with a two-pants suit. Now he wears the best, eats the best, sleeps the best. He walks down the street respected—the golden boy! They howl their heads off when Bonaparte steps in the ring . . . and I done it for him!

JOE: There are other things. . . .

EDDIE: There's no other things! Don't think so much—it could make you very sick! You're in this up to your neck. You owe me a lot—I don't like you to forget. You better be on your toes when you step in that ring tomorrow night. (EDDIE *turns and begins to dial phone.*)

JOE: Your loyalty makes me shiver. (JOE *starts for door.*)

EDDIE: Take the shirts.

JOE: What do I want them for? I can only wear one at a time. . . . (EDDIE *speaks into phone.*)

EDDIE: Meyer? . . . Fuseli is speaking. . . . I'm giving four to five on Bonaparte tomorrow. . . . Two? . . . Yeah. (*About to exit,* JOE *stands at the door and watches* EDDIE *as he calmly begins to dial phone again.*)

ACT III

SCENE 2

SCENE: *The next night.*

The lights fade in on an empty stage. We are in the same dressing room as seen in Act II, Scene 4. Far in the distance is heard the same roar of the crowd. The distant bell clangs menacingly. The room is shadows and patches of light. The silence here has its own ugly dead quality.

LORNA MOON *enters. She looks around nervously, she lights a cigarette; this reminds her to rouge her lips; she puffs the cigarette. The distant bell clangs again.* EDDIE FUSELI *enters, pale and tense. He sees* LORNA *and stops short in his tracks. There is an intense silence as they look at each other.*

LORNA: How's the fight?

EDDIE: I like to talk to you.

LORNA: Is Joe still on his feet?

EDDIE: Take a month in the country, Miss Moon.

LORNA: Why?

EDDIE (*repressing a murderous mood*): Give the boy . . . or move away.

LORNA: I get married tomorrow. . . .

EDDIE: You heard my request—give him or go!

LORNA: Don't Moody count?

EDDIE: If not for Bonaparte they'd find you in a barrel long ago—in the river or a bush!

LORNA: I'm not afraid of you. . . . (*The distant bell clangs.*)

EDDIE (*after turning his head and listening*): That's the beginning of the eighth. Bonaparte's unsettled—fighting like

82

a drunken sailor. He can't win no more, unless he knocks the Chocolate out. . . .

LORNA (*at a complete loss*): Don't look at me . . . what'd you . . . I . . .

EDDIE: Get outa town! (*The roar of the crowd mounts to a demand for a kill.* EDDIE, *listening intently.*) He's like a bum tonight . . . and a bum done it! You! (*The roar grows fuller.*) I can't watch him get slaughtered. . . .

LORNA: I couldn't watch it myself. (*The bell clangs loudly several times. The roar of the crowd hangs high in the air.*) What's happening now?

EDDIE: Someone's getting murdered. . . .

LORNA: It's me. . . .

EDDIE (*quietly, intensely*): That's right . . . if he lost . . . the trees are ready for your coffin. (*The roar of the crowd tones down.*) You can go now. I don't wanna make a scandal around his name. . . . I'll find you when I want you. Don't be here when they carry him in.

LORNA (*at a complete loss*): Where do you want me to go?

EDDIE (*suddenly releasing his wrath*): Get outa my sight! You turned down the sweetest boy who ever walked in shoes! You turned him down, the golden boy, that king among the ju-ven-iles! He gave you his hand—you spit in his face! You led him on like Gertie's whoore! You sold him down the river! And now you got the nerve to stand here, to wait and see him bleeding from the mouth!

LORNA: Fuseli, for God's sake—

EDDIE: Get outa my sight!

LORNA: Fuseli, please—

EDDIE: Outa my sight, you nickel whoore! (*Completely enraged and out of control,* EDDIE *half brings his gun out from under his left armpit.* JOE *appears in doorway. Behind him are* ROXY, MOODY *and a* SECOND.)

JOE: Eddie! (EDDIE *whirls around. The others enter the room. In the ensuing silence,* MOODY, *sensing what has happened, crosses to* LORNA.)

LORNA (*quietly*): What happened?

ROXY: What happened? (*He darts forward and picks up* JOE's *arm in the sign of victory. The arm drops back limply.*) The monarch of the masses!

EDDIE (*to the* SECOND): Keep everybody out. Only the newspaper boys. (*The* SECOND *exits and closes the door.* JOE *sits on a table. Physically he is a very tired boy. There is a high puff under one eye; the other is completely closed. His body is stained with angry splotches.*)

TOKIO (*gently*): I have to hand it to you, Joe. . . .

ROXY (*explaining to the frigid* EDDIE, *elaborately*): The beginning of the eighth: first the bell! Next the Chocolate Drop comes out like a waltz clog, confident. Oh, he was so confident! Haha! The next thing I know the Chocolate's on the floor, the referee lifts our arm, we got on our bathrobe and we're here in the dressing room! How do you like it?

EDDIE (*narrowly*): I like it.

TOKIO (*taking off* JOE's *gloves*): I'll have you feelin' better in a minute. (*He cuts the tapes.*)

JOE: I feel all right.

EDDIE (*to* TOKIO): Gimme his gloves.

MOODY (*wary of* JOE): That's a bad lump under your eye.

JOE: Not as bad as the Chocolate Drop got when he hit the floor!

ROXY: Darling, how you gave it to him! Not to my enemies!

JOE: 'Twas a straight right—with no trimmings or apologies! Aside from fouling me in the second and fifth—

MOODY: I called them on it—

ROXY: I seen the bastard—

JOE: That second time I nearly went through the floor. I gave him the fury of a lifetime in that final punch! (EDDIE *has taken the soggy boxing gloves for his own property.* TOKIO *is daubing the bruise under* JOE's *eye.*) And did you hear them cheer! (*Bitterly, as if reading a news report.*) Flash! As thousands cheer, that veritable whirlwind Bonaparte—that veritable cockeyed wonder, Bonaparte—he comes from behind in the eighth stanza to slaughter the

84

Chocolate Drop and clinch a bout with the champ! Well, how do you like me, boys? Am I good or am I good?

Roxy: Believe *me!*

Tokio (*attempting to settle* Joe): You won the right for a crack at the title. You won it fair and clean. Now lay down. . . .

Joe (*in a vehement outburst*): I'd like to go outside my weight and beat up the whole damn world!

Moody (*coldly*): Well, the world's your oyster now!

Tokio (*insistently*): Take it easy. Lemme fix that eye, Joe— (*Now a bustling little Irishman,* Driscoll, *hustles into the room.*)

Driscoll: Who's got the happy boy's gloves?

Eddie: Here . . . why? (Driscoll *rapidly takes gloves, "breaks" and examines them.*)

Tokio: What's the matter, Drisc?

Joe: What's wrong?

Driscoll (*handing the gloves back to* Eddie): Chocolate's a sick boy. Your hands are clean. (Driscoll *hustles for the door.* Joe *is up and to him.*)

Joe: What happened?

Driscoll (*bustling*): It looks like the Pride of Baltimore is out for good. Change your clothes.

Joe: How do you mean?

Driscoll: Just like I said—out! (Driscoll *pats* Joe's *shoulder, hustles out, closing door in* Joe's *face.* Joe *slowly sits on the nearest bench. Immediately* Tokio *comes to him, as tender as a mother.*)

Tokio: You didn't foul him—you're a clean fighter. You're so honest in the ring it's stupid. If something's happened, it's an accident. (*The others stand around stunned, not knowing what to do or say.*)

Moody (*very worried*): That's right, there's nothing to worry about.

Roxy (*very worried*): That's right. . . .

Joe: Gee . . . (Joe *stands up, slowly crosses the room and*

sits on the table, head in his hands, his back to the others.
No one knows what to say.)

EDDIE: (*to* MOODY): Go out there and size up the situation.
(MOODY, *glad of the opportunity to leave the room, turns*
to the door which is suddenly violently thrust open.
BARKER, *the* CHOCOLATE DROP'S *manager, pushes* MOODY
into the room with him, leaving door open. From outside
a small group of curious people look in. BARKER, *bereft of*
his senses, grabs MOODY *by the coat lapel.*)

BARKER: Do you know it? Do you know it?

MOODY: Now wait a minute, Barker— (BARKER *runs over to*
JOE *and screams.*)

BARKER: You murdered my boy! He's dead! You killed him!

TOKIO (*getting between* JOE *and* BARKER): Just a minute!

BARKER (*literally wringing his hands*): He's dead! Chocolate's dead!

TOKIO: We're very sorry about it. Now pull yourself together.
(EDDIE *crosses room and slams door shut as* BARKER *points*
an accusing finger at JOE *and screams.*)

BARKER: This dirty little wop killed my boy!

EDDIE (*coming to* BARKER): Go back in your room.

BARKER: Yes, he did! (EDDIE'S *answer is to shove* BARKER
roughly toward door, weeping.) Yes, he did!

EDDIE: Get out before I slug your teeth apart!

JOE (*jumping to his feet*): Eddie, for God sakes, don't hit
him! Let him alone! (EDDIE *immediately desists.* BARKER
stands there, a weeping idiot.)

MOODY: Accidents can happen.

BARKER: I know . . . know. . . .

MOODY: Chocolate fouled us twice.

BARKER: I know, I know. . . . (BARKER *stammers, gulps and*
tries to say something more. Suddenly he dashes out of the
room. There is a long silent pause during which JOE *sits*
down again.)

EDDIE: We'll have to wait for an investigation.

TOKIO (*to* JOE): Don't blame yourself for nothing. . . .

JOE: That poor guy . . . with those sleepy little eyes. . . .

ROXY (*solemnly*): It's in the hands of God, a thing like that. (LEWIS, *the sports writer, tries to enter the room.*)

EDDIE (*herding him out*): Stay outside. (*To* MOODY.) See what's happening? (MOODY *immediately leaves.*) Everybody out—leave Bonaparte to calm hisself. I'll watch the door.

TOKIO: Don't worry, Joe. (*He exits, followed by* ROXY. EDDIE *turns and looks at* LORNA.)

EDDIE: You too, Miss Moon—this ain't no cocktail lounge.

LORNA: I'll stay here. (EDDIE *looks at her sharply, shifts his glance from her to* JOE *and back again; he exits.*) Joe . . .

JOE: Gee, that poor boy . . .

LORNA (*holding herself off*): But it wasn't your fault.

JOE: That's right—it wasn't my fault!

LORNA: You didn't mean it!

JOE: That's right—I didn't mean it! I wouldn't want to do that, would I? Everybody knows I wouldn't want to kill a man. Lorna, you know it!

LORNA: Of course!

JOE: But I *did* it! That's the thing—I *did* it! What will my father say when he hears I murdered a man? Lorna, I see what I did. I murdered myself, too! I've been running around in circles. Now I'm smashed! That's the truth. Yes, I was a real sparrow, and I wanted to be a fake eagle! But now I'm hung up by my finger tips—I'm no good—my feet are off the earth!

LORNA (*in a sudden burst, going to* JOE): Joe, I love you! We love each other. Need each other!

JOE: Lorna darling, I see what's happened!

LORNA: You wanted to conquer the world—

JOE: Yes—

LORNA: But it's not the kings and dictators who do it—it's that kid in the park—

JOE: Yes, that boy who might have said, "I have myself; I am what I want to be!"

LORNA: And now, tonight, here, this minute—finding yourself again—that's what makes you a champ. Don't you see that?

JOE: Yes, Lorna—yes!

LORNA: It isn't too late to tell the world good evening again!

JOE: With what? These fists?

LORNA: Give up the fighting business!

JOE: Tonight!

LORNA: Yes, and go back to your music—

JOE: But my hands are ruined. I'll never play again! What's left, Lorna? Half a man, nothing, useless . . .

LORNA: No, *we're* left! Two together! We have each other! Somewhere there must be happy boys and girls who can teach us the way of life! We'll find some city where poverty's no shame—where music is no crime!—where there's no war in the streets—where a man is glad to be himself, to live and make his woman herself!

JOE: No more fighting, but where do we go?

LORNA: Tonight? Joe, we ride in your car. We speed through the night, across the park, over the Triboro Bridge—

JOE (*taking* LORNA'S *arms in his trembling hands*): Ride! That's it, we ride—clear my head. We'll drive through the night. When you mow down the night with headlights, nobody gets you! You're on top of the world then—nobody laughs! That's it—speed! We're off the earth—unconnected! We don't have to think! That's what speed's for, an easy way to live! Lorna darling, we'll burn up the night! (*He turns and begins to throw his street clothes out of his locker.*)

ACT III

SCENE 3

SCENE: *Late the same night.*

In the Bonaparte home, same as Act I, Scene 2, sit EDDIE
FUSELI, MOODY, ROXY *and* SIGGIE, *drinking homemade
wine, already half drunk.* BONAPARTE *stands on the other
side of the room, looking out of the window.* FRANK *sits
near him, a bandage around his head.*

MOODY *is at telephone as the lights fade in.*

MOODY (*impatiently*): . . . 'lo? Hello!

SIGGIE: I'll tell you why we need another drink. . . .

ROXY: No, I'll tell you. . . .

MOODY (*turning*): Quiet! For pete's sake! I can't hear myself
think! (*Turning to phone.*) Hello? This is Moody. Any
calls for me? Messages? No sign of Miss Moon? Thanks.
Call me if she comes in—the number I gave you before.
(*Hanging up and returning to his wine glass; to* BONA-
PARTE.) I thought you said Joe was coming up here!

BONAPARTE: I say maybe. . . .

MOODY (*sitting*): I'll wait another fifteen minutes. (*He
drinks.*)

SIGGIE: Here's why we need another drink; it's a night of
success! Joe's in those lofty brackets from now on! We're
gonna move to a better neighborhood, have a buncha kids!
(*To* BONAPARTE.) Hey, Pop, I wish we had a mortgage so
we could pay it off! To the next champ of the world!
(SIGGIE *lifts his glass; the others join him.*)

ROXY: Bonaparte.

EDDIE: Don't you drink, Mr. Bonaparte?

89

SIGGIE: You, too, Frank—it's all in the family. (BONAPARTE *shrugs and comes forward, accepting a glass.*)

ROXY: It's in the nature of a celebration!

BONAPARTE: My son'sa kill a man tonight—what'sa celebrate? What'sa gonna be, heh?

SIGGIE: Ahh, don't worry—they can't do him nothing for that! An accident!

EDDIE (*coldly, to* BONAPARTE): Listen, it's old news. It's been out on the front page two-three hours.

BONAPARTE: Poor color' boy . . .

MOODY: Nobody's fault. Everybody's sorry—we give the mother a few bucks. But we got the next champ! Bottoms up. (*All drink,* FRANK *included.*)

ROXY (*to* BONAPARTE): You see how a boy can make a success nowadays?

BONAPARTE: Yeah . . . I see.

EDDIE (*resenting* BONAPARTE's *attitude*): Do we bother you? If I didn't think Joe was here I don't come up. I don't like nobody to gimme a boycott!

BONAPARTE (*going back to window*): Helpa you'self to more wine.

SIGGIE (*to* EDDIE): Leave him alone—he don't feel social tonight.

MOODY: Don't worry, Mr. Bonaparte. Looka me—take a lesson from me—I'm not worried. I'm getting married tomorrow—*this afternoon!*—I don't know where my girl is, but I'm not worried! What for? We're all in clover up to our necks!

SIGGIE: Shh . . . don't wake up my wife. (MOODY *suddenly sits heavily; jealousy begins to gnaw at him despite his optimism.* ROXY *takes another drink.*)

EDDIE (*to* FRANK, *apropos of his bandaged head*): What's that "Spirit of '76" outfit for?

SIGGIE (*grinning to* EDDIE): Didn't you hear what he said before? They gave it to him in a strike—

EDDIE (*to* FRANK): You got a good build—you could be a fighter.

FRANK: I fight. . . .

EDDIE: Yeah? For what?

FRANK: A lotta things I believe in . . . (EDDIE *looks at* FRANK *and appreciates his quality.*)

EDDIE: Whatta you get for it?

ROXY (*laughing*): Can't you see? A busted head!

FRANK: I'm not fooled by a lotta things Joe's fooled by. I don't get autos and custom-made suits. But I get what Joe don't.

EDDIE: What don't he get? (BONAPARTE *comes in and listens intently.*)

FRANK (*modestly*): The pleasure of acting as you think! The satisfaction of staying where you belong, being what you are . . . at harmony with millions of others!

ROXY (*pricking up his ears*): Harmony? That's music! The family's starting up music again!

FRANK (*smiling*): That's right, that's music— (*Now* MOODY *emphatically stamps his glass down on table and stands.*)

MOODY: What's the use waiting around! They won't be back. (*Bitterly.*) Lorna's got a helluva lotta nerve, riding around in Long Island with him! Without even asking me!

SIGGIE: Long Island's famous for the best eating ducks.

EDDIE (*to* MOODY): You got the champ—you can't have everything.

MOODY: What's that supposed to mean?

EDDIE (*coldly*): That girl belongs to Bonaparte. They're together now, in some roadhouse . . . and they ain't eating duck!

MOODY (*finally, unsteadily*): You don't know what you're talking about!

EDDIE: Moody, what do you figger your interest is worth in Bonaparte?

MOODY: Why?

EDDIE (*without turning*): Roxy . . . are you listening?

ROXY: Yeah.

EDDIE: 'Cause after tonight I'd like to handle Bonaparte myself.

MOODY: Your gall is gorgeous! But I got a contract. . . .

ROXY: Eddie, have a heart—I'm holding a little twenty percent. (*Out of sheer rage* MOODY *drinks more wine;* ROXY
follows his example.)

FRANK (*to* EDDIE): How much does Joe own of himself?

EDDIE: Thirty percent. After tonight I own the rest.

MOODY: Oh, no! No, sir-ee!

EDDIE: You're drunk tonight! Tomorrow!

BONAPARTE (*coming forward*): Maybe Joe don't gonna fight
no more, after tonight. . . .

EDDIE: Listen, you creep! Why don't you change your tune
for a minute!

ROXY (*to* BONAPARTE): What're *you* worried about?

BONAPARTE: My boy usta coulda be great for all men. Whatta
he got now, heh? Pardon me fora nota to feel so confident
in Joe'sa future! Pardon me fora to be anxious. . . .

EDDIE (*standing up*): I don't like this talk!

SIGGIE: Sit down, Pop—you're rocking the boat! Shh! Shh!
(*He slips out of the room.*)

ROXY: Does anyone here know what he's talking about?

FRANK: He's trying to say he's worried for Joe.

ROXY: But why? Why? Don't he realize his kid's worth a
fortune from tonight on? (*After giving* EDDIE *a quick
glance.*) Ain't he got brains enough to see two feet ahead?
Tell him in Italian—he don't understand our language—this
is a festive occasion! To Bonaparte, the Monarch of the
Masses! (*Telephone rings.*)

MOODY (*triumphantly, to* EDDIE): That's my hotel! You see,
you were all wrong! That's Lorna! (*Speaking into telephone.*) Hello? . . . No. . . . (*Turning to* BONAPARTE.)
It's for you. (MOODY *extends telephone in* BONAPARTE'S
*direction, but the latter stands in his place, unable to move.
After a few seconds* FRANK *sees this and briskly moves to
telephone, taking it from* MOODY. *In the meantime* MOODY
has begun to address EDDIE *with drunken eloquence.
Wavering on his feet.*) There's a constitution in this country, Eddie Fuseli. Every man here enjoys life, liberty and
the pursuit of happiness!

FRANK (*speaking into telephone*): Yes? . . . No, this is his son. (BONAPARTE *watches* FRANK *mutely as he listens at telephone.*)

MOODY: There's laws in this country, Fuseli! *Contracts!* We live in a civilized world—!

FRANK (*loudly, to the others*): Keep quiet! (*Resumes listening.*) Yes . . . yes. . . .

ROXY (*to* EDDIE): And there's a God in heaven—don't forget it!

FRANK (*on telephone*): Say it again. . . . Yes. . . .

MOODY (*to* EDDIE): You're a killer! A man tries to do his best— but you're a killer! (FRANK *lowers telephone and comes down to the others.*)

FRANK: *You're all killers!* (BONAPARTE *advances a step toward* FRANK.)

BONAPARTE: Frank . . . is it . . . ?

FRANK: I don't know how to tell you, Poppa. . . .

BONAPARTE (*hopefully*): Yes . . . ?

FRANK: We'll have to go there—

EDDIE: Go where?

FRANK: Both of them . . . they were killed in a crash—

EDDIE: Who? What?

FRANK: They're waiting for identification—Long Island, Babylon.

EDDIE (*moving to* FRANK): What are you handing me? (EDDIE, *suddenly knowing the truth, stops in his tracks. Telephone operator signals for telephone to be replaced. The mechanical clicks call* FRANK *to attention, he slowly replaces the instrument.*)

MOODY: I don't believe that! Do you hear me? I don't believe it—

FRANK: What waste!

MOODY: It's a God damn lie!

BONAPARTE: What have-a you expect?

MOODY (*suddenly weeping*): Lorna!

BONAPARTE (*standing, his head high*): JOE . . . Come, we bring-a him home . . . where he belong. . . .

HIGH TOR

Introduction

When Maxwell Anderson's *High Tor* was produced in 1937, he had already won distinction with such successful plays as *What Price Glory?*, written with Laurence Stallings, *Both Your Houses*, *Mary of Scotland*, *Elizabeth the Queen* and several others. When he died in 1959, his dramatic career had spanned more than three decades from *White Desert*, in 1923, to *Barefoot in Athens*, in 1952. To the end of his writing career he maintained the qualities that George Jean Nathan aptly described:

No man writing for theatre has greater sincerity than Anderson, and no man a higher goal.[1]

Anderson continued to write throughout the 1940's and 1950's. Some plays did not meet with the critical or popular acclaim of his earlier successes. *The Eve of St. Mark* (1942) and *Storm Operation* (1944) dealt with World War II. *Joan of Lorraine* (1947) and *Anne of the Thousand Days* (1948), as well as *Barefoot in Athens* (1952), were biographical in the great tradition of *Mary of Scotland* and *Elizabeth the Queen*. On two occasions he ventured into the field of the musical drama: *Knickerbocker Holiday* (1938), with music by Kurt Weill, and *Lost in the Stars* (1950), based on Alan Paton's *Cry, the Beloved Country*.

High Tor has been described as a combination of "melodrama and farce, of Hudson River legend and contemporary satire, of smiling surface and serious depth."[2] Essentially it is the story of a pair of scoundrels who try to persuade the

---

[1] Quoted in Stanley J. Kunitz, *Twentieth Century Authors: First Supplement*, p. 300.
[2] Joseph T. Shipley, *Guide to Great Plays*, p. 30.

owner of High Tor mountain to sell it so that it may be broken into rock. Interwoven in this business transaction is the robbery of the Nanuet bank and the eventual capture of the robbers. All this is realism mixed with farce.

Fantasy and imagination enter into the play with the crew of the Dutch ship *Onrust,* who have been stranded in this vicinity for over three hundred years and are still hoping to go back to Amsterdam when their ship returns. Van Van Dorn, the idealistic owner of the mountain, finds a kindred spirit in Lise, the wife of the Dutch captain. DeWitt, a burly member of the crew, is more than a match for the bank robbers. Judith, Van Dorn's realistic and practical sweetheart, reconciles her differences with him.

Eventually Van Dorn sells the mountain for $50,000 and decides to settle down in the West. The two manipulators are caught red-handed with money stolen from the Nanuet bank. The crew of the *Onrust* return on their long-lost vessel.

A brief summary of *High Tor* cannot convey either the charm or the bitterness of the play. Maxwell Anderson was both a poet and a deeply serious thinker about man's problems and his relationships with his fellow men. In the words of John Mason Brown:

> Although he believes man builds only to erect ruins, he urges us to remember that for no mountain . . . should a man's life be sacrificed, regardless of how rich that mountain may be in associations with the past. Whether he wants to do so or not, man must recognize the present.[3]

THE PLAYWRIGHT

Anderson wrote his first play in verse (*White Desert,* 1923) and never faltered in his faith in the greater effectiveness of dramatic verse over dramatic prose. He said:

When I wrote my first play, *White Desert,* I wrote it in

---

[3] *Two on the Aisle,* p. 153.

verse because I was weary of plays in prose that never lifted from the ground. It failed and I did not come back to verse again until I discovered that poetic tragedy had never been successfully written about its own place and time. There is not one tragedy by Aeschylus, Sophocles, Euripides, Shakespeare, Corneille or Racine which did not have the advantage of a setting either far away or long ago. *Winterset* is largely in verse and treats a contemporary tragic theme, which makes it more of an experiment than I could wish, for the great masters themselves never tried to make tragic poetry out of the stuff of their own times. To do so is to attempt to establish a new convention, one that may prove impossible of acceptance, but to which I was driven by the lively historical sense of our day. . . . Whether or not I have solved the problem is probably of little moment. But it must be solved if we are to have a great theatre in America.[4]

It is not only as the greatest American protagonist of the use of verse in drama that Anderson claims our attention. He crystallized certain aspects of American life in such vivid forms that one could appropriately designate him, to paraphrase Matthew Arnold, as one who saw life steadily and saw it whole. In *Valley Forge* (1934) he portrayed George Washington. In the Pulitzer Prize-winner *Both Your Houses* (1933) he expressed his contempt for legislators who do not have a sense of public duty. In *Gods of the Lightning* (1928) and in *Winterset* (1935) he expressed his indignation against the Sacco-Vanzetti decision. *High Tor* (1937) mocked the crude materialism of money-mad businessmen, and *The Star Wagon* (1937) nostalgically reminisced about the comparative serenity of American life at the turn of the century. *Knickerbocker Holiday* made pointed references to contemporary events, although it concerned the life of Peter Stuyvesant.

---

[4] Quoted in Burns Mantle, *Contemporary American Playwrights*, p. 39.

Anderson did not confine his dramatic interests to American life, past or present. *Elizabeth the Queen* (1930) and *Mary of Scotland* (1933) were brilliant excursions into the realms of English royal history. *The Masque of Kings* (1937) was another of the many treatments of the tragic story of the Mayerling episode in Hapsburg history.

In a world that is forgetful of the mistakes and lessons of the past, mistrustful and fearful of the destructive elements of the present, Anderson believed in a theatre of the future that would help build a civilization more dedicated to beauty than is our own. As John Mason Brown wrote of *Winterset,* "his is the kind of play . . . upon which the hope and glory of the future theatre rest."[5]

What then was this theatre of the future that Anderson wanted to create? For one thing, he wanted his works to have permanence. He was frank about his desire to have his plays remembered after their period of box-office success. For this reason he preferred verse to prose as a medium in drama. He once told an interviewer:

All great plays I can remember were in verse. If we are going to have a great theatre in this country somebody has to write verse, even if it is written badly. It is at least a beginning.[6]

The play of the future was to be written in a language that was not a mere reproduction of the speech of everyday life. Its rhythm was to be richer in the power to evoke emotional responses in the audience. The various qualities of Anderson's dramatic language—the vocabulary, the verbal music, the rhythm—have already become subjects of analysis.

Yet his language alone did not give Anderson his position in American drama. He had definite ideas about the kind of themes that are worthy of permanent presentation in dramatic form. The playwright cannot hold himself aloof

---

[5] *Two on the Aisle*, p. 152.
[6] Quoted in Barrett H. Clark, *Maxwell Anderson* (New York: Samuel French, 1933, pp. 4–5.

Introduction

from beauty, and he must be aware of the soul-destroying elements of our times, which should be held up as objects of reproof and condemnation. Hence Anderson's preoccupation in two of his plays with the injustice of the notorious Sacco-Vanzetti trial of 1927. The chicanery and stupidity of inefficient and corrupt legislators stirred him to express his indignation in *Both Your Houses*. Certain unsavory aspects of American business life are condemned in *High Tor* and in *The Star Wagon*. The drabness of contemporary civilization, which destroys the very rare islands of beauty in the sea of ugliness, is pictured in *Saturday's Children* (1927). The grim realities of the World War were incorporated into *What Price Glory?* (1924). Throughout his dramatic career, which began in 1923, Anderson kept faith with his ideals as a playwright. He always wrote with strength and sincerity, with tenderness rather than bitterness, with a feeling for the beauties in life that are always present though often obscured.

FURTHER READING

Brown, John Mason. *Broadway in Review*. New York: W. W. Norton, 1940, pp. 40-42, 67-71.

———. *Seeing Things*. New York: McGraw-Hill, 1946, pp. 300-302.

———. *Still Seeing Things*. New York: McGraw-Hill, 1950, pp. 207-213, 227-232.

———. *Two on the Aisle*. New York: W. W. Norton, 1938, pp. 152-155.

Clurman, Harold. *The Fervent Years*. New York: Knopf, 1945.

Flexner, Eleanor. *American Playwrights, 1918–1938*. New York: Simon and Schuster, 1938, pp. 78-129.

Gagey, Edmond M. *Revolution in American Drama*. New York: Columbia, 1947.

Gassner, John. *Masters of the Drama*. 3rd ed. New York: Dover, 1954, pp. 678-683.

Hewitt, Barnard. *Theatre U.S.A.: 1668–1957*. New York: McGraw-Hill, 1959, pp. 358-360, 394-396.

Krutch, Joseph Wood. *The American Drama Since 1918*. New York: Random House, 1939, pp. 286-318.

Kunitz, Stanley J. *Twentieth Century Authors: First Supplement*. New York: H. W. Wilson, 1955, pp. 19-20.

———, and Haycraft, Howard. *Twentieth Century Authors*. New York: H. W. Wilson, 1942, pp. 23-24.

Mantle, Burns. *Contemporary American Playwrights*. New York: Dodd, Mead, 1938, pp. 37-46.

Morehouse, Ward. *Matinee Tomorrow*. New York: McGraw-Hill, 1949.

O'Hara, Frank Hurburt. *Today in American Drama*. Chicago: University of Chicago, 1939.

Shipley, Joseph T. *Guide to Great Plays*. Washington: Public Affairs, 1956, pp. 22-37.

HIGH TOR

MAXWELL ANDERSON

ACT I

SCENE 1

SCENE: *A section of the broad flat traprock summit of High Tor, from which one looks out into sky and from which one might look down a sheer quarter mile to the Tappan Zee below. A cluster of hexagonal pillared rocks masks the view to the left and a wind-tortured small hemlock wedges into the rock floor at the right. Light from the setting sun pours in from the left, and an ancient* INDIAN, *wearing an old greatcoat thrown round him like a blanket, stands in the rays from a cleft, making his prayer to the sunset.*

INDIAN: I make my prayer to you, the falling fire,
      bearing in mind the whisper in my ears

from the great spirit, talking on the wind,
whispering that a young race, in its morning,
should pray to the rising sun, but a race that's old
and dying should invoke the dying flame
eaten and gulfed by the shark-toothed mountain-west,
a god that dies to live. As we have died,
my race of the red faces and old ways,
and as we hope to rise. I give you thanks
for light, for quiet on the hills
where the loud races dare not walk for fear
lest they be lost, where their blind hunters pass
peering with caps and guns, but see no game
and curse as they go down. I am fed
and sheltered on this mountain where their hands
are helpless. But I am old as my race is old;
my eyes hunt day and night along the ground
the grave where I shall lie; my ears have heard
dead women calling upward from the earth,
mother and wife and child: "You are welcome here;
you are no longer welcome where you walk,
but here you are most welcome." I shall go
and lie and sleep, and I shall give you thanks,
O God that dies, that my last night is dark
and long, for I am tired. And this is then my prayer,
that I sleep soundly, hear no step,
hear only through the earth your step in spring,
O God of the dying fire!

(VAN DORN and JUDITH *come in,* JUDITH *carrying lunch.*)

VAN: Evening, John.

INDIAN: Evening.

VAN: How'll the fishing be tomorrow?

INDIAN: There'll be a storm tonight.
     We could try the lake tomorrow.

VAN: Would you go along?

INDIAN: If you'll be here at sunrise.

VAN: Fine. I'll be here. About that other matter.
     Had any luck so far?

104

INDIAN: Luck?

VAN: I mean, have you found it?

INDIAN: Not yet, but I will.

VAN: O.K., John, let me know.
     Let me know in time.

INDIAN: I will. Good night.

VAN: Good night. (INDIAN *slips away through the rocks.*)

JUDITH: Who is it, Van?

VAN: Just an Indian.

JUDITH: Are there Indians?
     I didn't know there were any Indians left.

VAN: Well, *there's* one. There's not much left of him,
     and he's the last around here.

JUDITH: He's hunting something?
     You asked him if he'd found it.

VAN: Um—yes, you see,
     he's looking for a place to make his grave,
     and he's kind of captious about it—folks get that way
     along toward the end, wanting their bones done up
     in some particular fashion. Maybe because
     that's all you've got to leave about that time
     and you want it the way you want it.

JUDITH: Did he tell you this?

VAN: We've got an understanding. When he feels it
     coming over him he's going to die
     he'll let me know, and I'll go dig him in
     so the crows and foxes can't get at him. See,
     he's all alone in the world. We fixed this up
     a couple of years ago.

JUDITH (*digging in ground*): But you couldn't, Van,
     without a permit. A burial permit.

VAN: Oh,
     I guess you could. This getting old and dying
     and crawling into the ground, that was invented
     back before medical examiners
     and taxes and all that. The old boy's clean.
     He'll go right back to dirt.

JUDITH: But, Van, you can't!
    People can't die that way!
VAN: I guess they can.
    What the hell good's being wrapped in cellophane?
    You don't keep anyway.
JUDITH: You're impossible
    to live with! Why do you say such things? If I
    should die—you'd get a pine box—!
VAN: If you should die
    the old boy that drives the sun around up there,
    he'd unhitch, and put the cattle out
    to grass, and give it up. He'd plumb lose interest
    if you should die. Maybe I would myself,
    I don't say. Maybe I would— Fetch out that supper.
    We want to see what we eat.
JUDITH: It's dinner, Van, not supper.
VAN: That's what I said. Fetch out that dinner.
    When it gets a little darker what's black's pepper
    and what's green's parsley; still you can't be sure.
    It might be ants.
JUDITH: Just the same we'll quarrel.
    We'll always quarrel.
VAN: Oh, no. We've both got sense.
    What's the sense fighting?
(*He looks at newspaper that was round lunch.*)
JUDITH: And you shouldn't read at table.
VAN: I never do. The Nanuet bank's been robbed.
    My God, there's not enough money in Nanuet
    to buy their gas for a getaway. One night
    Pap and me sat in on a poker game
    in Nanuet and took twenty-seven dollars
    out of town. Next day they couldn't do business.
    The place was clean.
JUDITH: There were troopers at the train
    tonight, and sirens going through Haverstraw,
    but the robbers got away.
VAN: They took twenty-five thousand.

How'd twenty-five thousand get to Nanuet?
It's against nature.

JUDITH: It didn't stay there long.

VAN: No—I understand that.
But just to have it there in passing, just
to look at, just to fool the customers,
how do they do it?

JUDITH: Maybe it wasn't real.

VAN: Federal money, that's all.
Only now you see it
and now you don't.

JUDITH: They say it buys as much
as if you earned it.

VAN: Bad for the stomach, though,
to live on humble pie.

JUDITH: I'd rather work.

VAN: Well, as I said, don't work if you don't feel like it.
Any time you want to move up in the hills
and sleep with me, it's a bargain.

JUDITH: Van!

VAN: Why not?
We'll get married if that's what you mean.

JUDITH: You haven't any job. And you make it sound
like animals.

VAN: I'm fond of animals.

JUDITH: You shoot them all the time.

VAN: Well, I get hungry.
Any man's liable to get hungry.

JUDITH: Van,
I want to talk to you seriously.

VAN: Can't be done.
Listen, things get serious enough
without setting out to do it.

JUDITH: Van, this spring
you had three weeks' work, laying dry wall.
You could have had more, but you didn't take it.
You're an expert mason—

VAN: I'm good at everything.

JUDITH: But you work three weeks in the year—

VAN: That's all I need—

JUDITH: And all the rest of the year you hunt or fish
or sleep, or God knows what—

VAN: Ain't it the truth?

JUDITH: Last fall I came looking for you once, and you
were gone—gone to Port Jervis hunting—deer,
you said on the post card—

VAN: Sure, I was hunting deer—
didn't I bring you half a venison?

JUDITH: But not a word to me until I got the post card
ten days later—

VAN: Didn't have a minute—

JUDITH: Then last winter there's a note nailed to a tree
and you're in Virginia, down in the Dismal Swamp
tracking bear. Now, for God's sake, Van,
it's no way to live.

VAN: Jeez, it's a lot of fun.

JUDITH: Maybe for you.

VAN: You want me to take that job.

JUDITH: Why don't you, Van?

VAN: Porter in a hotel, lugging up satchels,
opening windows, maybe you get a dime.
I'd choke to death.

JUDITH: I'd see you every day.

VAN: Yeah, I could see you on the mezzanine,
taking dictation from the drummer boys,
all about how they can't get home. You can stand it,
a woman stands that stuff, but if you're a man
I say it chokes you.

JUDITH: We can't live in your cabin
and have no money, like the Jackson Whites
over at Suffern.

VAN: Hell, you don't need money.
Pap worked that out. All you need's a place to sleep
and something to eat. I've never seen the time

I couldn't find a meal on the mountain here,
rainbow trout, jugged hare, something in season
right around the zodiac.

JUDITH: You didn't like
the Chevrolet factory, either?

VAN (*walking toward cliff edge*): Look at it, Judy.
That's the Chevrolet factory, four miles down,
and straight across, that's Sing Sing. Right from here
you can't tell one from another; get inside,
and what's the difference? You're in there, and you work,
and they've got you. If you're in the factory
you buy a car, and then you put in your time
to pay for the God damn thing. If you get in a hurry
and steal a car, they put you in Sing Sing first,
and then you work out your time. They graduate
from one to the other, back and forth, those guys,
paying for cars both ways.

JUDITH: But one has to have a car.

VAN: Honest to God now, Judy, what's the hurry?
Where in hell are we going?

JUDITH: If a man works hard,
and has ability, as you have, Van,
he takes a place among them, saves his money,
works right out of the ruck and gets above
where he's safe and secure.

VAN: I wouldn't bet on it much.

JUDITH: But it's true.

VAN: All right, suppose it's true. Suppose
a man saves money all his life, and works
like hell about forty years, till he can say:
good-by, I'm going, I'm on easy street
from now on. What's he do?

JUDITH: Takes a vacation.

VAN: Why should I work forty years to earn
time off when I've got it?
I'm on vacation now.

JUDITH: It's not always easy,

you know it's not. There was that time last winter
when I helped you out.

VAN: Why, sure, you helped me out.
Why wouldn't you? But if you didn't help me
I'd get along.

JUDITH: Yes, you would. I know you would.
You won't take it
when they bring it to you.

VAN: When did they bring me any?

JUDITH: And what if there was a child?

VAN: Why, he'd be fine—
the less they have the better they like it— Oh,
you mean the traprock company, wanting to buy
High Tor? They offered seven hundred dollars—
and they offered Pap ten thousand before he died,
and he wouldn't sell.

JUDITH: He wouldn't?

VAN: They want to chew
the back right off this mountain, the way they did
across the clove there. Leave the old Palisades
sticking up here like billboards, nothing left
but a false front facing the river. Not for Pap,
and not for me. I like this place.

JUDITH: But, Van Van Dorn!
Ten thousand dollars!

VAN: Well, it's Federal money.
Look, Judy, it's a quarter mile
straight down to the Tappan Zee
from here— You can see fifteen miles of river
north and south. I grew up looking at it.
Hudson came up that river just about
three hundred years ago, and lost a ship
here in the Zee. They say the crew climbed up
this Tor to keep a lookout for the ship
that never came. Maybe the Indians got them.
Anyway, on dark nights before a storm,
they say you sometimes see them.

JUDITH: Have you seen them?

VAN: The Dutchmen? Maybe I have. You can't be sure.
It's pretty wild around here when it storms.
That's when I like it best. But look at it now.
Every night I come back here like the Indian
to get a fill of it. Seven hundred dollars
and tear it down? Hell, no.

(BIGGS *and* SKIMMERHORN *come in from the right, a bit
bedraggled, and wiping their brows.* SKIMMERHORN *carries
a briefcase. It is growing darker.*)

BIGGS (*to* VAN): Hey listen, Mac, any houses round here?

VAN: Guess you're off the beat, buddy; never heard of any
houses on the mountain.

SKIMMERHORN: Come on, Art; we're doing well if we're down
at the road before dark.

BIGGS: Look, Mac, maybe you can help us out. You familiar
with this region, at all?

VAN: I've been around here some.

BIGGS: Well, we're all afternoon hunting a cabin that's somewhere along the ridge. Ever hear of it?

VAN: Anybody live in it?

BIGGS: Fellow named Van Dorn.

VAN: Oh, yes, sure.

BIGGS: You know where it is?

VAN: Sure. You climb down the face of the cliff here and
keep left along the ledge about a hundred yards, then you
turn sharp left through a cleft up the ridge. Follow the
trail about half a mile and there you are.

SKIMMERHORN: Down the face of the cliff?

VAN: Down through the rocks there, then turn left—

SKIMMERHORN: A monkey couldn't go down there, hanging
on with four hands and a tail!

VAN: Well, you can always walk along back toward Little
Tor, and cut down from there through the gulch. There's
a slough at the bottom of the ravine, but if you get through
that you can see the cabin up on the sidehill. About four
miles that way.

111

SKIMMERHORN: Yeah, we'll set right out. I always did want
  to get lost up here and spend a night in the hills.
VAN: Oh, you'll get lost, all right.
SKIMMERHORN: Thanks.
VAN: Don't mention it. (BIGGS *and* SKIMMERHORN *go out.*)
JUDITH: But they were looking for you!
VAN: Yeah.
JUDITH: Why didn't you tell them?
VAN: What?
JUDITH: Who you were!
VAN: They didn't ask about that.
JUDITH: But out of common courtesy!
VAN: Well, you see, I know who they are.
JUDITH: Who are they?
VAN: Art J. Biggs, Junior, and Skimmerhorn,
  Judge Skimmerhorn.
JUDITH: But why not talk to them?
VAN: Oh, we communicate by mail. I've got
  a dozen letters stacked up from the firm:
  Skimmerhorn, Skimmerhorn, Biggs and Skimmerhorn.
  They're realtors,
  whatever that is, and they own the traprock company,
  and one of the Skimmerhorns, he's probate judge,
  and goes around condemning property
  when they want to make a rake-off.
JUDITH: But they're the traprock men!
VAN: That's what I said.
JUDITH: I'll call them!
VAN: Oh, no; oh, no!
  I've got nothing to say to those two buzzards
  except I hope they break their fat-back necks
  on their own traprock.
JUDITH: You take a lot for granted.
VAN: Do I?
JUDITH: You think, because I said I loved you once,
  That's the end; I'm finished.
VAN: Oh, far from it.

JUDITH: Oh, yes—you think because a girl's been kissed
   she stays kissed, and after that the man
   does her thinking for her.
VAN: Hell, it's all I can do
   to handle my own thinking.
JUDITH: If we're married
   I'll have to live the way you want to live.
   You prefer being a pauper!
VAN: Get it straight!
   I don't take money nor orders, and I live
   as I damn well please.
JUDITH: But we'd live like paupers!
   And you could have a fortune!
VAN: Seven hundred dollars?
JUDITH: You could get more!
VAN: I don't mean to sell at all.
JUDITH: You see; it's your place, and your thinking! You
      decide,
   but I'd have to stand it with you!
VAN: What do you want?
JUDITH: Something to start on; and now, you see,
      we could have it,
   only you won't!
VAN: I can't, Judy, that's the truth.
   I just can't.
JUDITH: They'll get it anyway.
   They've worked right up to where your land begins,
   and they won't stop for you. They'll just condemn it
   and take it.
VAN: They'll be in trouble.
JUDITH: You can't make trouble
   for companies. They have a dozen lawyers
   and ride right over you. I've worked for them.
   It's never any use.
VAN: Well, I won't sell.
JUDITH: We'll call it off then.
VAN: What?

JUDITH: Between you and me.
VAN: Only you don't mean it.
JUDITH: I know I do, though.
>   You haven't thought about it, and so you think
>   I couldn't do it. But it's better now
>   than later.
VAN: You don't know what it means to me
>   if you can say it.
JUDITH: It means as much to me,
>   but I look ahead a little.
VAN: What do you see?
JUDITH: Two people growing old
>   and having children, running wild in the woods
>   with nothing.
VAN: There's no better place to run.
>   But I've been counting on you. More than you know.
>   More than— Judy, this is the kind of night
>   we've been in love most.
JUDITH: Yes, we could be in love,
>   but that's not everything.
VAN: Well, just about.
>   What else do we get?
JUDITH: I think I'd better go.
>   It's getting dark.
VAN: You could find your way by the beacon.
JUDITH: I'd better go. (BIGGS *and* SKIMMERHORN *come back.*)
BIGGS: Listen, Mac, would you do something for us?
VAN: I don't know.
BIGGS: Could you take a paper round to Van Dorn and leave
   it with him?
VAN: A summons?
BIGGS: A sort of notice.
VAN: Yeah, a notice to appear. No, I couldn't.
BIGGS: It's worth a dollar to me.
VAN: I'd be cheating you.
SKIMMERHORN (*comes over to* BIGGS): Make it two dollars.
BIGGS: All right, make it two dollars.

VAN: You'd be throwing away money.

SKIMMERHORN: Never mind that part of it. Will you do it?

VAN: You'll take a running jump over the edge of the cliff and think things over on the way down before I serve any papers for you.

BIGGS: What's the matter with us?

VAN: My rule in life is keep away from skunks.

BIGGS: You'll get the tar kicked out of you one of these days.

VAN: Make it today.

JUDITH: If you gentlemen care to know, this is Mr. Van Dorn.

BIGGS: Say, are you Van Dorn?

VAN: Sure I am.

BIGGS (*extending a hand*): Oh, in that case, forget it—you're the fellow we want to see! Boy, we apologize—(*crosses to* JUDITH; *takes off his hat*)—and to the lady, too! Listen, I don't know what to say but you've got us all wrong. We want to buy this place!

VAN: You like the view, I suppose?

BIGGS: Certainly is a view.

VAN: You wouldn't spoil it, of course? You wouldn't move in with a million dollars' worth of machinery and cut the guts out of the mountain, would you?

SKIMMERHORN: We always leave the front—the part you see from the river.

VAN: But you take down all the law allows.

SKIMMERHORN: Well, we're in business.

VAN: Not with me.

JUDITH: Do you mind if I ask how much you're offering?

BIGGS: We said seven hundred, but I'll make it a thousand right here and now.

SKIMMERHORN: As a matter of fact, we'll make it two thousand.

BIGGS: Yeah, all right. Two thousand for the hundred and seven acres. (*Takes checks from his pocket.*)

JUDITH: But you offered Mr. Van Dorn's father ten thousand before he died.

SKIMMERHORN: His father had a clear title, right down from

the original Dutch patroon to the original Van Dorn. But unfortunately the present Mr. Van Dorn has a somewhat clouded claim to the acreage.

VAN: My father's title was clear, and he left it to me.

SKIMMERHORN: The truth is he should have employed a lawyer when he drew his will, because the instrument, as recorded, is faulty in many respects. It was brought before me in my capacity as probate judge at Ledentown.

VAN: And in your capacity as second vice-president of the traprock company you shot it full of holes.

SKIMMERHORN: Sir, I keep my duties entirely separate.

VAN: Sure, but when your left hand takes money your right hand finds out about it. And when there's too much to carry away in both hands you use a basket. You're also vice-president of the power company, and you stole right-of-ways clear across the county north and south—

SKIMMERHORN: We paid for every foot of land—

VAN: Yes, at your own price.

BIGGS: Let's not get in an argument, Mr. Van Dorn, because your father died intestate. Now we've found twenty-seven Van Dorns living at Blauvelt, and all willing to sign away their rights for a consideration.

VAN: The best you can do you'll need my name on your little paper, and you won't have it.

SKIMMERHORN: To put it straight, you'll take three thousand dollars, and I'll hold the will valid. (*Comes closer to* VAN.)

VAN: I'm still waiting to hear what you do about my signature.

SKIMMERHORN: It's quite possible you'll be held incompetent by the court and a guardian appointed.

VAN: Me incompetent?

SKIMMERHORN: But I've got the validation in my pocket, naming you executor, if you'll sell.

BIGGS: And by God, anybody that won't take money when it's offered to him is incompetent! And you'll take it now or not at all! I don't go mountain-climbing every day with a blank check in my pocket! (*A pause. Starts out, then stops.*)

Come on. It's bad enough sliding down that trail by daylight.

VAN: Well, I wouldn't want to make you nervous,
    a couple of eminent respectables
    like you two—but a dog won't bite a Dutchman—
    maybe you've heard that—and the reason is
    a Dutchman's poison when he don't like you. Now,
    I'm Dutch and I don't like you.

SKIMMERHORN: That's a threat?

VAN: Not at all. Only don't try to eat me
    or you'll curl up. I'm poison to a hound-dog,
    and you're both sons-of-bitches.

BIGGS: Come on. (*Starts further left, but stops. The daylight
is now gone. The airplane beacon that stands on top of
High Tor lights scene from the right for a moment.*)

VAN (*stands on rocks*): What's more,
    there's something funny about this mountaintop.
    It draws fire. Every storm on the Tappan Zee
    climbs up here and wraps itself around
    High Tor, and blazes away at what you've got,
    airplane beacon, steam shovels, anything
    newfangled. It smashed the beacon twice. It blew
    the fuses on your shovel and killed a man
    only last week. I've got a premonition
    something might happen to you.

BIGGS: God, he's crazy.

SKIMMERHORN: Yeah, let him talk. (*There is a sudden rum-
bling roar of falling rock.*)

BIGGS: What's that?

VAN: That's nothing much.
    That's just a section of the cliff come down
    across the trail. I've been expecting it
    this last two years. You'd better go down this way.

BIGGS: No, thanks.

VAN: All right.
    Only don't try that trail in the dark.

You think High Tor's just so much raw material, but
   you're wrong.
A lot of stubborn men have died up here
and some of them don't sleep well. They come back
and push things round these dark nights. Don't blame me
if anything falls on you.

SKIMMERHORN. Oh, what the hell!
   Let's get out of here.

(BIGGS *and* SKIMMERHORN *go out.*)

JUDITH: What do you mean?

VAN: I don't know.

JUDITH: They'll say you threatened them.
   Good-by, Van.

VAN: You'll be up tomorrow?

JUDITH: No.

VAN: You'd better let me see you down.

JUDITH: Oh, no.
   I can climb. Stay here and guard your rock—
   you think so much of it.

VAN: When will I see you?

JUDITH: Never. We'll call it off.
   You haven't thought much about it, so you think I
      couldn't do it.

VAN: Will you listen, Judy? I love you.
   I can explain it, but these fellows that drive up and down
   the road in cars, they don't care where they live,
   but I have roots down here, roots right down in the rock,
   so I don't know whether I'd live at all if I pulled up
   and left. I don't know what it's like anywhere else—
   down there in the towns they got two rooms and a bath.
   It's hard to breathe down there when you've lived
   here in the hills.

JUDITH: I know how it is, Van. We'll forget about it.
   You're in love with your mountain.
   Well, keep your mountain.

VAN: All right.

JUDITH: Good night.

VAN: Good night. (JUDITH *disappears down the rocks.* VAN
*sits in the shadow, looking into darkness. After a moment
a barely perceptible* FIGURE *enters from the gloom and
crosses toward the rocks. At the foot of the climb he
pauses and his face is caught in the light of the beacon.
He is seen to be young or middle-aged, bearded and
wearing the costume of a Dutch sailor of the sixteen
hundreds. He climbs the rocks, and another* SAILOR, *a
small cask strapped to his shoulder, follows. Three more
cross the stage similarly, then the* CAPTAIN *and his wife,*
LISE, *pause, like the others, in the light of the beacon.
The* CAPTAIN *is like his men, only younger perhaps, his
wife is a tiny figure, with a delicate girlish face looking
out from under the Dutch bonnet. They too pass up the
rocks, and are followed by a rolling silenus of a man in
the same garments. As they vanish* VAN *rises, looking
after them.*) Uh-huh—going to rain.

ACT I

SCENE 2

SCENE: *The same, though location of rocks suggests a different part of the mountaintop. The curtain goes up on
complete darkness enfolding the summit of the Tor. There
is a long, cumbrous rolling, as of a ball going down a
bowling alley, a flash of white light, a crackling as of falling
pins and a mutter dying into echo along the hills. The flash
reveals the outline of the Tor, black against the sky, and on
it the figures of the* DUTCH CREW *in the midst of which
is a large old beer keg. They are gathered about it, drinking. Again the roll, the flash, the break and the dying away.
The beam of the beacon steals into the scene sufficiently to
suggest the bowlers, some of them standing, some sitting
about the keg, the* CAPTAIN's *wife,* LISE, *a little apart from*

*the rest. Beyond the peak is a moving floor, the upper side
of blown cloud.*

LISE (*to* CAPTAIN): Asher! When you drink
there should be one on guard to watch the river
lest the ship come, and pass, and we must haunt
the dark another year!

CAPTAIN: To humor her,
Pieter, old son, climb down and post the Zee,
and mind you keep good lookout.

PIETER: Ships, aye, ships—
when the ball's rolling and there's gin in hand
I go to post. My luck!

CAPTAIN: When you shipped with me
you signed the voyage.

PIETER: Is this sea or land?
I'm no foot soldier!

CAPTAIN: March!

PIETER: Aye-aye. I'm going. (PIETER *detaches himself from
group and goes down rocks and off.*)

CAPTAIN: Are you content?

LISE: When the ship returns
and we have boarded her, and the wind scuds fair
into the east—yes, when we see the wharves
of Texel town across the Zuider Zee,
with faces waiting for us, hands and cries
to welcome our returning, then
I shall be content.

A SAILOR: Now, God for Texel town!

ANOTHER SAILOR (*rising*): I'll drink no more.

DEWITT: Drink up, lads, and forget.
It's a long way to the Texel. Drink your drink
and play your play.

CAPTAIN: Drink up and play it out.

LISE: Have you forgotten how the cobbled street
comes down by cranks and turns upon the quay
where the *Onrust* set sail? There your wives

120

wait for you, their sharp roofs in Amsterdam
cut on a rainy sky.

CAPTAIN: Be quiet, Lise.
You were so much in love you must come with me;
you were so young that I was patient with you,
but now day long, night long you carp and quarrel,
a carping wife.

LISE: We stay so long—so long;
Asher, at first the days were years, but now
the years are days; the ship that set us down
to watch this river palisade becomes
alike with supper stories round a hearth
when we were children. Was there this ship at all,
was there a sailor-city, Amsterdam? Will the ship return,
and shall I then see the Netherlands once more,
with sabots clattering homeward from the school
on winter evenings?

CAPTAIN: Aye, there was a ship,
and we wait here for her, but she's long away,
somewhere upriver.

LISE: And now you drink and drink,
distil your liquor on the mountaintop
and bowl against the light. But when you break it
these new strange men come build it up again;
and giant shovels spade the mountain down.
We must go back. There's no safety here.

SAILOR: We must go back.

CAPTAIN: These muttering fools!

LISE: Oh, Asher, I'm afraid!
For one thing I have known, and never told
lest it be true, lest you be frightened too.
Sometimes in a morning
when all the crew come down the rocks together,
holding my breath I see you in the light,
and back of you the gray rock bright and hard,
seen through figures of air! And you, and you

121

and you were but cloud-drift walking, pierced by the
   light,
translucent in the sun.

DeWitt: Now, damn the woman!

Captain: Why, then, I knew it. The land and sea
   about us on this dark side of the earth
   is thick with demons, heavy with enchantment,
   cutting us off from home.

Lise: Is it enchantment?
   Aye, we were warned before we came away
   against the cabalistic words and signs
   of those who dwell along these unknown waters;
   never to watch them dance nor hear them sing
   lest their powers weave a weird medicine throughout the
      air,
   and we be chained invisibly, our eyes darkened,
   our wrists and breasts pulseless, anchored in time,
   like birds blown back in a wind. But we have listened,
   and we are stricken through with light and sound,
   empty as autumn leaves; stripped of bone and will,
   the chrysalids of locusts staring here
   at one another.

Captain: And yet
   what we're to have we shall have here. Years past
   the demons of this air palsied our hands,
   fixed us upon one pinnacle of time,
   and on this pinnacle of stone. These new strange men
   are like the gods, work miracles, have power
   to pierce the walls with music.
   They have changed us. We may take
   the fireballs of the lightning in our hands
   and bowl them down the level floor of cloud
   to wreck the beacon, yet there was a time
   when these were death to touch. The life we keep
   is motionless as the center of a storm,
   yet while we can we keep it; while we can,
   snuff out to darkness their bright sweeping light,

    melt down the harness of the slow machines
    that hew the mountain from us. When it goes
    we shall go, too. They leave us this place, High Tor,
    and we shall have no other. You learn it last.
    A long while now we've known.
    Come, we'll go down.
    (CAPTAIN *and his* MEN *go out, leaving only* DEWITT
    and LISE.)

LISE: That's why they drink.

DEWITT: It's enough to drive a sailorman to drink, by the great jib boom, marooned somewhere on the hinder parts of the earth and degenerating hourly to the status of a flying Dutchman, half-spook and half God-knows-what. Drink? Why wouldn't we drink? A pewter flagon of Holland's gin puts manhood into the remnants and gives a sailor courage to look out on these fanciful new devils that ride sea, land and air on a puff of blue smoke.

LISE: If I had known. It's not too late.
    The sun still rises in the east and lays a course
    toward the old streets and days. These are my hands
    as when I was a child. Some great magician,
    binding a half-world in his wiles, has laid
    a spell here. We must break it and go home.
    I see this clearly.

DEWITT: Lise, little heart, the devils are too much for us. The very points of the compass grow doubtful these latter years, partly because I'm none too sober and partly because the great master devil sits on top of the world stirring up north and south with a long spoon to confuse poor mariners. I've seen him at it, a horned bull three times the size of the Dunderberg and with more cloven feet than the nine beasts in Revelations. Very clearly I saw him, too, as clear as you see the east and a path across the waters.

LISE: Are we to wait till all the color steals
    from flower and cloud before our eyes; till a wind
    out of the morning from the Tappan Zee
    lift us, we are so light, for all our crying,

and all we are becomes a voiceless cry
heard on the wind.

DeWITT: Aye, we'll see the time, if they continue to work
on us, when we'll be apparent in a strong light only by the
gin contained in our interior piping. You tremble, little
Lise, and you weep, but look now, there's a remedy I've had
in mind. Fall in love with one of them. Fall in love with
one of these same strange new-world magicians. I shall
choose me out one of their female mermaid witches, and set
my heart on her and become a man again.

LISE: I gave my love long ago, and it's no help.
I love enough.

DeWITT: Aye, but he's in a worse case than you are, the
Captain. Saving his captaincy, there's not enough belief in
him to produce half a tear in a passion of sobbing. Look
now, it may not sit easy on the stomach to love these new
winged demons, or their unfrocked women either, but it's
that or disintegrate, child; and who knows—with a little
practice a man might even acquire a taste for bob-haired
skinny witches in pantaloons. We can't go on forever,
here on these spellbound rocks, drawing up water from
time past—the well growing deeper, and the water lower,
till there be none.

ACT I

SCENE 3

SCENE: *Another section of the Tor, change of place indicated
by a slight alteration of positions of rocks, in darkness save
for the airplane beacon. A large steam shovel reaches in
from an adjacent excavation and hangs over the rock, the
control cables dangling. VAN is alone on the stage looking
at the machinery. He reaches up, catches a cable, and
swings the shovel a little. BIGGS and SKIMMERHORN enter.*

BIGGS: Hey, what are you doing with that shovel?

VAN: Did you know you're trespassing? Also when a man owns land he owns the air above it and the rock below. That means this damn shovel of yours is also trespassing.

BIGGS: Oh, it's Van Dorn. We'll have that moved tomorrow, Mr. Van Dorn. Somebody's made a miscue and left it hanging over the line.

SKIMMERHORN: By the way, that trail's gone out completely, Mr. Van Dorn; there's a fifty foot sheer drop there now, where it was. Now we've got to get off, if you can think of any way to manage it.

VAN: I'm not worrying about it. Spend the night. No charge.

SKIMMERHORN: The truth is I have to be in court early to-morrow, and a man needs his sleep.

VAN: Afraid you'd doze off on the bench and somebody else might take a trick? Oh, you'd wake up before they got far with anything. The Skimmerhorns are automatic that way.

BIGGS: You don't know any other trail down?

VAN: I showed you the one I knew, and you both turned green looking at it. What am I supposed to do now? Pin wings on you? (*He goes out.*)

SKIMMERHORN: I think I'll swear out a warrant for that squirt. He's too independent by half.

BIGGS (*sits*): On what grounds?

SKIMMERHORN: He threatened us, didn't he?

BIGGS: And where'll that get us?

SKIMMERHORN: He might be easier to talk to in jail.

BIGGS: That's true.

SKIMMERHORN (*sitting on a rock*): This is a hell of a mess.

BIGGS: You're explaining to me?

SKIMMERHORN: What did we ever come up here for?

BIGGS: Twenty-two thousand dollars.

SKIMMERHORN: Will we get it?

BIGGS: The old man will never know. It'll look all right on the books.

SKIMMERHORN: It's not good enough, though.

BIGGS: What are you squawking about?

SKIMMERHORN: Because I want my dinner, damn it! And because I'm tired of taking forty per cent and giving you sixty on all the side bets! I want half!

BIGGS: You're a damn sight more likely to get your dinner. You're overpaid already.

SKIMMERHORN: The will's perfectly good. I could find holes in it, but I've probated plenty much the same.

BIGGS: What of it?

SKIMMERHORN: A judge has some conscience, you know. When he sets a precedent he likes to stick to it.

BIGGS: I never knew your conscience to operate except on a cash basis. You want half.

SKIMMERHORN: Yes, I want half.

BIGGS: Well, you don't get it. Any other judge I put in there'd work for nothing but the salary and glad of the job. You take a forty per cent cut and howl for more. The woods are full of shyster lawyers looking for probate judgeships and I'll slip one in at Ledentown next election.

SKIMMERHORN: Oh, no, you won't, Art; oh, no, you won't. You wouldn't do that to an old friend like me; because if you did, think what I'd do to an old friend like you.

BIGGS: Well, maybe I wouldn't. Not if you're reasonable. Look, what's the difference between forty per cent and fifty per cent? Practically nothing!

SKIMMERHORN: Then why don't you give it to me?

BIGGS: Because, try and get it!

SKIMMERHORN: Damn it, I'm hungry. I ought to telephone my wife, too.

BIGGS: Why don't you?

SKIMMERHORN: Maybe it's fun for you—nothing to eat, no place to sleep, cold as hell, black as Tophet and a storm coming up! Only (gets up) I'm not used to it!

BIGGS: You're pulling down forty per cent of twenty-two thousand dollars for the night's work. I say it's worth it.

SKIMMERHORN: Think we could slide down one of those cables?

BIGGS: Maybe you could, Humpty Dumpty, but not me.

SKIMMERHORN: I'm going to look at it. (*He goes out,* BIGGS *following. After a moment* THREE MEN *climb in through the rocks, one of them carrying a small zipper satchel. They throw themselves down wearily on the rock. They are, in brief, the Nanuet bank robbers,* ELKUS, DOPE *and* BUDDY.)

DOPE: God, I got no wind. (*A siren is heard faintly, far down on the road.*)

ELKUS: Sons-a'-bitches a' troopers. (*Follows and stands on rock.*)

DOPE: What'd you want to wreck the car for?

ELKUS: Want to get caught with the stuff on you?

BUDDY: We'll get four hundred years for this.

ELKUS: Shut up!

DOPE: You didn't need to wreck the car, though.

ELKUS: Didn't you hear the trooper slam on the brakes when he went by? You'd be wearing bracelets right now if I hadn't dumped the old crate over the embankment. (*Siren sounds again.*) The way it is he thinks he's following us, and he'll blow that fire alarm all the way to Bear Mountain Bridge.

DOPE: What I want to know is where we go from here.

ELKUS: Down the other side and pick up a car. We tried every road out of Nanuet and they're all covered. (*Siren is heard receding.*)

BUDDY: We'll get four hundred years for this.

ELKUS: What do you think you are, a chorus? Go on back to St. Thomas's and sing it to the priest. You're about as much help as a flat tire.

BUDDY: I never wanted to be in it. I was only lookout—you're both witness to that.

ELKUS: What good do you think that does you, you poor fish? Brace up and take it like a man. There's twenty-five thousand in that bag and some of it's yours.

DOPE: How do you know it's twenty-five thousand?

ELKUS: It's the Orangeburg payroll. (BUDDY *looks offstage.*)

BUDDY: Before God, it's Judge Skimmerhorn!

ELKUS: What? Where?

BUDDY: There. Coming round the rocks. Judge Skimmerhorn
of Ledentown.

ELKUS: Does he know you?

BUDDY: Sure, he knows me.

ELKUS: We're out climbing, see? Hikers, see? On a picnic.
(*They sit.* ELKUS *puts the satchel behind rock casually.*
BIGGS *and* SKIMMERHORN *come in.*)

BIGGS: Hello.

ELKUS: How are you?

BIGGS: Out walking?

ELKUS: That's right. Climbed up on a bet.

SKIMMERHORN: Isn't that Buddy?

BUDDY: Yes, sir. Evening, Judge.

SKIMMERHORN: You're a long way from home.

BUDDY: Yes, sir.

BIGGS: Think you could show us a way down? We're stuck up
here.

BUDDY: There's a path down the cliff. Yes, sir.

SKIMMERHORN: No, thanks. I saw that one. Going to camp
here?

ELKUS: Might as well. Sure.

SKIMMERHORN: Bring anything to eat?

ELKUS: Matter of fact, we didn't.

SKIMMERHORN: Not a thing?

ELKUS: Not a thing.

SKIMMERHORN: That's funny. Camping with nothing to eat.

ELKUS: Yeah, it is kinda funny.

DOPE: We ate before we started. (*He smiles cunningly.*)

ELKUS: That's right. The Dope's right for once. We ate before we started.

SKIMMERHORN: Wish I had.

BUDDY: You—you staying up here tonight, sir?

SKIMMERHORN: Seems that way. We came up looking for
somebody.

ELKUS: Looking for somebody?

SKIMMERHORN: That's what I said.

ELKUS: Who was it?

BIGGS: That's our business.

ELKUS: I see.

SKIMMERHORN (*coming near the three*): Listen, Buddy, you're young and ambitious. Would you do something for me if you got well paid?

BUDDY: I guess so, Judge.

SKIMMERHORN (*sitting on rock and incidentally over satchel*): We're done in, traipsing around the rocks. Would you climb down the Tor and get to Haverstraw and telephone my wife I can't come home?

BUDDY: I guess so, wouldn't I, Elkus?

ELKUS: Up to you.

SKIMMERHORN: And while you're there will you buy a dozen sandwiches and some beer?

BUDDY: Yes, sir.

SKIMMERHORN: There's another thing you could do. Call up the state troopers for me, and tell them I'm here and I want them to come up and make an arrest.

BUDDY: You—want to arrest somebody?

SKIMMERHORN: You get it. What do you say?

BUDDY: I—I guess so. Is it all right, Elkus?

DOPE: Oh—no. Oh—no.

ELKUS: Sure it's O.K. Why not?

BUDDY: It'd take about five hours—to get down and back.

SKIMMERHORN: Damn it—I'll starve to death.

DOPE: What do you want to make an arrest for?

BIGGS: That's our business.

BUDDY (*crosses to* SKIMMERHORN, *takes money*): All right. I'll go.

SKIMMERHORN: Here's five dollars for you. And another when you get back. And make it fast, will you?

BUDDY: Yes, sir. (*He starts out.*)

ELKUS: Just a minute, Bud. (ELKUS *and* DOPE *follow* BUDDY *on the way out to converse with him.*)

BIGGS: You might have made it two dozen sandwiches. (*Crosses to* SKIMMERHORN.)

SKIMMERHORN: I guess I will. (*He starts to rise, places his hand on satchel and jumps.*) Christ, what's that? (*He kicks satchel.* DeWitt *appears.*)

BIGGS: Yeah?

SKIMMERHORN: I thought it was a snake. Somebody's mouldy luggage. People are always throwing truck around. (*Calls.*) Say, for God's sake, get started, will you? (DeWitt *disappears again.*)

BUDDY (*offstage*): Yes, sir. Right away. (ELKUS *and* DOPE *return.*)

ELKUS: I guess we'll all go. (*He looks nonchalantly where satchel was.*)

SKIMMERHORN: Fine. Will you make it two dozen sandwiches?

ELKUS: What the hell's going on here?

SKIMMERHORN: We're hungry, that's all.

ELKUS: Are you two finagling with us? Because if you are—!

BIGGS: What are you looking for?

ELKUS: Nothing. Who said I was looking for anything? (DeWitt *appears again as before.*)

DOPE: Hey, Elkus! They got the troopers up here! (DeWitt's *broad Dutch hat appears above rocks in rear, looking, for the moment, remarkably like that of a state trooper.* ELKUS *and* DOPE *freeze, looking at it.*)

ELKUS (*drawing a gun*): Why, you fat pimps! (DeWitt *disappears again.*)

DOPE: Beat it, you fool! (ELKUS *and* DOPE *scatter out.*)

BIGGS (*looking at rocks*): What was all that about? What did he mean by troopers?

SKIMMERHORN: Want to take a look?

BIGGS: I'm plenty unhappy, right where I am. (SKIMMERHORN *climbs up rocks.*)

SKIMMERHORN: Wish to God I did see a trooper. (*Going to rocks.*)

BIGGS: Nobody there?

SKIMMERHORN: Not a thing. Hey! Hey, you! (*A silence.*) Nope. Nobody. Looks to me as if we just missed being stuck up by a couple of lunatics.

BIGGS: They're not bringing back any sandwiches, those two. Well, if we can't get down off here I'm going to try and get some sleep.

SKIMMERHORN: Maybe you've never tried adjusting yourself to igneous limestone.

BIGGS: I'm about to try it now.

SKIMMERHORN: You have my sympathy. (BIGGS *takes off his coat for a pillow and prepares to lie down.*)

BIGGS: Thanks.

SKIMMERHORN: Beautiful shape you have. A lot of slop tied up with a piece of string.

BIGGS: God, it's cold. Listen, we could use one coat for a pillow and put the other one over us.

SKIMMERHORN: What other one?

BIGGS: Yours.

SKIMMERHORN: A proposition, huh?

BIGGS: You going to sit up all night? (*Gets down from rocks where he had climbed.*)

SKIMMERHORN: In some ways it might be preferable.

BIGGS: You can't prop yourself on end forever, like a duck on a rock.

SKIMMERHORN: Pull yourself together then. You stick out behind like (*lying down*) a bump on a duck. All right. Move over.

BIGGS: Your coat's bigger than mine. (*They pull* BIGGS' *coat around them and lie down.*)

SKIMMERHORN: Just a couple of perfect forty-nines.

BIGGS: Where the hell am I supposed to put my hipbone?

SKIMMERHORN: You juggle your own hipbones. (DEWITT *appears on rocks at rear, looking down.*)

BIGGS: If you snore, you probate judge, I'll have you disbarred.

SKIMMERHORN: Go to sleep.

BIGGS: Wish I thought I could. On bedrock. Wake me early, Mother dear, for I'm to be Queen of the May.

SKIMMERHORN: Shut up. (DEWITT *meanwhile has opened satchel and now brings it into the light to examine the contents. He takes out packages of bills, shakes satchel, then begins to go through inner pockets. He finds a roll of pennies, which he breaks open.*)

DeWITT: Copper pieces, by the great jib boom, enough to purchase a new wig, if a man ever got back to a place where money was useful to him. I might even try ships—buy a ship from one of these semi-demi-demi-semi-devils. (*Two snores rise in concert from* BIGGS *and* SKIMMERHORN. DeWITT *goes over to them, looking down on them.*) What kind of demi-semi-devil do you think you are, with four legs and two faces, both looking the same direction? Jesu Maria, it's a kind of centaur, as big one way as another, no arms, and feet the size of dishpans.

BIGGS: What's that?

DeWITT (*backing away*): It's the rear end that talks, evidently, the front being fast asleep in the manner of a figurehead.

BIGGS: Who's there? Did somebody speak?

DeWITT (*sits next to them*): None too clear in the back thinker, I should say, which would be a natural result of lugging two sets of brains, fore and aft. I'd incline to communicate with the front end, but if necessary I'll converse with the posterior.

BIGGS (*sitting up, looking at* DeWITT): Skimmerhorn!

SKIMMERHORN: What's the matter?

BIGGS: I'm damned if I know.

SKIMMERHORN: Go to sleep, then.

BIGGS: Do you believe in apparitions?

SKIMMERHORN: No.

BIGGS: Well, there's a figure of fun sitting talking to me, right out of a masquerade ball.

SKIMMERHORN: You been drinking?

BIGGS: What would I find to drink?

DeWITT: If the forecastle wakes now I shall play both ends against (*stands*) the middle, like a marine auctioneer. I want to buy a boat.

BIGGS: You've come to the wrong shop, sailor. I'm in the real-estate business, and it's a long mile down to sea level.

DEWITT: You have no boats?

BIGGS: No boats.

SKIMMERHORN: What in the hell—? (*Looks at* DEWITT.)

BIGGS: I told you I'm damned if I know.

DEWITT: And the front end has no boats?

BIGGS: You're the front end, see. He wants to know if you've got boats.

SKIMMERHORN: No, stranger, no boats.

DEWITT: Ah. (*He shakes his head mournfully, turns himself about and goes to the right, still muttering.*) The great plague on them, the lying, two-headed fairies out of a witch's placket. What chance has an honest man against a two-faced double-tongued beast, telling the same tale— (*He disappears through rocks.*)

BIGGS (*on knees*): Did you see what I saw?

SKIMMERHORN: Not if you saw what I saw. What I saw wasn't possible. Did you fake that thing?

BIGGS: Fake it? I saw it.

SKIMMERHORN: Oh, no—! Nobody saw that—what I saw. I didn't either. I've got a family to support. They aren't going to put me away anywhere.

BIGGS: Whatever it was, it left a calling card. Looks as if he ate his lunch here, supposing a thing like that eats lunch.

SKIMMERHORN: I don't want any of that.

BIGGS: You know what this is?

SKIMMERHORN: Probably a sheaf of contracts with the devil.

BIGGS: No, it's money.

SKIMMERHORN (*leaping to his feet*): Money!

BIGGS: Fives and tens.

SKIMMERHORN: Well, bless the poor little Dutchman's heart —after all we said about him, too!

BIGGS: Think he left it?

SKIMMERHORN: It wasn't there before.

BIGGS: No.

SKIMMERHORN: Were you born with a caul, or anything?

BIGGS: Always before I had to work for it, or steal it. Never till tonight have I been waked up by a little man in a big hat, fetching it to me in packages.

SKIMMERHORN: Are you asleep?

BIGGS: I probably am, asleep and dreaming.

SKIMMERHORN: If you're dreaming, you're dreaming that I found money.

BIGGS: Oh, you found it now?

SKIMMERHORN: Fifty-fifty!

BIGGS: Wait a minute. You know what money this is?

SKIMMERHORN: No.

BIGGS: It came out of the Nanuet bank. (SKIMMERHORN *takes envelope from him.*)

SKIMMERHORN: If that little guy's a bank robber he's certainly careless with the proceeds.

BIGGS: That's where it came from.

SKIMMERHORN: In that case we ought to give it back. For the reward. (*Puts money down.*)

BIGGS: No reward offered yet.

SKIMMERHORN: Maybe we ought to give it back anyway.

BIGGS: Think so?

SKIMMERHORN (*both pick up money*): Might be *marked* bills.

BIGGS: No, it's not. I was talking with the president of the bank on the phone. Made up for a payroll. No marks on any of it.

SKIMMERHORN: It ought to be returned, though.

BIGGS: Sure, it should. Question is, will it be? (*Holds* SKIMMERHORN's *eye.*)

SKIMMERHORN: I think so, don't you?

BIGGS: I'm inclined to think so. Bank robbing's way out of my line.

SKIMMERHORN: Mine, too, as a matter of fact. The president of the bank's a friend of yours?

BIGGS: Yes, he is, in a way. Oh, he's gypped me a couple of times, same as you would.

SKIMMERHORN: He wouldn't lose anything.

BIGGS: Oh, no, he's insured.

Skimmerhorn: Has it occurred to you the little Dutchman that was here might not mean any good to us?

Biggs: Did you see a little Dutchman?

Skimmerhorn: I thought I did, there for a minute.

Biggs: I don't believe that any more.

Skimmerhorn: Certainly doesn't sound very likely.

Biggs: We'd better count it. Man never ought to carry money around without knowing how much it is.

Skimmerhorn: Yeah, let's count it. It said twenty-five thousand in the paper.

Biggs: You know, nobody in the world would ever know who had it?

Skimmerhorn: No, they wouldn't.

Biggs: What do you say?

Skimmerhorn: I say fifty-fifty.

Biggs: Damn you, Skimmerhorn, if I hadn't been in business with you for twenty years I'd say you were a crook!

Skimmerhorn: There's nothing crooked about it; I want fifty per cent and it's perfectly fair.

Biggs: What's fifty per cent of twenty-five thousand? Twelve thousand five hundred! And what's forty per cent? Ten thousand. Are you going to hold up the deal for two thousand five hundred?

Skimmerhorn: I certainly am.

Biggs: All right then, take it. Fifty-fifty on this one deal.

Skimmerhorn: And on the Van Dorn deal, too.

Biggs: Why, you wizened louse— (Van Dorn *comes in.*)

Van: Sorry to bother you gentlemen—

Biggs: Where the hell did you come from?

Van: There's a storm coming up and I thought I might show you where you could keep dry under a ledge.

Biggs: Much obliged.

Van: Want me to show you the way?

Biggs: No, thanks. (Biggs *and* Skimmerhorn *go out.* Van *looks after them.* Lise *comes up rocks in rear and stands looking out to the river, shading her eyes from the beacon.*)

Lise: You who have watched this river in the past

135

till your hope turned bitterness, pity me now,
my hope gone, but no power to keep my eyes
from the mocking water. Never in all days,
never, though I should watch here without rest,
(*Comes forward.*)
will any ship come downward with the tide
flying the flag we knew.
(VAN *crosses into the light.* LISE *draws back an instant, then
steps toward him.*)
Do you hear my voice?

VAN: Yes, lady.

LISE: Do you see me?

VAN: Yes.

LISE: You are one of those
the earth bears now, the quick, fierce wizard men
who plow the mountains down with steel, and set
new mountains in their sky. You've come to drive
machines through the white rock's heart.

VAN: Not I. I hate them all like poison.

LISE: You're against them—the machines?

VAN: I'd like to smash the lot,
and the men that own them.

LISE: Oh, if there were a friend
among so many enemies! I wish
I knew how to make you friend.
I have seen you. I know you. You are kind.

VAN: How do you know?

LISE: Once when I was most lonely in the spring
I made a wild-flower garden; none of these I knew,
for none I know are here, little and lovely, nameless,
flowers of the woods. I saw you then
come on this garden and drew my breath in dread
that you should laugh and trample it. You smiled
and then went on. But when I came again
there was a new flower growing with the rest,
one I'd not seen. You brought and placed it there.
What was this flower?

136

VAN: Wild orchid. It was your garden?
LISE: Yes. You know
    the names of all the flowers?
VAN: Yes.
LISE: But then
    you'd teach them to me?
VAN: Yes.
LISE: Teach me the names.
    What is the tall three-petaled one that's black
    almost, the red's so dark?
VAN: That's trillium.
    Speaking of flowers, tell me your name.
LISE: It's Lise,
    or used to be.
VAN: Not now?
LISE: I'm weary of it,
    and all things that I've seen. You have a lover?
    She'll be angry?
VAN: She's angry now. She's off
    and gone. She won't come back.
LISE: Love me a little.
    Enough to save me from the dark.
VAN: I've seen you on the hills
    moving with shadows. But you're not shadow.
LISE: No. Could one live and be shadow?
VAN: Take my hand.
LISE: I dare not.
VAN: Come, let me see your garden.
LISE: No,
    I dare not. Never put out your hand
    to touch me, lest some magic in your blood
    reach me and I be nothing.
    I know not, under these spells, if I be cloud
    or dust. Nor whether you dream of me, or I
    make you of light and sound. But I know you're kind.
    Love me a little!
    Be gentle. You were gentle with the orchid.

Take my hand now.

VAN: You're cold.

LISE: Yes.

VAN: Here on the Tor
the sun beats down like murder all day long
and the wind comes up like murder in the night.
I'm cold myself.

LISE: How have I slipped so far
from the things you have? I'm puzzled here and lost.
Is it so different for you? Keep my hand
and tell me. In these new times are all men shadow?
All men lost?

VAN: Sometimes I stand here at night
and look out over the river when the fog
covers the lights. Then if it's dark enough
and I can't see my hands or where the rock
leaves off against the cloud, and I'm alone,
then, well I'm damned if I know who I am,
staring out into that black. Maybe I'm cloud
and maybe I'm dust. I might be as old as time.
I'd like to think I knew.

LISE: Then it's the same for you! Here on this verge
where your life dips in dusk and my gray days
lift to the light a moment, we walk here
and our eyes meet. Is it the light I feel
come flooding back in me? Light or their charms
broken here, seeing your face?

ELKUS (*offstage*): Somewhere around here it was. Over toward the crane.

DOPE (*offstage*): What'd you go and put down the satchel
for?

ELKUS (*offstage*): How did I know he'd sit on top of it? (VAN
and LISE *slip out.*)

DOPE (*entering*): That's where. Under that rock.

ELKUS (*also entering*): Keep your eye peeled. They're probably beating the woods for us.

DOPE: What's this? (*He picks up envelope that had been dropped by* BIGGS.)

ELKUS: They got it.

DOPE: God damn the rotten business! Now we will get four hundred years.

ELKUS: Now you're saying it—

DOPE: What are we going to do?

ELKUS: I'm going to send Buddy back with sandwiches to see if the Judge got the money. If he did we'll stick him up.

DOPE: Hey, how about the troopers?

ELKUS: If that was troopers I'm Admiral Dewey. Troopers woulda used the artillery. Come on.

DOPE: O.K. Some pennies here.

ELKUS: To hell with 'em. (DOPE *flings pennies to the right.*)

DOPE: Get going. (ELKUS *and* DOPE *run out.* BIGGS *and* SKIMMERHORN *come in.*)

BIGGS: Now it's raining money. I got the price of a morning paper square in the eye.

SKIMMERHORN: I've got two thousand five hundred in a breast pocket, five thousand in a side pocket, and five thousand in the billfold. (*He slaps his rear.*) How do I look?

BIGGS: You could get stuck in a revolving door. I've got five thousand in each side pocket and two thousand five hundred in the back. How do I look?

SKIMMERHORN: No different. Just a lot of slop tied up with a piece of string. All we need now's a pair of wings.

BIGGS: Wish I could find the little guy with the big heart that gave us the money. Maybe he'd help us down off this devil's belfry.

SKIMMERHORN: How about that shovel? Any possibility of making it pick us up and set us down below there?

BIGGS: Sure—if anybody was running it. If it swung us over on that dump we could slide the rest of the way. You might wear out that last five thousand of yours, the five thousand that's bringing up the rear there.

SKIMMERHORN: When do they come to work in the morning?

BIGGS: They won't come to work tomorrow. They can't do any more till we buy this land.

SKIMMERHORN: That's fine. That's just dandy.

BIGGS: Nice idea though. Somebody might come along that could run the engine.

SKIMMERHORN: You don't think that boy's coming back with the sandwiches?

BIGGS: No, I don't.

SKIMMERHORN: The way I feel inside I may never live to spend the money.

BIGGS: Who you going to leave it to?

SKIMMERHORN: Yeah?

BIGGS: Oh, all right. Nothing personal. (*They sit facing the audience.* CAPTAIN *and his* CREW, *including* DEWITT, *seep in through rocks about them and stand quietly looking on.*) There was something in that—what you said about needing a pair of wings.

SKIMMERHORN: I should say that wings was the last thing likely to grow on you. You might grow horns, or a cloven hoof, or a tail, but wings, no. Not unless somebody slipped up behind you and bashed you over the head.

BIGGS: You know, you'd murder *me* for what I've got in my pockets!

SKIMMERHORN: You thought of it first. Who am I going to leave it to, you said.

BIGGS: Just the same I wouldn't feel right if you were standing (CREW *start coming toward them*) behind me with a rock in your hand. (CREW *move in a little.*)

SKIMMERHORN: You wouldn't?

BIGGS: No. At the moment I wouldn't like to think anybody was creeping up behind me. (*He stiffens.*) And by God there is somebody behind me!

SKIMMERHORN (*without turning*): What makes you think so?

BIGGS (*running a hand over his head*): I just feel it. Turn around, will you? Take a look.

SKIMMERHORN (*shivering*): I will not. Now you've got me worried. Or else I'm getting lightheaded for lack of food.

(Biggs *ducks suddenly, as if from an imaginary blow.* Skimmerhorn *dodges in sympathy, and with their heads drawn in like turtles they creep forward on hands and knees.*) What are you dodging? Want to scare me to death? Go on, turn around and face it like a man!

Biggs: Now!

Skimmerhorn: Now! (*They whirl in concert, on their knees, facing* Crew. *They look at each other.*)

Biggs: You're crazy!

Skimmerhorn: I certainly am. And so are you.

Biggs: That isn't there at all. There's nothing there.

Skimmerhorn: All right, you go up and hit it. I'll stay right here, and you go punch it in the nose. (Biggs *stands up.*)

Biggs: Uh—how do you do? Maybe you—wanted to give us something, huh? (*To* DeWitt, *as* Crew *start forward.*) Uh—I see you brought your friends with you. If you want the money back you can have it, you know. We don't want the money. (*He sticks a hand in his pocket.*) How much was it, now? (Crew *look at each other gravely, tapping their foreheads.* Skimmerhorn *rises.*) Anything we can do, you know, we'd be glad to do. We're just trying to get down off here.

Skimmerhorn: You know what it is, Art; it's a moving-picture company. And have they got the laugh on us! Thinking they're real. It's all right, boys, we're on to you.

Biggs: Is that so? Say, I guess that's so. Was that moving-picture money you gave us, you fellows? We thought that was real. Ha, ha! That's a good one. I guess you must have thought we were pretty funny, backing up that way and jumping around. You had us scared stiff! (Crew *shake their heads at each other.*)

Asher: Lay a hand to it.

DeWitt: Lay a hand to it, lads. Heave. (Crew *catch cable hanging from steam shovel and haul on it, sailor-fashion. Shovel begins to descend.*)

Crew (*pulling down*): Heave! Heave! Heave! Heave!
    Coming a blow, coming a blow,

Sea runs black, glass runs low;
Heave! Heave!
Yardarm dips; foam's like snow!
Heave!

(*Shovel touches ground.*)

BIGGS: Say, that's an act if I ever saw one. What kind of picture you putting on? (CAPTAIN *points to interior of shovel, looking at* BIGGS *and* SKIMMERHORN. CREW *close in on them.* SKIMMERHORN *gets up first.*) What's up, anyway? Want us to go aboard? You know, we were just saying if somebody could run that thing we might get across to the dump and slide down out of here. Think you could swing it across there? (SAILORS *maneuver behind the two, edging them into machine.*) Sure, I'll get in. I'll try anything once. (CAPTAIN *gives gesture to* CREW *to hoist shovel.* BIGGS *steps in,* SKIMMERHORN *follows reluctantly.* CAPTAIN *and* DEWITT *guard their retreat.* SAILORS *catch hold of cable.* CAPTAIN *goes back to shovel.*)

CREW: Hoist! Hoist! Hoist! Hoist!
Tar on a rope's end, man on a yard,
Wind through an eyebolt, points on a card;
Hoist! Hoist!
Weevil in the biscuit, rats in the lard,
Hoist!

(*They haul* SKIMMERHORN *and* BIGGS *up as far as seems necessary, and swing crane out over the abyss. Then they stop to contemplate their handiwork.*)

BIGGS: I'll tell you what—if you catch that line over there some of you can hold back while the rest pull, and that'll swing it around. If that don't work you'd better pull it down again and we'll just wait till morning. (CREW *continue to stare silently.*)

SKIMMERHORN: You better make it snappy, boys. It gives me the megrims to look down this way. (*Draws his feet up suddenly.*) I'm going to be sick.

BIGGS: Hey, don't rock the boat, you fool! It's a thousand miles straight down!

SKIMMERHORN: I'm going to be sick.

BIGGS: You better take us down, fellows. It's no good. You can't make it.

DEWITT: How about a game of bowls? (CAPTAIN *nods.*)

PIETER: Aye, a game of bowls. (*Led by* CAPTAIN, CREW *begin to file out.*)

BIGGS: Hey, you wouldn't leave us up here, would you? Hey, listen! You! You can have that money back, you know! We don't want the money! What in the name of time? Listen, what did we ever do to you? A joke's a joke, after all, but this thing might let go any minute! What's more you're responsible if anything happens to us! There's such a thing as laws in this country! (*But they have all gone.*)

SKIMMERHORN: I'm sick.

BIGGS: You'll be sicker before you're out of this mess. What do you think they meant by that?

SKIMMERHORN: I don't know. Quit kicking me, will you? I'm sick.

BIGGS: Well, keep it to yourself.

SKIMMERHORN: I wish I thought I could.

BIGGS: Help, somebody! Help! We're stuck up here!

SKIMMERHORN: What good's that going to do?

BIGGS: You don't think they'll leave us here, do you?

SKIMMERHORN: I don't know. I don't care. I wish I was dead! Say, keep away from me, will you? What are you trying to do, pick my pocket?

BIGGS: Pick your pocket, you fish? All I ask is keep your feet out of my face.

SKIMMERHORN: Well, where in hell's my billfold?

BIGGS: How do I know? Do you think I took it?

SKIMMERHORN: Come on, now. Where is it? (*He searches his clothes frantically.*)

BIGGS: You're probably sitting on it. You are sitting on it. There it is.

SKIMMERHORN (*finding it*): Jeez, I might have lost it.

BIGGS: Now you'd better count it. Just to make sure it's good.

SKIMMERHORN: I think I will. (*He begins to count bills.*) It's good money, Art. Look at it.

BIGGS: Not a bad idea, either. (*He takes out money and counts it. There is a flash, a long roll and a crash of thunder. Then another and another.*) Isn't that coming pretty close?

SKIMMERHORN: What?

BIGGS: The lightning, you fool! Put your money away before you get it wet.

SKIMMERHORN: There's one thing about money you find. You don't have to pay income tax on it.

BIGGS: That's true. (*Crash of thunder.*) You know what I think?

SKIMMERHORN: No.

BIGGS: There's something up there taking pot shots at us. (*There is a terrific flash, a crash, and stage is in darkness.*) That one got the beacon! (*Another flash runs right down the crane.*) Good God, will you quit that? That's close enough! Say, do you know any prayers?

SKIMMERHORN: I know one.

BIGGS: Say it, will you?

SKIMMERHORN: Matthew, Mark, Luke and John,
Bless the bed that I lie on.

BIGGS: That's not much good, that one.

SKIMMERHORN: It's the only one I know. Hey, catch it—hey!

BIGGS: What? (*The lightning is now an almost perpetual illumination, the thunder a constant roll.*)

SKIMMERHORN: I dropped fourteen ten-dollar bills!

BIGGS: Do you know we're going to die here? (*Pulls him back.*)

SKIMMERHORN: We're going to what?

BIGGS: Will you quit counting money? We're going to be killed! We're going to die right here in our own steam shovel!

SKIMMERHORN: Oh, no, I can't die now. I'm not ready to die!

BIGGS: I wish you'd put up your money, then, and pray!

SKIMMERHORN: I don't know how to pray. (*A crash.*)

BIGGS (*on his knees*): Oh, God, I never did this before, and I

don't know how, but keep me safe here and I'll be a better
man! I'll put candles on the altar, yes, I'll get that Spring
Valley church fixed up, the one that's falling down! I can
do a lot for you if you'll let me live! Oh, God— (*A crash.*)
SKIMMERHORN (*on his knees, his hands full of money*): Oh,
God, you wouldn't do a thing like that, hang us up in our
own steam shovel, wet through, and then strike us with
lightning! Oh, God, you've been kind to us tonight, and
given us things we never expected to get so easy; don't
spoil it now! God damn it, there goes another batch of bills!
(*He snatches at the falling money, and is hauled back by*
BIGGS.) I don't know how to pray! (*Another crash.*)
BIGGS: Say the one you know, then, for God's sake—say it!
SKIMMERHORN: Matthew, Mark, Luke and John,
    Bless the bed that I lie on!
BIGGS: Matthew, Mark, Luke and John,
    Bless the bed—
Why don't you tell him you'll give the money back?
SKIMMERHORN: Because I won't! And you won't, either! (*Big
crash.*)
BIGGS: Now you've done it! Can't you keep anything to your-
self? There's such a thing as being politic, even when you're
talking to God Almighty! (*Thunder again.*)

ACT II

SCENE 1

SCENE: *The same. The Tor and the steam shovel as before,
only five or six hours later. It's still pitch dark, and* BIGGS
and SKIMMERHORN *are still in the shovel. They are, how-
ever, fast asleep in much the same postures they took
formerly on the ground. Under the shovel sits* DEWITT,
picking up and smoothing on his knee a few bills which

*he has found blowing loose on the rock. The beacon light
flashes into the scene.*

DeWitt: There comes on the light again, too, the sweeping
light that withers a body's entrails. No sooner out than lit
again. (*Two snores rise from the sleeping pair.*) Aye, take
your ease and rest, you detachable Doppelgangers, swollen
with lies, protected by the fiends, impervious to lightning,
shedding rain like ducks—and why wouldn't you shed rain?
Your complexions being pure grease and your insides blub-
ber? You can sleep, you can rest. You of the two-bottoms.
You make nothing for the lightning playing up and down
your backbones, or turning in on cold iron, but a poor
sailor out of Holland, what rest has he? (*He smooths a bill.*)
These will be tokens and signs, these will, useful in magic,
potent to ward off evil or put a curse on your enemies.
Devil's work or not, I shall carry them on me, and make
myself a match for these fulminating latter-day spirits. (*He
pouches the bills.*) I'm hanged if it's not noticeable at
once, a sort of Dutch courage infused into the joints and
tissues from the mere pocketing up of their infernal
numbered papers. (*He takes out bill and looks at it.*) That's
sorcery, that's witchcraft; why, this stuff would make a man
out of a cocked hat and a pair of crutches! (*He slaps his
chest.*) Now I shall face destiny and take it like a pinch
of snuff! Which reminds me I could use a pinch of snuff.
(*He takes out his snuffbox.*) Snuff? When have I reached
for snuff? It would seem to me I haven't gone after snuff in
something like two hundred years! (*He ladles into both
nostrils and sneezes violently.*) Aha, DeWitt! You're a man,
DeWitt! A man and a devil! And what shall we wish for
now that we have wishing papers in the pockets of our
pantaloons? What but a woman, one of these new female
furies of theirs, wearing pants like a man, and with nothing
to indicate her sex but the general conformation! (*He draws
out the bills.*) Let my woman appear, god of the numbered
papers, and let her wear what she likes, so long as a man

can make out how she's made. Let her appear within this next three minutes, for God knows how long this mood will last in an old man! (*He takes another pinch of snuff.* BUDDY *enters, carrying beer and sandwiches.*)

BUDDY: Hello.

DEWITT: What answer would a man make to that now? That's a strange greeting.

BUDDY: Seen a couple of old fat men around anywhere?

DEWITT: Boy, I have seen nothing else all night.

BUDDY: Where are they?

DEWITT: You wish to find a couple of old fat men?

BUDDY: That's right.

DEWITT: I begin to doubt the supernal powers of these new angel-demons. Here he stands in their presence and asks very foolishly if old DeWitt has seen them.

BUDDY: What's foolish about that?

DEWITT: A cabin boy.

BUDDY: What's the matter with you?

DEWITT: What do you carry in the bag?

BUDDY: That's my business.

DEWITT: He has a business, then? He is not perhaps so witless as he appears.

BUDDY: Are you going to tell me where those two are, or do you want me to blow your brains out?

DEWITT: Is my carcass so thin you think to puff my brains out with a breath? Look, 'prentice devil, I am one of you. I bear your signs and symbols. Here you see your own countersign, a cabalistic device of extreme rarity and force. What have you in the bag?

BUDDY: Nothing but sandwiches. What do you mean, you're one of us?

DEWITT: You should recognize the insignium.

BUDDY: Where'd you get it?

DEWITT: It blew away from these same two fat men, 'prentice devil; but now I have it, and it's mine and I obtain power over you. Let me see these sandwiches.

BUDDY: It blew away from the fat men, huh? All right, that's what I want to know. It's mine, see? Hand it over. (*Places bag on rocks.*)

DEWITT: You reveal yourself a very young and tender 'prentice.

BUDDY: Hand it over or I'll fill you full of holes. (*He sets down his packages and draws a gun, but* DEWITT *is beforehand with two flintlock pistols.*)

DEWITT: You will drop your child's armory on the ground, cabin boy, or I shall pull both triggers at once and blast you halfway to the water. (BUDDY *drops gun.*) I tell you I am now a great devil and violent. When I wish merely I have my way. (BUDDY *suddenly takes to his heels. Goes out.* DEWITT *pulls triggers one after another, hammers click but there is no explosion.*) I am left in possession of the field! (*He picks up* BUDDY's *automatic.*) They fight with the weapons of children. Why, this world begins to be mine to do with as I please. Whatever kind of witch a sandwich may be, come out and let me interrogate you. (*He takes out sandwiches.*) If it be the food eaten by witches and wizards, so much the better, for I am now a wizard myself, and by the great jib boom I haven't tasted food in God knows when. (*He eats.*) A sweet and excellent morsel, very strong with garlic and salami, medicinal for the veins and bladder. (*He examines bottle of beer.*) I will eat your rations, cabin boy out of the new age, and I will master you all, men and maids, now that my strength comes back, but I will not drink your feeble drink.

JUDITH (*entering*): Van! Van!

DEWITT: A woman! By the great tropical cross, a savage woman, come in answer to these printed charms! (*She starts to go off.*) Don't run away, please. You're seeking someone—you're seeking a certain lad, I know—but he's lost and past praying for.

JUDITH (*pausing*): He's lost? What do you mean? I'm looking for Van Van Dorn.

DEWITT: That may well be his name. But he's lost and gone,

ma'am, lost the way a woman loses her man, a mere shift of partners—easily remedied—

JUDITH: Do you know him?

DEWITT: I've seen him about.

JUDITH: Where is he?

DEWITT: If you hunt out a very pretty little mistress named Lise in a bonnet somewhat behind the fashion, and look under the bonnet, you may chance to find him there.

JUDITH: You live on the mountain?

DEWITT: I maintain a residence here, though the situation eludes me at the moment.

JUDITH: Van told me about you. You're a shadow, and not real at all. I'm not afraid of you. You're a shadow.

DEWITT: Aye, but grown, God knows how, to something of a person this last quarter hour.

JUDITH: Forgive me, I shall look elsewhere.

DEWITT: Now a pretty lass like yourself should have no trouble replacing one sailorman with another in these stirring times. They come and go like a run of salmon. Could you find it in your heart to love me?

JUDITH: I'm sorry, no.

DEWITT: To save a sad and desperate man from such a death as the lines of frost on a window? I'm a blunt man, but constant, and of considerable substance on my own wharf. This is a kindly face, this of mine, and a kindly heart under a worn jerkin. These are real tears on my cheeks, too, and I weep them for you, lady.

JUDITH: They're not real at all, and you're not real.

DEWITT: But you could save me from their sorcery, and I'm a sad and broken man, lady, lost here among the lesser known peaks on the west side of the world, and looking only for a hand to help me.

JUDITH: Isn't there someone coming there now?

DEWITT: If there be, watch what soldierly stand old DeWitt makes in defense of a lady! Come out, children of the new Satan, show yourselves in the light! (ELKUS *and* DOPE *creep in, and* JUDITH *runs out.*)

ELKUS: Stick 'em up, bo! (*They train automatics on him.*)

DEWITT: More toys! Stand back, you cheap new devils!

ELKUS: Keep your hands down or I'll let you have it!

DEWITT: Watch now how a man holds off the fiends. (*He lifts his pistols.*)

ELKUS: Give it to him! (*They fire a fusillade at* DEWITT, *who stands unmoved.*)

DEWITT: Firecrackers! You think me a devil like yourselves, to be exorcised with firecrackers?

ELKUS: Give it to him again! (*They fire once more.*)

DEWITT: Look, you puny devils, I'm a patient man, but in one moment I shall blow you both into the Tappan Zee!

ELKUS: Too bad about you! (*To* DOPE.) Take the money off him.

DOPE: There's something funny about this guy! I can see right through him!

ELKUS: No wonder. He's full of holes as a tennis racket.

DOPE: No, by God, I can see through him! Look! (*They step back together.*)

ELKUS: What kind of a thing are you?

DEWITT: I'm not a man to be daunted by loud noises and firecrackers, Beelzebub! Go seek your place with the new father of hell before I send you there! Wizards!

ELKUS: Where's the money?

DEWITT: I have a talisman and I ate a sandwich, devils!

DOPE: Look, he's a moving picture! He's a regular church window! Look!

DEWITT: Disperse or I fire! (*Pointing at* DOPE.)

ELKUS: Keep out of the way of that sawed-off shotgun! (DOPE *suddenly runs in and shoots* DEWITT *through the head, then retreats.*)

DEWITT: I warn you, I begin to be annoyed!

DOPE: It's no use, chief. I blew his brains out, and he's standing right there!

BIGGS (*looking over the side of shovel*): It's a war.

ELKUS: Who said that?

DOPE: Damned if I know.

ELKUS: Beat it.

DOPE: Yeah, beat it. Let the money hang. I'm for Canada.

ELKUS: You said it. (*They turn tail. As they are going out
DeWitt fires his pistols in the air.*)

DeWITT: Now am I master of the world of things,
    a buccaneer, a devil and a rake!
    Women love mastery, and they ran from me;
    they ran, these minor devils, ran from DeWitt!
    Look where they go there, sweetheart!

(*He turns.*)

    God, she's gone!
    Lady! New-world lady! Are you lost?

(*He follows her.*)

    Look now, I've dispersed them, brats and wizards,
    spawn out of hell, they ran! I'm master here,
    I'm master of the world! Look, lady!

(*He goes out.*)

SKIMMERHORN: Are you awake?

BIGGS: I hope not. I hope this is a nightmare and I wake up
at home in bed.

SKIMMERHORN: How did we get here?

BIGGS: It must have been something we ate.

SKIMMERHORN: I didn't eat anything.

BIGGS: There are some sandwiches down there on the ground.

SKIMMERHORN: That's a pleasant thought.

BIGGS: Look for yourself.

SKIMMERHORN: You're right. There are sandwiches.

BIGGS: Didn't we send somebody for sandwiches and beer,
way back before all this started?

SKIMMERHORN: I don't know. I'm all wet, and I'm stuck to
the shovel.

BIGGS: If any of your constituency sees you in this condition
you're out of office for good.

SKIMMERHORN: I don't care. I feel terrible. How in hell did
those sandwiches get there?

BIGGS: How in hell did we get here?

SKIMMERHORN: You haven't got a fishhook on you, have you?

BIGGS: No, I haven't. (*They sit gloomily looking at sand-wiches. VAN and LISE come in.*)

VAN: We can go through this way—

LISE: But there I dare not walk. I'm frightened here where the
    great machines come down.

VAN: Why, Lise?

LISE: When the wizards come to tear the mountain down,
    I'll have no place. I'll be gone then.

VAN: Child, they won't get our mountain!
    Not if I have to shoot them as they come,
    they won't get our mountain! The mountain's mine.
    All their world's made up of fat men doing tricks with laws
    to manage tides and root up hills. The hills
    can afford to laugh at them.

LISE: And yet—don't go too near!
    Never see them or hear their words.
    Already they may have touched you.
    I was once here as you are, loving the light,
    and my waking day was day, and my sleep was dreams,
    but now all days and nights are one waking dream—
    as yours may be now you walk here with me.
    You are not like these men;
    you are their enemy. Then lest they find you out
    and reach you, and we be helpless here together,
    don't go too near.

VAN: How could they hurt us, Lise?

LISE: I don't know, but you walk here in my night,
    and your dream's mine!

VAN: These fellows you call wizards,
    they're all asleep, and the power's turned off, and the bucket's
    empty—even if they were all awake
    they can't hurt us, Lise. Right over there
    my line begins, and they have nothing to say

    this side that line. But we'll give it a wide berth
    if it frightens you.
(They start to go out as they came.)
BIGGS: Hey—who's that, Van Dorn!
VAN: What are you doing on the roost, you birds?
    Building a nest?
BIGGS: We can't get down.
VAN: I'd say
    it ought to be just as easy to get down
    as it was to get up there.
SKIMMERHORN: Will you help us out?
VAN: You look all right to me. What happened to you?
BIGGS: It's a long story!
VAN: You've been there all night?
BIGGS: Yes, all night.
VAN: I wouldn't want to spoil it.
    It's too good to be true. You see those two,
    Lise, there in the scoop?
LISE: They're pitiful.
    Shouldn't you help them?
VAN: No. Since time began
    there haven't been two fatguts that deserved
    a hoisting like those two. In their own machine—
    that makes it perfect.
LISE: What have they done?
VAN: They've been themselves, that's all. Two thieves.
    They want High Tor among other things, and mean
    to carve it down, at three cents a square yard.
LISE: Those two old men?
VAN: Those two old men.
LISE: Let them hang there, then!
VAN: They'll hang there for all me.
SKIMMERHORN: I'll tell you what,
    Van Dorn, I'll let you have the validation
    If you'll help me down.
VAN: That means my title's clear?
SKIMMERHORN: Sure.

VAN: Only you'd cancel it,
    once you got home.
SKIMMERHORN: To tell the truth I couldn't,
    not if you had the paper.
VAN: Toss it over;
    I'd like to see it.
(SKIMMERHORN *takes out both papers and throws one to*
    VAN.)
BIGGS: You're a simple judge!
    Now the land's his.
VAN: There's a bond goes with this,
    a bond signed by the court. Oh, I looked it up.
    I've read that much law.
SKIMMERHORN: Yes. I'll keep the bond
    till we're on your level.
VAN: Then I'd advise you both
    to make yourself a nest with two-three sticks,
    like a couple of crows, and settle down to see
    what you can hatch—or maybe lay an egg—
    you'll have plenty of time.
BIGGS: Come now, Van Dorn, we're in a bad way.
    Out of common humanity, lean on that cable
    and pull us in.
(VAN *pulls. Shovel dips.*)
VAN: Now, here my—
    Toss me the bond,
    or I'll give this line a yank
    and you won't even hang.
SKIMMERHORN: You wouldn't do it!
VAN: Oh wouldn't I? Just for a taste, how's the incline now?
    A little steep?
(*He pulls line. Shovel tips as before.*)
SKIMMERHORN: Straighten it up.
VAN: Do I get the bond?
SKIMMERHORN: Hell, yes!
(VAN *restores their equilibrium.* SKIMMERHORN *throws down
    bond.*)

154

BIGGS: And now you've got it, how's five thousand sound?
　　Settle for it, and let us down in the bargain.
VAN: Bid against them, Lise.
　　What would you say?
　　They offer me five thousand.
LISE: Pieces of silver?
VAN: Pieces of silver.
LISE: But I'll give you more!
　　I offer you nine thousand!
　　To be paid in silver!
VAN: You hear? I've got nine thousand;
　　what am I offered?
BIGGS: Make it ten thousand.
VAN: Yes? Ten thousand?
　　A mountain for ten thousand? Hear them, Lise.
　　In their despair they lift it by a grand!
　　Should it go for ten?
SKIMMERHORN: We'll never get it back—
　　but that's all right.
VAN: Yes, Lise?
LISE: A hundred thousand, sir, in silver.
　　This is my offer!
VAN: Come, now, meet it, boys—
　　I have a hundred thousand!
BIGGS: She's a fraud! She's
　　no dealer; she's a ringer, primed
　　to put the price up! What do you mean by silver?
VAN: Coinage of the moon,
　　but it's current here!
SKIMMERHORN: Ten thousand, cash, and that's
　　the last. Five thousand out of my pocket, see,
　　and five from Biggs!
(*He pulls out bundle of bills.* BIGGS *does same.*)
　　Take a good look at cash,
　　see how that operates!
(*He tosses down both rolls.*)

VAN: You go well heeled
   when you go mountain-climbing. Is it real?
SKIMMERHORN: Well, look it over. Count it.
(VAN *takes up one packet, then other.*)
VAN: Where did this come from?
SKIMMERHORN: Where would you think?
VAN (*studying bills again*): I don't want this money.
BIGGS: What's wrong with it?
VAN: Didn't I tell you I had a hundred thousand?
   Take the stuff back. Put up your mitts!
(*He tosses bundles back.*)
   It's no sale. What's more,
   I never meant to sell.
   The auctioneer's about to take a walk.
SKIMMERHORN: You won't do that, Van Dorn?
   Just leave us here?
VAN: Watch me, if you don't think so. Sweet dreams!
SKIMMERHORN: We'll run you out of the state, Van Dorn.
VAN: You'll have to get down first!
(*He gives an arm to* LISE.)
   Let me tell you about those thieves.
(*They go out.*)
SKIMMERHORN: Is he going away and leave us sitting?
BIGGS: Looks like it.
SKIMMERHORN: He got away with that bond.
BIGGS: Yeah.
SKIMMERHORN: Looks as if we wouldn't make anything on
   Van Dorn.
BIGGS: That's what it looks like.
SKIMMERHORN: Christ.
BIGGS: Well, we've still got the windfall.
SKIMMERHORN: Yeah, we've got that.
BIGGS: And here he comes again.
SKIMMERHORN: Who?
BIGGS: Our mascot, our rabbit's foot, our good luck token—
(DEWITT *comes in.*)
DEWITT: Magic again! More devil's work. The woman

gone, slipped round a turn, and the scent was cold
for an old dog like me. By the mizzen yards,
it's wearing to the temper of a man
even if he's not choleric!—And those two,
those buzzards of evil omen, brooding there
on how they'll cut the mountain like a pie
and sell it off in slices!
(*He takes out his pistols.*)
　　　One apiece.
It should be just enough, and it's a wonder
I never thought of it.
(*He lifts his pistols.*)
　　　Now then, damn you, blow 'em off their perch!
(*As he starts to fire, his eye catches something out on the
　　Zee. He stands transfixed for a moment, watching.*)
　　　The ship! It can't be there!
It's there! It's gone! I saw it! Captain Asher!
Captain! Captain! Captain! the river! Captain Asher!
(*He rushes out.*)

ACT II

SCENE 2

SCENE: *Another part of the Tor, a scene similar to the others.
　　LISE is sitting up on a ledge, looking into the west. VAN
　　stretches on ground beside her.*

VAN: It's almost morning.
LISE: How do you know?
VAN: See that star,
　　that heavy red star back in the west? When that
　　goes down, then look for the morning star across
　　Long Island Sound, and after that the lights
　　dim down in the gray.

LISE: When did you part from Judith?
VAN: Judith?
LISE: When did she go away?
VAN: Last evening.
    But it seems longer.
LISE: Why?
VAN: Why, a lot's happened—
LISE: You loved her very much?
VAN: Yes.
LISE: I loved someone, too. I love him still.
VAN: No, you're mine now.
LISE: See the great gulf that lies
    between the heavy red star down the west,
    and the star that comes with morning? It's a long way.
    There's that much lies between us.
VAN: Not for me.
LISE: Even for you. You're weary?
    Put your head down.
    I'll hold you.
VAN: Well, the truth is
    I sometimes sleep at night.
(He lays his head on her knees and stretches out.)
LISE: Now I'll wish that I could sing
    and make you sleep. Somehow they're all forgotten,
    the old songs.
    May I ask you something?
VAN: Yes.
LISE: There's so much that's changed now men can fly
    and hear each other across seas, must men
    still die—do they die still?
VAN: Oh, yes, they die.
    Why do you ask?
LISE: Because I'm still so young,
    and yet I can't remember all the years
    there must have been. In a long night sometimes
    I try to count them, but they blow in clouds
    across the sky, the dancing firefly years,

incredible numbers. Tell me how old you are
before you go to sleep.

VAN: Lying here now
there's not much logic in arithmetic.
Five or six maybe. Five or six thousand, maybe.
But when I'm awake I'm twenty-three.

LISE: No more?

VAN: No more.

LISE: Have I been enchanted here?
I've seen the traprock men, there in the shovel, seeming
so stupid and so pitiful. Could these
use charms and rites to hold wrecked mariners
forever in a deep cataleptic spell
high on a mountain-fringe?

VAN: The traprock men?
They're no more wizards than I am. They buy
and sell, and when they've had their fill of dust
they die like the rest of us.

LISE: But they laid spells
about us?

VAN: There are no wizards and no spells.
Just men and women and money and the earth,
the way it always was. The traprock men
don't know you're here.

LISE: It's not sorcery, then? If I had died
and left my bones here on the mountaintop
but had no memory of it, and lived on
in dreams, it might be as it is. As children
sure we were told of living after death,
but there were angels there, and on stone
paving an angel city, no darkness and no sun,
nothing of earth. Now can it be men die
and carry thence no memory of death,
only this curious lightness of the hands,
only this curious darkness of the mind,
only to be still changeless with the winters
passing, drifting among men,

till one by one forgotten, fading out
we lose our hold and go?
Could it be true? Could this be how men die?

VAN (*half asleep*): I love you when you speak.

LISE: And I love you.
But I am dead, and all the crew is dead—
and we have clung beyond our place and time,
on into a world unreal as sleep, unreal as this
your sleep that comes upon you now. Oh you were cruel
to love me and to tell me I am dead
and lie here warm and living. You haven't heard.
Sleep, sweet. When you wake we shall be parted.
You will have a world but I'll have none.

(JUDITH *comes up rocks.*)
You are Judith?

JUDITH: Yes.

LISE: The lad's asleep, but when he wakes
you'll have him back.

JUDITH: Do you dispose of him
just as you please?

LISE: It's not what I please.
It's what will happen.
He'll wake and he'll be yours,
all as it was.

JUDITH: Why are you crying?

LISE: Am I crying?
Well, they're not for him, nor you, these tears;
something so far away, so long ago,
so hopeless, so fallen, so lost, so deep in dust
the names wash from the urns, summons my tears,
not love or longing. Only when you have him,
love him a little better for your sake,
for your sake only, knowing how bitterly
I cried for times past and things done.

JUDITH: You're strange—I'm afraid of you.

LISE: Afraid of tears
and a voice out of long ago? It's all I have.

JUDITH: No—no—I'm not afraid. Only for him.
　　I've done my crying, too. Shall I come back?
LISE: Don't wake him now. Come back at dawn. You'll find
　　him here alone.
CAPTAIN (*offstage*): Lise! Lise! Lise!
(CAPTAIN *comes in at rear with* DEWITT.)
　　Lise, the ship's on the river! Quick, there's haste!
　　She must catch the tide downstream!
LISE: Hush! Hush! You'll wake him!
CAPTAIN: But look across the Zee! The *Onrust's* in
　　and waiting for us!
LISE: But you say it, Asher,
　　only to comfort me. There is no ship,
　　nor are we caught in spells here, or enchanted.
　　There is no ship, only a phantom haunting down the Zee
　　as we still haunt the heights.
CAPTAIN: Look! The *Onrust!*
　　Look, Lise!
LISE: Yes, I see it.
CAPTAIN: Will you come?
LISE: Why should I stay? Why should I go? For go
　　or stay, we're phantoms still.
CAPTAIN (*going out*): Come, Lise, we must go quickly!
LISE: Yes, it's better that I go.
VAN (*wakening and sitting up*): Where must you go?
LISE: The *Onrust's* on the river
　　and we must catch the tide.
VAN: Would you leave me now?
LISE: Yes, I must leave you!
VAN: You'll go back with him?
LISE: Yes.
VAN: And was nothing meant of all we said?
LISE: What could we mean, we two? Your hurt's quite cured,
　　and mine's past curing.
VAN: Let me go with you, then.
　　Any world you have I'll make it mine.
　　Give me your hand again!

LISE: The world I have is a wraith of yesterdays,
    burnt out and cold, and you must live today,
    play now with fire while fire will burn,
    bend down the bough and eat before the fruit falls.
    For there comes a time when the great sunlit pattern
    of the earth shakes like an image under water, darkens,
    dims, and the clearest voices that we know are sunken
      bells,
    dead, sullen, undersea, receding.

VAN: I'll be alone here.

LISE: No, not alone. She'll come back
    and she'll be yours.

CAPTAIN (*offstage*): Lise, come!

LISE: When you must walk the air,
    as all must walk it sometime, with a tread
    that stirs no leaf, and breathe here with a breath
    that blows impalpable through smoke or cloud,
    when you are as I am, a bending wind
    along the grain, think of me some time then.

CAPTAIN (*offstage*): Lise!

LISE: See, the dawn points
    with one purple finger at a star
    to put it out. When it has quite gone out
    then we'll be gone.

(VAN *looks at dawn, then turns back to* LISE.)

VAN: Lise! Lise!

(*But even as he speaks she moves off down the cliff.*)

LISE: This is your age, your dawn, your life to live.
    The morning light strikes through us, and the wind
    that follows after rain tugs at our sails—
    and so we go.

DEWITT: And welcome you are to the age, too, an age of
    paper, an age of paper money and paper men, so that a
    poor Dutch wraith's more man than the thickest of you!
    (*He disappears down cliff.*)

VAN: There is a ship. The canvas casts no shadow;

the light sifts through the spars. A moonlight rig
no doubt they call it.

SAILORS (*sounds of wisp of chantey in the distance*):
Coming a blow, coming a blow,
Sea runs black, glass runs low.

VAN: Just voices down the wind.
Why, then they were all mist, a fog that hangs
along the crevices of hills, a kind
of memory of things you read in books,
things you thought you'd forgotten. She was here
and she was real, but she was cloud and gone
and the hill's barren of her. There are no ghosts,
I know, but these were ghosts, or I'm a ghost,
and all of us. God knows where ghosts leave off
and we begin, God knows where we leave off
and ghosts begin. Maybe I'm ghost myself,
maybe we're all the same, these ghosts of Dutchmen,
clinging to what's been lost three hundred years,
and one poor superannuated Indian,
and one last hunter, clinging to his land
because he's always had it. Trying to hold
an age back with his hands. Trying to hold
an age back with his hands.

ACT III

SCENE: *The same as preceding scene.*
The shovel still hangs over the verge, and BIGGS *and* SKIM-
MERHORN *still occupy it. The rising sun sends level rays
across the rock, lighting their intent faces as they stare
downward.* BIGGS *has torn a handkerchief into strips and
tied them together into a string. He appears to be fishing
for something which lies below the ledge, out of view of
the audience. Over and over he tries his cast.*

SKIMMERHORN: Little to the left.

BIGGS: You don't say?

SKIMMERHORN: Little to the right.

BIGGS: Put it to a tune and sing it, why don't you?

SKIMMERHORN: There! Almost!

BIGGS: I don't need any umpire.

SKIMMERHORN: Let me try it.

BIGGS: Oh, no. You always were a butterfingers. (*The string tightens.*) By Golly!

SKIMMERHORN: It's on!

BIGGS: You're explaining to me? (*He pulls up. A bottle of beer emerges from below.*)

SKIMMERHORN: Fifty per cent!

BIGGS: What? (*He pauses, bottle in air.*)

SKIMMERHORN: You tore up my handkerchief! Fifty per cent! That's the natural division between capital and labor.

BIGGS: Oh, now I'm labor and you're capital! (*He pulls up carefully.*)

SKIMMERHORN: Fifty per cent!

BIGGS: I get the first pull at it. That's all I ask. (*The string parts, and the bottle descends silently into the void.*) That's that.

SKIMMERHORN: (*Sits.*) You shoulda let me handle it.

BIGGS: Yeah. No doubt. Here's your handkerchief.

SKIMMERHORN: Thanks. Am I thirsty?

BIGGS: Wait till the sun gets up a little. We'll be pan-fried in this thing.

SKIMMERHORN (*stands*): Look! (*He points down the rocks.*)

BIGGS: If it's more of those little people, I give up.

SKIMMERHORN: It's a trooper.

BIGGS: What do you know? Up early for a trooper, too. Listen, about that stuff in our pockets?

SKIMMERHORN: Yeah?

BIGGS: Do we say anything about it?

SKIMMERHORN: Do you?

BIGGS: Do you?

SKIMMERHORN: No.

BIGGS: Neither do I, then. (*A* TROOPER *climbs in, followed by* SKIMMERHORN, SENIOR.)

TROOPER (*outside*): Hello!

BIGGS: Hello, Patsy!

PATSY (*entering*): Say; you boys had the wives worried down in Ledentown. Been looking for you all night. There they are, Mr. Skimmerhorn.

SENIOR (*winded*): Good God! And I climbed up here. We thought you were under that rock slide.

SKIMMERHORN: I guess you're disappointed.

SENIOR: The next time you two go on a bat and spend a night up a tree you can stay there and sober up.

SKIMMERHORN: We haven't been drinking.

SENIOR: What were you doing? You came up here to buy Van Dorn's property; you're gone all night, and the whole damn town's up all night hunting for you! And we find you up in a steam shovel enjoying a hang-over!

BIGGS: I tell you we didn't even have a drink of water.

SENIOR: I believe that. Now tell me what you were doing last night. Did you see Van Dorn?

SKIMMERHORN: Sure we saw him.

SENIOR: Well, what did he say?

SKIMMERHORN: He said no.

SENIOR: And I suppose that took all night?

SKIMMERHORN: We had an argument.

SENIOR: And then he chased you up the crane, I suppose?

SKIMMERHORN: No.

SENIOR: Well, how did you get up there?

SKIMMERHORN: We were hauled up.

SENIOR: All right. Who hauled you up?

SKIMMERHORN: You tell him, Art.

BIGGS: Oh, no. You tell him.

SKIMMERHORN: As a matter of fact, I don't think it happened.

SENIOR: You're there, aren't you?

SKIMMERHORN: Yes, we're here.

SENIOR: Well, if you weren't drunk how did you get there?

MAXWELL ANDERSON

SKIMMERHORN: Well, you see, first we tried to negotiate with Van Dorn.

SENIOR: And he wouldn't take the money?

SKIMMERHORN: That's right.

SENIOR: Then what happened?

SKIMMERHORN: Well, we couldn't get down because of the slide, so some sailors offered to let us down in this thing.

SENIOR: Sailors—up here?

SKIMMERHORN: Funny little men, in big hats.

SENIOR: Any elephants? Or snakes?

SKIMMERHORN: Are you going to let us down out of this basket?

SENIOR: No. Not till you come across with what's been going on.

SKIMMERHORN: All right. I'll talk when I'm down. (VAN DORN *comes in.*)

SENIOR: Who are you?

SKIMMERHORN: That's Van Dorn.

SENIOR: Mr. Van Dorn, I'm A. B. Skimmerhorn, President of Igneous Traprock.

VAN: Are these friends of yours?

SENIOR: One's a nephew and one's a partner. Why?

VAN: Well, swing them back on your own property.

SENIOR: Look, Mr. Van Dorn, there must have been some misunderstanding. Those two were hardly in condition to negotiate. But I can offer you a fair price for your land, and if you don't take it we may have to push you a little, because we want this acreage and we intend to have it.

SKIMMERHORN: He's got the validation papers.

SENIOR: You gave him the validation papers? (SKIMMERHORN *nods.*) That puts us in a sweet mess, that does. Will you take twenty-five thousand?

VAN: No.

SENIOR: Will you take fifty thousand?

VAN: No. (INDIAN *comes in.*)

INDIAN: Ready, Van?

VAN: I was looking for you.

166

SENIOR: Look, Van Dorn. You know the saying,
    every man has his price. I've heard it said
    God has His price, if you'll go high enough.
    Set a figure.

VAN: I'm not thinking of prices.
    I don't want to sell. Hell, fifty thousand's
    too much money for me.

SENIOR: We'll give you less.

VAN: I don't want less or more. It's not a matter
    of money.

SENIOR: Good God, what do you want?

VAN: I want to have it back the way it was
    before you came here. Will you get out! I know
    what kind of fool I look to all of you,
    all but old John there. But I'll be a fool
    along with John, and keep my own, before
    I let you have an inch. John, fifty thousand
    or this old hilltop. Is it worth keeping?

INDIAN: No.

VAN: No?

INDIAN: It's gone already. Not worth keeping.

VAN: I thought you'd say it was. I counted on you
    to be my friend in that.

INDIAN: It's an old question,
    one I heard often talked of round the fire
    when the hills and I were younger. Then as now
    the young braves were for keeping what was ours,
    whatever it cost in blood. And they did try,
    but when they'd paid their blood, and still must sell,
    the price was always less than what it was
    before their blood was paid.

VAN: Well, that may be.

INDIAN: I wish now I had listened when they spoke
    their prophecies, the sachems of the tents;
    for I have heard them say that other races,
    out of the east, will live here in their time,
    one following another. Each will build

its cities, and its monuments to gods
we dare not worship. Some will come with ships,
and some with wings, and each will desecrate
the altars of the people overthrown,
but none will live forever. Each will live
its little time, and fly before the feet
of those who follow after. Let them come in
despoiling, for a time is but a time
and these will not endure.

SENIOR (*to* BIGGS *and* SKIMMERHORN): That's a smart Indian.
A little pessimistic about the aims
of civilization, but wise anyway.
What do you say, Van Dorn?

INDIAN: You too will go
like gnats on the wind. Build monuments
and worship at your temples. But you too
will go.

SENIOR: You're on my side, so I don't mind,
but you have a damned uncomfortable way
of speaking. I'm a Republican myself,
but I don't go that far! Will you sell, Van Dorn?

(TROOPER *appears with* ELKUS, DOPE *and* BUDDY.)

BUDGE (TROOPER): Help me keep an eye on these guys, will
you, Patsy? I've got a confession out of them on the Nanuet
bank robbery, and they say the money's up here.

PATSY: Up here? Whereabouts?

BUDGE: They left it in a satchel.

PATSY: There's the satchel, all right. (*He examines it.*)
Empty. (SKIMMERHORN *and* BIGGS *look at each other.*)

BUDGE: Looks like a stall, you guys. You buried it.

ELKUS: Didn't keep a cent, officer. Somebody up here got it.

BUDGE: Well, who?

ELKUS: Last time I saw it one of those birds sat down on it.
(*He points to* BIGGS *and* SKIMMERHORN.)

PATSY: You know who they are? That's Judge Skimmerhorn
of the probate court, and Arthur Biggs of the Traprock
company.

ELKUS: Well, one of them sat down on it.

BUDGE: Why didn't he pick it up?

ELKUS: I don't know whether he saw it.

DOPE: And then there was a funny guy in a big hat that had some of it.

BUDGE: So now we have to look for a funny guy in a big hat! Any other description?

ELKUS: Short and fat, had two sawed-off shotguns, and wore plus fours.

DOPE: And you could see right through him. (BUDGE *is writing in notebook which he has taken from his pocket.*)

PATSY: What?

DOPE: You could see right through him.

BUDGE: I'm beginning to think I can see right through you.

PATSY: Take 'em away, Budge. They're nuts.

ELKUS: But he had the money! Buddy saw him with the money!

PATSY: Van Dorn, did you see a funny guy in a big hat?

VAN: Six or seven of them.

BUDGE: What!

VAN: Six or seven of them.

PATSY: I suppose you could see right through *them?*

VAN: Once in a while.

BUDGE: I'm going to quit writing this down. There's enough here to get me fired already.

PATSY: Didn't one of you say something about sailors in big hats? (*The two look at each other.*)

SKIMMERHORN: Why, yes, we did.

BUDGE: Well, if they say so, he must have been here.

PATSY: Do you know where they went?

SKIMMERHORN: No. (*He points to* ELKUS *and* DOPE.)

PATSY: If you saw anything else that might give us a clue—?

SKIMMERHORN: No, not a thing.

PATSY: It beats me. I'll think up my own questions, feller. Well, we might as well trundle the yeggs back to jail, Judge. Whoever got the stuff, it's gone.

SKIMMERHORN, SENIOR: Aren't you going to help the boys down before you go?

PATSY: Sure. That's what we came up for.

BIGGS: Oh, don't bother. We'll get down.

SKIMMERHORN: No hurry. We're all right. You take care of your prisoners.

PATSY: Might as well lend a hand while we're here.

BIGGS: Run along, boys. We're all right. Don't worry about us.

VAN: Oh, we can't leave those poor fellows up in that bucket! They've been there all night!

SKIMMERHORN: We're fine. You run along. (VAN *and* PATSY *haul shovel down.*) No need to go to all this trouble.

PATSY: No trouble at all.

VAN: A pleasure. They've been asking me all night to get them out of this. (*Shovel touches ground. The two sit still.*)

PATSY: What's the matter?

SKIMMERHORN: Guess my legs are asleep.

BIGGS: Mine, too.

PATSY: I'll help you up. (*They are pulled to their feet, staggering. Their pockets are very obvious.* PATSY *helps both down.*)

BUDGE: How about it? O.K.?

PATSY: All set. Say, you are loaded down. Carried plenty of lunch, I guess?

BIGGS: Oh, we brought plenty.

ELKUS: Couldn't be money, could it?

BIGGS: As a matter of fact, some of it is. We were carrying cash to pay Van Dorn for his farm.

ELKUS: And it wouldn't have the Orangeburg stamp on it, would it?

BIGGS (*looking at money*): Well, hardly. As a matter of fact, it has. Take it.

SKIMMERHORN: You're right.

PATSY: Budge, take those muggs back down.

DOPE: But what about the funny guy with the big hat? What about him?

BUDGE: I'll tell you about him. It's entirely possible there wasn't any funny guy in a big hat.

DOPE: But we all saw him!

BUDGE: Oh no, you didn't see him. You saw right through him. And the reason was, he wasn't there.

SKIMMERHORN: Must be some mistake. They must have got the money mixed at the bank.

PATSY: Sure. Well, if that's all, we can easily check on that.

SKIMMERHORN: Are you under the impression that we robbed the bank?

PATSY: Here's the money and you've got to explain it somehow.

BIGGS: I wish to God I could explain it. Explain it, we've been doing nothing else. You were right, Van Dorn, this mountain with people you could see through hauling us up in buckets, a crew of pirates using us for ninepins in a God damned bowling alley.

PATSY: If you can't explain it, I guess we'll have to put you both under arrest.

BIGGS: I'd rather be under arrest than try to explain it. (*All go out.*)

SKIMMERHORN: I'd like to keep it out of the papers, if possible. It might be very embarrassing. You see, I have political enemies.

SENIOR: That's the first time I ever knew those boys to rob a bank. I don't blame you for not doing business with them. Whenever you make up your mind to sell, Van Dorn, come down to Ledentown and get your money. I'll be waiting for you. (*Goes off.* JUDITH *enters.*)

JUDITH: Hello, Van.

VAN (*upon a rock*): Judith?

JUDITH: I came to tell you
that I was wrong—I mean about the land.
Your way was best.
I think it always would be.

VAN: You mean it, Judith?

JUDITH: I'm sorry I went, I'm sorry this happened.

I came to say if only I could keep you
you should keep the Tor, or what you wished.
VAN: Shall I keep the Tor?
INDIAN: Let them have this little hill
and find your peace beyond, for there's no hill
worth a man's peace while he may live and find it.
VAN: Maybe it's true,
God knows they haven't left me much of it.
Look where the new road winds along the ledge.
Look at the jagged cut the quarries make
down to the south, and there's a Boy Scout trail
running along the ridge Mount Ivy way,
where they try out their hatchets. The crusher underneath
dumps road rock into barges all day long,
and sometimes half the night. Their damned shovel
hangs across my line, ready to gouge the peak we're
  standing on.
It's better than fighting out a grudge, I guess.
What will you do, John?
INDIAN: The hills will take care of me.
I've found my place.
JUDITH: I'd remember Lise.
VAN: Was there a Lise?
I think she was my dream of you and me,
and how you left the mountain barren once
when you were gone. She was my dream of you
and how you left the Tor. Say you'll come with me.
JUDITH: Yes, I'll come. (*They kiss.*)
VAN: One last look at the rock. Think of the gouge
they'll make across these hills. Let them
come, we won't be here.
INDIAN: And there's another comfort.
There is nothing made,
and will be nothing made by these new men,
quarries, machines, or steel work in the sky,
that will not make good ruins.
JUDITH: This will be ruins.

INDIAN: Why, when the race is gone, or looks aside
  only a little while, the white stone darkens,
  the wounds close, and the roofs fall, and the walls
  give way to rains. Nothing is made by men
  but makes in the end good ruins.
VAN: If you live long enough.
  But I can hardly wait for that.

THE MAGNIFICENT YANKEE

Introduction

In an interview with Lucius Beebe of the *New York Herald Tribune* shortly after *The Magnificent Yankee* opened, Arthur Hopkins, the producer, explained his purpose in presenting Emmet Lavery's drama of the Great Dissenter:

We are living in extraordinarily cynical and unsympathetic times. So I produced the Holmes play as a sort of gesture of faith, and a symbol of loyalties and kindnesses which are, momentarily, at a great discount in the world. I regard *The Magnificent Yankee* as a great deal more than entertainment. It is a permanent and abiding enrichment to many people who see it. It is, I feel, like a good friendship, well worth the investment of time, money and labor that has gone into it.[1]

Biographical plays are nothing new on the Broadway stage. Such successes as Dore Schary's *Sunrise at Campobello*, Laurence Housman's *Victoria Regina*, Rudolf Besier's *The Barretts of Wimpole Street* and Robert E. Sherwood's *Abe Lincoln in Illinois* are only a few of the most successful in recent decades. They are difficult to write if they are to be true to the lives of the protagonists and at the same time aspire to be good drama. Most biographical plays have failed on the stage because they were neither good biography nor good drama.

Emmet Lavery's play could not possibly have encompassed the ninety-four years of one of the most brilliant legal

---

[1] Quoted in John Mason Brown, *Seeing Things*, pp. 237–238.

minds of recent times. Nor could the author have done much to dramatize the many epoch-making decisions that the Great Dissenter wrote. That might have made interesting American legal history but poor drama. What Lavery has done so well is to present seven scenes from the thirty-one years that Justice Holmes spent in Washington—from 1902, when he was first appointed to the United States Supreme Court, to 1933, when President Franklin D. Roosevelt visited him one hour after his inauguration. Selectivity is one of the hallmarks of dramatic construction, as it is in other literary forms. What Lavery has selected from a life of almost a century seemed to him characteristic of Justice Holmes the man, the devoted husband, the trainer of younger men and the loyal friend.

In addition to the two main characters, Justice and Mrs. Holmes, three other historical figures are introduced: Justice Louis D. Brandeis, Owen Wister, author of *The Virginian*, and the ever-complaining Henry Adams. These are presented as vignettes rather than complete portraits, but they serve to bring out certain traits of Justice Holmes. The Brandeis relationship shows the deep friendship between these two great liberal legal philosophers, as well as their concern over individual rights in such famous cases as the Abrams and the Rosika Schwimmer decisions. Owen Wister serves as a bridge between the first Roosevelt in the White House, fuming over one of Justice Holmes' opinions, and the Holmeses as personalities. Henry Adams, the eternal pessimist, is in contrast to Holmes who is not forever looking backwards, but is always growing with the times, both as a person and as a jurist.

Now and then some of the words of famous decisions are incorporated in the dialogue, but for the most part the language of the play is that of cultured, urbane citizens of whom America should well be proud. Occasionally an epigram or witticism shines out.

Critics have commented on the lack of plot and conflict and hence the weakness of the play from the point of view of structure. It is true that there are no dramatic clashes—physical, mental or emotional—to sustain our attention. But our interest is held nevertheless by the very humanity and simplicity of this far from simple person. Such a scene as the surprise party on the Justice's eightieth birthday is handled with excellent taste and tenderness. Likewise, Holmes' conversation with Brandeis about the illness of his wife, Fanny Dixwell Holmes, is extremely touching and expresses the basic feeling of all partners of a long marriage, when the partnership is in imminent danger of being broken up after half a century. The final pantomime of Holmes at ninety-one straightening himself in soldier fashion as he prepares to meet the newly inaugurated President Roosevelt is a magnificent moment in the theatre.

It is interesting to compare Emmet Lavery's treatment of Holmes' life with the treatment by two biographers: Francis Biddle in his *Mr. Justice Holmes* and Catherine Drinker Bowen in her *Yankee from Olympus*. The playwright has acknowledged his indebtedness to Mr. Biddle. Yet we must always keep in mind that a carefully documented biography does not make for living theatre. What the dramatist must do is keep the artistic (if not literal) truth and at the same time present that truth in a form that is convincing on the stage.

The essence of the play is summed up succinctly by John Mason Brown in his review:

> *The Magnificent Yankee* is a success story in which the success is never in doubt. It approaches national issues in fireside terms, revealing the life of an outstanding jurist, not as the nation knew him on the bench, but as he was known to his wife at home. Above all, it is the saga of a happy marriage; of two people, prosperous, cultivated, wise and good. . . .[2]

Those who had the good fortune to witness the late Louis

[2] *Op. cit.*, p. 239.

Calhern in the title role of Justice Holmes and Lillian Gish as Mrs. Holmes were treated to one of the great performances of the past twenty years. Although the newspaper critics may have caviled here and there about the construction of the play, there was almost unanimous consent about the superb performances. It was almost as if Lavery had written his play with these two actors in mind.[3] It was the kind of acting triumph that Helen Hayes achieved in *Victoria Regina* as she changed from the nineteen-year-old queen to the aging grandmother in her last scene.

THE PLAYWRIGHT

Emmet Lavery was born of Irish parents in Poughkeepsie, New York, in 1902. After attending schools there, he became sports editor and later court reporter of the *Eagle-News* of that city. He studied law in New York City and practiced there for a time, writing occasionally for the press. This lasted for ten years, but his interest in the drama could not be satisfied either by the law or by journalism. In Poughkeepsie, he acted in the local community theatre and worked in the Experimental Theatre at Vassar College, at a time when it had inspiring leadership. Lavery began his playwriting career there, with *The First Legion,* a play about the Jesuits, which had considerable success in New York City and was later produced as one of the offerings of the Federal Theatre Project. It has been translated into twelve languages and has played abroad. A stint in Hollywood followed, where he worked as a scenarist. He also directed the National Service Bureau of the Federal Theatre Project. His other plays include: *Second Spring,* a play about Cardinal Newman, *Brief Music, The Gentleman from Athens* and *Kamiano, the Story of Damien,* written in collaboration with Grace Murphy.

[3] *See* the reviews listed in *New York Theatre Critics' Reviews,* January 23, 1946, pp. 477–480.

Introduction

FURTHER READING

Brown, John Mason. *Seeing Things*. New York: McGraw-Hill, 1946, pp. 237-243.

Mantle, Burns. *The Best Plays of 1945–1946*. New York: Dodd, Mead, 1946, pp. 141-175.

Nathan, George Jean. Review of Emmet Lavery's *The Magnificent Yankee*, in *New York Theatre Critics' Reviews* (New York), VII (January, 1946), p. 477.

———. *The Theatre Book of the Year, 1945–1946*. New York: Knopf, 1946, pp. 286-289.

THE MAGNIFICENT YANKEE

EMMET LAVERY

ACT I

SCENE 1

SCENE: *The library of Mr. Justice Holmes—an afternoon in December, 1902.*

The room, as the curtain goes up, is deserted. It has a pale, ghostly air, heightened by the fact that only a little light filters through tall windows, where the curtains are two-thirds drawn.

There are a few odds and ends of furniture in the room but they are draped in furniture covers.

Double doors, with a broken pediment, divide the room and open on a pleasant hall.

*Great rows of bookshelves flank the doors but the shelves,
like the rest of the furniture, are completely covered.*

*At rear left there is a generous doorway and below it, worked
into the corner of the room, are a beautiful fireplace and
mantel.*

*As the curtain goes up, we hear the faint murmur of voices
offstage. The door at left opens and a* REAL-ESTATE BROKER
steps in. He is a man of about forty.

BROKER (*moving in*): Ah, here we are, sir. You won't find a
better house in Washington. No, sir—nor in Georgetown,
either. (*A tall figure of a man, bundled comfortably in a
big winter overcoat, strides into the room with the brisk
air of a general reconnoitering a bit of important ground.
He wears a smart black fedora, with a rather high crown,
and is smoking a large black cigar. Despite the touches
of white in his hair and mustache, there is a youthful,
elastic quality to his walk. He stops and looks about him
with a searching, quizzical glance. He is impressed with the
place but with true Yankee caution is not prepared to say
so too soon.*)

BROKER (*anxiously*): You only have to look at it for yourself, sir.

HOLMES (*drily*): Thank you, young man. I'd like to. (BROKER
falls back a bit, as HOLMES *strides about the room.*)

BROKER: The painters will be out in the morning, sir—and
then—

HOLMES: Hmmm . . . not bad . . . not bad. This room is all
right. So is that one over there—

BROKER: The view is very nice too, sir.

HOLMES (*moving to window*): I am a little curious about the
air out here, if you don't mind. (*Lifts window, sniffs air.*)
Hmmm. Not bad at all, especially for December. Tell me,
can you really smell spring out here—when it is spring, I
mean?

BROKER: Why, I don't know, sir. . . . I mean . . . well, no one's
ever asked that before, sir.

HOLMES: You see, that's the trouble with you real-estate fellers. No imagination. You have your feet on the ground when it ought to be your nose.

BROKER: Of course, it will look even better with your own things, Mr.— Mr.—

HOLMES: Holmes—Oliver Wendell Holmes.

BROKER: Of course—of course. I never forget a name, Mr. Holmes! But, you see, this isn't one of my regular listings.

HOLMES (*airily*): That's perfectly all right, Mr.— Mr.—

BROKER: Dixon is the name, sir.

HOLMES (*taking out cigar*): Have a cigar, Mr. Dixon?

BROKER: Oh, thank you, sir. Thank you very much.

HOLMES: Tell me, Mr. Dixon—what are the winters like down here?

BROKER (*virtuously*): Oh—why a Washington winter is hardly a winter at all, sir.

HOLMES (*with a sigh*): That's good. Mighty good. I think I've had enough of New England winter for a while.

BROKER: Then you'll take the house, sir?

HOLMES: Well, young man, that all depends—on what my wife says and if you know what a woman is going to say when it comes to a house, you're a smarter gent than I am. Ought to be here any minute now.

BROKER (*shivering*): V-v-v-ery g-g-g-ood, sir. Would you mind, if I shut the window, sir?

HOLMES: Young man, it's the air out here that's selling me this house. (HOLMES *breathes deeply and walks about the room approvingly.*)

BROKER (*still shivering*): Of course, sir. Do you—do you expect to be in Washington for long, sir?

HOLMES (*drily*): Oh, I give myself ten years if I'm lucky.

BROKER: Pardon me—but would it be impertinent—to ask what your line of work is?

HOLMES: It certainly would but I'll tell you just the same. You might say I was a missionary sort of—(*then with a great chuckle*)—a missionary from Boston! (*At this moment the small trim figure of* FANNY DIXWELL HOLMES *appears in the doorway. She is not a pretty woman in the accepted sense of the word: but at sixty-one she has an inner fire and radiance which match and at times surpass that of her illustrious husband. The Washington adventure for FANNY, no less than for the judge, is a new lease on life. There's an inner excitement to the new march of events which she cannot always conceal. In time she will bloom with the dash and color of a brilliant Washington hostess. But for the moment she is, to outward appearance at least, the rather modest wife of a Yankee judge recently down from Boston—modest but with spirit.)*

FANNY *(from doorway)*: Wendell, you ought to be ashamed of yourself. (HOLMES *takes off his hat and bows with a gallant gesture.* BROKER *follows suit.*) A missionary indeed! Pay no attention to him, Mr. Dixon.

BROKER: But if he isn't a missionary—?

FANNY *(moving across room)*: It would be a lot closer to the truth to say he was a traveling salesman, with a consuming passion for naughty French novels.

HOLMES: Come, come—my dear. Not necessarily French!

FANNY: Heavens, Wendell—do you want to freeze us out of house and home before we even have one? (FANNY *shuts window firmly, then turns eagerly to* HOLMES.) Oh, Wendell—you do like it, don't you?

HOLMES *(flicking cigar ash away with jaunty air)*: Well, it isn't exactly the New Willard—but—

FANNY *(advancing on him)*: Oh, I suppose you'd like to buy the New Willard? Then you could scatter ashes to your heart's content in every room of the house. Then you could— *(Suddenly a voice from offstage breaks in. It is* HENRY ADAMS, *now a man of fifty-eight. He speaks with the voice of destiny—and a very tired and weary voice it is.)*

ADAMS *(offstage)*: Hello, Holmes—is that you, Holmes?

HOLMES *(going to* ADAMS, *as he comes in door)*: By the eternal—it's Adams—Henry Adams! (ADAMS, *inclined to be a little diffident and awkward, is pleased at the warmth of the greeting.)*

ADAMS: I live only a few blocks away—and I wanted to be the first to say "welcome to Washington."

FANNY (*coming to* ADAMS): Why, thank you—Mr. Adams. Thank you very much. That's very thoughtful of you.

ADAMS: The postman told me Mrs. Holmes had already given him this number as your new address . . . so . . . so I thought you wouldn't mind . . . if . . .

FANNY (*a little flustered*): Of course we don't mind. Not at all—but will you excuse me for just a moment, Mr. Adams? Will you step this way, Mr. Dixon, please? (BROKER *moves out left.*) My, it's good to see you again, Mr. Adams. You know how it is when you're in a strange place. It's good to see anybody . . . I mean . . . Oh, dear . . . I'm so excited I don't know what I mean (FANNY *whisks off.*)

HOLMES: Sit down, Adams—if you can find a seat.

ADAMS: No, thank you. I can't stay. I just wanted to stop by to say—to say—

HOLMES (*in a kindly fashion*): Well, what is it, man—out with it.

ADAMS: I'm worried—terribly worried. It's—it's that man in the White House!

HOLMES (*drily*): Mr. Roosevelt? I thought you were good friends?

ADAMS: We still are. I was one of the first to congratulate him when he named you to the Court.

HOLMES: Then what's the trouble?

ADAMS (*moodily*): He's doing too many things . . . and saying too many things. Do you know what he said only the other day? That no nation could be great that was ruled by clerks, women and lawyers. Why, the man is beginning to attack the very law itself!

HOLMES (*chuckling*): Adams—did you ever hear of a strong President who *didn't* think all lawyers were damned pests?

ADAMS (*hardly hearing him*): And I don't like the tone of the country, Holmes. Cabot Lodge says the Spanish War has made us a nation. But I think it has only made us like the old nations—selfish, grasping, imperialist.

HOLMES: Oh, I don't know . . . I look around me and I see more faith and enthusiasm in the young men than in our day. At least, they are building their America on hopes—not on regrets.

ADAMS: But it's all so crude . . .

HOLMES (*reflectively*): Crude? Maybe . . . but it's real . . . it's alive . . . and it isn't always selfish. Why, every day I meet boys still capable of denying the material order of things—still capable, by God, of doing the spontaneous, uneconomic thing!

ADAMS: Yes, but the President is trying to do too many things too fast. Every day he's stirring up the people about something new . . . and where is it all going to end?

HOLMES: Cheer up, Adams. I think this country is young enough and strong enough to survive almost anything . . . including Theodore Roosevelt.

ADAMS: Well, I hope so—I certainly hope so. But I wish he'd remember that this isn't the millennium. This is only the year 1902—and he might leave a few things for someone else to do.

HOLMES (*with a grin*): I'll tell him that the next time I see him.

ADAMS: Watch out, Holmes—or he'll swallow you up just as he has everyone else in Washington.

HOLMES: I'll take my chances on that.

ADAMS (*extending hand*): Well, good-by for a while—and the best of good fortune to you.

HOLMES: Thank you— (ADAMS *starts out left, stops at door and turns to* HOLMES.)

ADAMS: I wish I knew what it is that always makes you so infernally unworried about everything.

HOLMES: Listen, Adams—when I was mustered out of the Civil War—almost forty years ago—people told me the country was going to the dogs. When I went on the bench in Massachusetts, twenty years ago, they told me the same

The Magnificent Yankee

thing. Well, we may not be out of the trenches yet, Adams, but we're a long way from the dogs!

ADAMS: Maybe—but I hear them barking. (*He goes out.*)

FANNY (*offstage*): Good-by, Mr. Adams.

ADAMS (*offstage*): Good-by, Mrs. Holmes.

HOLMES (*vigorously*): All right, you can come out now—you deserter!

FANNY (*moving to* HOLMES): I'm sorry, Wendell—really I am. But you know I can take just so much of the Adamses.

HOLMES (*exploding*): Damm it to hell, Fanny—what's the matter with Henry Adams anyway? Everything he touches has a way of turning to ashes. Why, forty-one years ago he was telling me the same things at Harvard—and he hasn't changed one damned bit.

FANNY: Wendell, stop your swearing.

HOLMES: Listen to me, milady. In a democracy a man can swear at an Adams any damn time he pleases.

FANNY: Then why don't you, instead of swearing at me?

HOLMES (*softly*): I don't know . . . (*then vigorously*) . . . but what's he got to grouse about anyway? This country did all right by the Adamses, didn't it? His grandfather a President and his great-grandfather as well. Humph, if Henry isn't equal to the strain of being an Adams, it only means *he's* going to the dogs—not the country. Damn it to hell, Fanny, I don't believe in sudden ruin any more than I believe in sudden reform. I don't believe—

FANNY: Hush, Wendell. Mr. Dixon will hear you. I left him in the kitchen downstairs . . . waiting for your verdict.

HOLMES (*with mock severity*): My verdict? Look here my good woman—(*something familiar about the shape of the covered table at the right catches the judge's eye and he begins to lift the covering from it*)—who found this house anyway? Who told the postman we had decided to take it? Who?—(HOLMES *throws back the covering and is pleasantly surprised at what he sees. But he pretends to be put out*) —my good woman, do you have any idea what this piece of furniture happens to be?

189

FANNY (*with nice naturalness*): Why, of course, Wendell—it's your desk!

HOLMES (*uncovering an item that stands behind a shrouded sofa*): And this?

FANNY: Why, Wendell, I do believe—it's my rocker!

HOLMES (*gesturing with cigar*): And all the rest of this—ah—concealed artillery? I suppose that's ours, too?

FANNY: Why, I hope so, Wendell—I certainly hope so. It would be dreadful if the railroad didn't send us our own things!

HOLMES: A fine state of affairs, I must say. You not only take a house without consulting me—you even move in the furniture. You conspire with this estimable Mr. Dixon—you connive with him—you—

FANNY (*with disarming directness*): What's the matter, Wendell? Don't you like the house?

HOLMES (*with a slow grin*): Like it? My dear, I'm enchanted with it. Enchanted—only—

FANNY: Only what?

HOLMES: You might have let me have the fun of thinking I was the commanding officer around here . . . just once. (FANNY *turns away from him a little and sits down on the covered sofa which faces the audience squarely a little right of center.*)

FANNY: Oh, it's happened, Wendell—it's really happened—the thing I've dreamed of so often . . . you in Washington.

HOLMES: Queer. I would have sworn my life was all wrapped up in blue ribbon and finished—somewhere back in Boston.

FANNY: You'll have a chance at greatness here.

HOLMES: I'll be only a side judge here and I was Chief in Massachusetts.

FANNY: Yes. But now you'll have the chance to sum up the work and thought of twenty years.

HOLMES (*sitting down beside her*): Yes. But a man might fool himself at sixty-one and not know it. Not a chance of us having arrived in Washington just a bit too late, is there?

FANNY: You know there isn't. Here you'll have a chance to work things out on a scale you never had in Massachusetts.

HOLMES (*with rising excitement*): Yes, you're right, Fanny. This is the promised land and I'm as excited as if I were a boy seeing it all for the first time. Only it isn't the first time. Why, this town is my home, too. . . . I fought for this town once—and, by Jove, we won that fight, too—even if I did have to tell my Commander-in-chief, Mr. Lincoln, to "get the hell down" when he popped up on the ramparts at Fort Stevens! (HOLMES *chuckles softly, then grows more serious.*) We'll win this fight too. Only we won't win it in a day or a year. I saw that just now talking with Henry Adams. Right now, Fanny, you and I stand alone. We're a couple of generals without an army. Up till now your family and mine have always been on the firing line . . . fighting Indians, before there was a union . . . my great-grandfather a judge in Boston when the British entered Old South Church in 1776 . . . and now—well, we're at the bottom of the barrel. (FANNY *places her hand lightly on* HOLMES'.) Oh, yes, we are . . . the truth is the Holmeses are really ending with us and we might as well face it. There's no one left to carry on for us the way there is for the Adamses . . . funny, you could always find an Adams somewhere if you looked far enough . . . I wonder why. . . .

FANNY (*taking her hand away from his*): I don't know, Wendell . . . maybe it's just that the Lord wanted a few more Adamses than Holmeses. . . . (HOLMES *comes out of his reverie. There's an edge in* FANNY'S *voice that brings him to. He pats her hand, gets up briskly and moves forward.*)

HOLMES: Now, now—Fanny . . . I was just daydreaming, that's all . . . I've nothing to complain of . . . I've had a full life and a merry one . . . and I've had the most wonderful wife an undeserving Yankee could ever hope for.

FANNY: Yes. We could almost make an epitaph of it, couldn't we? "Here lies Fanny Dixwell, wonderful wife of Oliver Wendell Holmes, Jr."

HOLMES (*turning back to her*): Fanny, please—

FANNY (*getting up and moving to the left*): But you know and I know that a Yankee wife is only a good wife . . . when she's a good mother too.

HOLMES (*crossing to her*): Steady, Fanny—you're stronger than I and always have been. Why, you have the joy of living in you and you've shared it with me. It wasn't your fault that we couldn't have passed some of it along. That . . . that . . . Oh, damn Adams! We'll carry on somehow and we'll win through, too, on our own. We'll— (*There is a discreet tap at the door at left. They look up and there is the eternally correct Harvard man, vintage of '02. This is the first of the thirty secretaries and he is a nice mixture of proper deference and genteel self-assurance.*)

SECRETARY (*a little breathless*): I beg your pardon, sir,— but could you tell me, sir—where I may find Mr. Justice Holmes, sir? It is most urgent, I assure you, sir—and—

HOLMES: Young man, if you'll just take a deep breath and stop saying "sir" every two seconds, I'll be happy to direct you. (*The interruption has brought* FANNY *out of her dark mood in the most natural way in the world: there's a job to be done . . . the judge is teasing a nice boy . . . and it's time she took a hand.*)

FANNY: Wendell, behave yourself! (*Then to the boy.*) This is Justice Holmes. I am Mrs. Holmes.

SECRETARY (*to* FANNY): Oh, forgive me, please— (*Then to* HOLMES.) My deepest apologies, sir.

HOLMES (*triumphantly*): There, you see—he's gone and said it again.

FANNY (*with increasing emphasis*): Wendell—

SECRETARY (*eagerly*): I'm Copeland, sir—I mean, Mr. Holmes —I mean, Mr. Justice—

HOLMES (*smiling*): My friends call me Judge.

SECRETARY: Professor Gray said I was to seek you out at once. . . .

FANNY: Oh, then you're the new secretary, of course?

SECRETARY: Well, I hope to be, ma'am—I— (FANNY *crosses to left. At the doors she stops and looks back.*)

FANNY (*to* HOLMES): I'll be waiting for you in the kitchen—with Mr. Dixon! (FANNY *goes out*.)

HOLMES (*looks* SECRETARY *over, then sits down on sofa*): Hmmm. One of Harvard's bright boys, eh?

SECRETARY (*proudly*): Law School—1902, sir. (HOLMES *raises his head as if to challenge the "sir"—then lets it pass*.)

HOLMES: Law Review, no doubt?

SECRETARY: Yes, sir. Notes Editor!

HOLMES: Hmmm. Well, Mr. Copeland, I'm not sure I really require a law editor. What I really need is someone who can handle writs of certiorari, balance a checkbook—and listen to my tall talk. Think you can do that?

SECRETARY (*confidently*): I think so, sir.

HOLMES: You understand, the job is good only for a year. Professor Gray has suggested that it might be a good idea to take a *different* man from the Law School each year. (*Then reflectively.*) Bound to be hell on me, of course, but it ought to be fine for the Law School.

SECRETARY: Yes, sir.

HOLMES: Look here, young man—I don't mind your saying "sir" all the time but it doesn't have to be "yes," if you don't mean "yes"—understand?

SECRETARY: Yes, sir!

HOLMES: Just why do you want to be my secretary?

SECRETARY: Well, I don't hold with everything you say about the law, sir.

HOLMES: Well—that's a promising beginning anyway. Go on.

SECRETARY (*with a rush*): But you're on the right track, sir —whether the rest of the country knows it or not. The law isn't just the dead hand of precedent—it's a living thing and it has to grow with the time in which it lives—it has to. It— (*Suddenly diffident.*) Sorry, sir. I didn't mean to appropriate your ideas! (*There's something very appealing about the unleashed eloquence of the boy.* HOLMES *rises quite pleased.*)

HOLMES: Well, this is most interesting, Copeland. Most interesting. But I want to be quite frank with you. My needs are few but my rules are fixed—fairly fixed.

SECRETARY (*hopefully*): Yes, sir?

HOLMES: My philosophy, on the other hand, is rather complex . . . part of your duties will be to listen to it during the next few months!

SECRETARY: Very well, sir. Am I to consider myself employed?

HOLMES: Report to me at the New Willard at ten in the morning.

SECRETARY: Thank you, sir. Thank you very much. I am deeply honored, sir. (HOLMES *and* SECRETARY *bow with nice courtesy.* SECRETARY *starts out left, then comes back.*) Just one thing more, sir. You mentioned certain rules?

HOLMES: Oh yes, I almost forgot. The Government will pay you two thousand dollars a year but there are certain conditions. Do you have a girl you're in love with?

SECRETARY (*almost too fervently to suit* HOLMES): Oh, no, sir. No—indeed, sir.

HOLMES: Well, there's no harm in having one. Nice thing, girls. But just make sure you don't marry one while you're in my employ. Understand?

SECRETARY: Very good, sir.

HOLMES: Hmmm. I don't know how good it is but it's the way I prefer to work. Well, there you are, Copeland—not a bad arrangement any way you look at it. If you're a credit to me and I'm a credit to you, we'll both have something to brag about. On the other hand, if you disappoint me and I disappoint you, no harm is done. You see, my boy, I intend to have all the pleasures of parenthood without any of the responsibility. If there is anything there, perhaps I can enrich it and you will go away not altogether ungrateful. Perhaps— (*Suddenly the words "boy" and "parenthood" seem to re-echo in* HOLMES' *ear. He breaks off abruptly.*)

SECRETARY: Yes, Mr. Justice?

HOLMES: Never mind, son. (*With a start* HOLMES *realizes he has used the word "son" with special emphasis.*) Run

194

along. I'll see you in the morning. (SECRETARY *goes out left.* HOLMES *watches him off, then starts to strut and whistles "Yankee Doodle."* FANNY *returns and takes in these cheerful antics with raised eyebrows.*)

FANNY: Wendell Holmes—whatever do you think you're doing?

HOLMES (*with a flourish*): Quiet, woman—quiet. I've just discovered that I'm going to have lots of children—lots of 'em—and they're going to be *all* boys!

==

ACT I

SCENE 2

SCENE: The library of Justice Holmes on an afternoon in March, 1904.

There is a bright tone to the room now, in sharp contrast to the previous scene. It has a lived-in look and a clean sweep of line that is inevitably New England, even in Washington. The law books stretch about halfway to the ceiling. But they are not all books about the law. Blackstone rubs elbows with paper-backed French novels.

In the foreground, at right angles to the footlights, is HOLMES' *large desk. Near it are two beautiful Chippendale chairs which balance a pleasant sofa on the opposite side of the room. A beautiful large lamp on a little table behind the sofa matches one of similar design on* HOLMES' *desk.*

There are a few flowers in the room, but they know their place. The brass at the fireplace has a lovely sheen to it but it too is discreet: it is not too bright.

As the curtain goes up a new SECRETARY *is examining the afternoon editions of the Washington newspapers. He puts one down, picks up another—then compares them with the printed report of* HOLMES' *decision in the Northern Securities case.* HOUSEKEEPER *enters with more newspapers.*

HOUSEKEEPER: Here are the New York papers, sir. They just came in. But what about all those reporters downstairs? They just won't go away.

SECRETARY: Well, I guess we'll just have to leave them to the Judge when he gets home from Court.

HOUSEKEEPER: He won't like that either, will he?

SECRETARY: Oh, I don't know. The Judge hasn't anything against reporters. He just doesn't like the things they write for the papers, that's all!

HOUSEKEEPER: Well, I wish they'd go away, just the same. (SECRETARY *turns back to the papers and the* HOUSE-KEEPER *goes out, very much puzzled.* SECRETARY *reaches eagerly for the New York papers and a moment later* FANNY *comes on. There's a considerable change in* FANNY. *Washington has been kind to her and she has literally had a second blooming. It isn't that she wasn't striking before. But now her whole manner is a little easier, a little more relaxed; she's more sure of herself and the Judge. Her style in clothes has changed too and the afternoon dress she is wearing has, like* FANNY *herself, a subtle but definite sparkle.*)

FANNY (*eagerly*): Well, Mr. Mason—what do the papers say?

SECRETARY: Oh, they are quite flattering, all things considered. But the President seems to be a bit angry.

FANNY (*examining papers at table*): But what does Mr. Roosevelt have to be angry about? The Court voted his way, didn't it? He can still go around busting all the trusts he wants to, can't he?

SECRETARY (*drily*): Yes, but it was close. Five to four . . . and it seems he had rather counted on the Judge.

FANNY: Oh . . . I see.

SECRETARY: And the fact that the Judge's dissenting opinion gets almost as much space as the majority won't make the President any happier.

FANNY (*shocked at an item she has found in a paper*): Why,

the very idea—how dare he—how dare he—even if he *is* the President?

SECRETARY: What's the matter, Mrs. Holmes? (FANNY *takes paper and stalks away from table. She's as angry as a wet hen.*)

FANNY: Why, just listen to this. "When asked to comment on the unexpected dissent of Mr. Justice Holmes, one of his own appointees to the Court, President Roosevelt replied with a bark: 'I could carve a man with more backbone out of a banana!' " (FANNY *puts paper down and looks over grimly at* SECRETARY.) Well, merciful heavens, what does the President want—a judge or a banana?

SECRETARY: If you don't mind my saying so, ma'am, I think the President would be content with a banana.

FANNY: Well, just wait till I see Mr. Roosevelt. (HOUSEKEEPER *comes in with the afternoon mail. She is still disturbed over developments below.*)

HOUSEKEEPER: Here is the afternoon mail, Mrs. Holmes.

FANNY (*taking the mail*): Oh, thank you, Mary. (HOUSEKEEPER *starts out uncertainly, as* FANNY *turns to* SECRETARY.)

FANNY: Maybe it's just as well that the Judge never reads the newspapers.

HOUSEKEEPER (*coming back*): I beg your pardon, ma'am—

FANNY: Yes, Mary?

HOUSEKEEPER: There's a gentleman below—in the kitchen— well, he really *is* a gentleman—not at all like the others at the front door—and he insists he must have a word with you.

FANNY: Why, Mary! I wouldn't dare.

HOUSEKEEPER (*starting out*): Very well, ma'am. But he was mighty nice spoken . . . if you could have heard the way he said: "*I am the Boston Transcript!*"

FANNY (*quickly*): The *Transcript*?

HOUSEKEEPER: Yes. He said it like you might say: "*I am the Archangel Gabriel.*"

FANNY (*intrigued*): Well, of all things—the *Transcript!* That's different, Mary. Show him up—show him up right away.

HOUSEKEEPER: Yes, indeed, ma'am. (HOUSEKEEPER *goes out.*)

FANNY: Now, Mr. Mason, don't look like that. I know the Judge never gives interviews but this isn't going to be an interview. I just haven't seen an Archangel around in a long time—especially one from Boston. (SECRETARY *starts out with newspapers.*) Oh, you might as well take the afternoon mail with you. Nothing important, I guess—except—(FANNY *starts to run through the few letters, gives a curious little start when she discovers a rather flossy envelope, addressed to the Judge in a feminine hand*)—except this one perhaps. It's—it's marked "personal." I'll leave it for the Judge on his desk. (SECRETARY *goes out.* FANNY *moves across room with the letter. She stops along the way, holds it up and sniffs: no question about it, there is a trace of perfume in the letter. Amused and piqued,* FANNY *continues across the room to the Judge's desk, pretending for herself that the letter means nothing to her. She puts it down firmly on the Judge's desk and turns away resolutely. But temptation is too much for her. A second later, she turns back to the desk, takes the letter and holds it up to the light which is pouring in the tall windows in back of the desk. At this moment there is a knock on the door leading into hall and* FANNY *whirls around quickly, the letter still in her hand. But she is safe. The door has not yet opened.*) Yes—come in. (*The door opens and* HOUSEKEEPER *shows in* MR. PALMER *of the* Transcript. *He answers the housekeeper's description: there is a deliberate condescension about the man which is almost regal.*)

HOUSEKEEPER (*proudly*): Mr. Palmer of the *Transcript!*

FANNY: How do you do, Mr. Palmer?

MR. PALMER (*with a lordly bow*): Mrs. Holmes— (HOUSEKEEPER *goes out.* FANNY *looks at* MR. PALMER *with cool poise.*)

FANNY: Well, Mr. Palmer? (FANNY *is unexpectedly young in appearance.* MR. PALMER *is troubled.*)

MR. PALMER: Your pardon, madame, but you *are* Mrs. Holmes, are you not?

FANNY: Why, Mr. Palmer! Is there any doubt of it?

MR. PALMER: Well, the fact is—I had been given to understand—that is, I was under the impression—that the Judge's wife was a much older woman. Very much older, I might say.

FANNY (*sweetly*): Oh, I see. That must have been the Judge's first wife.

MR. PALMER: First wife? But I had always understood that Justice Holmes had married only once.

FANNY: Ah, it only goes to show—you never *can* tell about people from Boston, can you, Mr. Palmer?

MR. PALMER (*very stiffly*): My apologies, Mrs. Holmes. I assure you—

FANNY: Oh, it's quite all right, Mr. Palmer. It's quite the nicest compliment I have had in a long time. (FANNY *whirls about and gives* MR. PALMER *a ravishing smile.*) And how is Mrs. Palmer these days?

MR. PALMER (*miserably*): Please, Mrs. Holmes—there is *no* Mrs. Palmer.

FANNY: Oh, I'm so sorry—so sorry for the nonexistent Mrs. Palmer, I mean. A woman like that misses so much.

MR. PALMER (*starting to back out*): Excuse me, please. I've just remembered something I forgot. I'll come back later when the Judge is here. I—

FANNY: But, Mr. Palmer, you can't leave so soon. Are you sure I can't help you?

MR. PALMER (*desperately*): Mrs. Holmes, I want to know only one thing.

FANNY: Yes, Mr. Palmer?

MR. PALMER: Does Justice Holmes know that President Roosevelt has said he will throw him out of the White House if he ever sets foot there again?

FANNY (*honestly aghast*): Why, Mr. Palmer—Mr. Palmer—! (*The door flies open and* SECRETARY *comes in hurriedly.*)

SECRETARY: Oh, Mrs. Holmes—the Judge is coming up the walk now—

FANNY: Thank you, Mr. Mason. Here, Mr. Palmer—you go out through here—and down the back stairs into the kitchen. Quick—with you now. (FANNY *starts to edge* MR. PALMER *out.*)

MR. PALMER: But, Mrs. Holmes—

FANNY: Now—now, Mr. Palmer. Just say that we love Washington—and that we adore Mr. Roosevelt at all times.

MR. PALMER: Adore him, Mrs. Holmes?

FANNY: Yes. We adore everything about him—except his taste in bananas. Good-by, Mr. Palmer. (FANNY *gently pushes* MR. PALMER *out and draws the door to behind him.* SECRETARY *is at table down right sorting mail.*) Well, Mr. Mason, anything exciting in the mail?

SECRETARY: Oh, no . . . just the usual things. But I did want to ask—what time are you and the Judge dining at the White House tonight?

FANNY (*with a gasp*): This evening? Surely it isn't tonight. Why, it can't be.

SECRETARY: But it is, Mrs. Holmes. It's written down here in the Judge's calendar.

FANNY: Good heavens, so many things have happened today, I forgot all about it. But I don't feel like going to dinner with—with that man in the White House. Not now anyway.

SECRETARY: But, Mrs. Holmes, one doesn't decline invitations to the White House, especially at the last minute. One— (*Over the scene we hear a cheerful whistle from the hall.* HOLMES *throws open the door with a flourish. He is wearing a smart dark suit, with a white vest, and he's feeling very gay. In his lapel is a little fresh crocus which he picked on the way home.*)

HOLMES (*saluting*): Captain Holmes reporting, madame. We have met the enemy below and silenced them with Mary's biscuits. (*Then coming into room.*) No interviews. But all the sugar buns they can make away with. (HOLMES *kisses* FANNY *with a dashing air and moves over to desk. She*

can't be sure whether he's seen MR. PALMER *or not.*)
Mason, what are you doing indoors on a day like this? Take
the rest of the afternoon off and get out of here, before I
think of something for you to do.

SECRETARY: Very well, sir—if you insist. But there is quite a
little mail and—

HOLMES: My boy—on a day like this the mail can wait.

FANNY: Well, Mr. Holmes, may I ask the meaning of this
extraordinary behavior?

HOLMES: Fanny, my love, hasn't anyone told you? Why, you
poor child, it's all over town.

FANNY (*apprehensively*): What's all over town?

HOLMES: Spring, my love—it's everywhere! You can't get
away from it. Even the birds are yelling their heads off
about it. And there are crocuses blooming on the White
House lawn— (HOLMES *takes crocus from his lapel and
gives it to* FANNY.) Here, I picked this one—just for you.
It's all right, my love. Mr. Roosevelt was not looking.

FANNY: Oh, Wendell, you can be a dear—at times.

HOLMES (*to* SECRETARY, *still fussing at desk*): Haven't you
gone yet, Mason?

SECRETARY: No, sir. I wanted to ask—shall I get you a cab
for a little before eight, sir? If you're dining at the White
House tonight—

HOLMES (*jovially*): My boy, what do you mean "if"? Of
course, we're dining at the White House tonight. Company
is bound to be a bore but the food is sure to be good.

FANNY: But, Wendell, what about Mr. Roosevelt?

HOLMES (*blandly*): Well, what about him?

FANNY: I mean—suppose he makes good his threat to throw
you out of the White House. Suppose—

HOLMES (*slyly*): Well, my dear, in that event, I shall simply
say to myself: "Holmes, what would a man from the Boston
Transcript do in a situation like this?"—and then be sure
to do the opposite.

FANNY: Oh . . . then you saw Mr. Palmer?

HOLMES (*grinning*): Yes . . . I saw Mr. Palmer. (HOLMES

looks up to find SECRETARY *smiling too. He addresses the young man briskly.*) Good afternoon, Mason.

SECRETARY: Oh, good afternoon, sir. Good day, Mrs. Holmes. (SECRETARY *goes out.* HOLMES *turns to* FANNY *with mock severity.*)

HOLMES: Now, you little she-devil, what do you mean going around telling people that you are the *second* Mrs. Holmes?

FANNY (*backing across the room in front of him*): Well, how do I know you don't wish there *had* been a second Mrs. Holmes?

HOLMES: Now, Fanny—

FANNY: Besides, I didn't tell Mr. Palmer anything. He just drew his own conclusions. Being so overcome at *not* finding the great man's wife with one foot in the grave, he naturally assumed—

HOLMES: I see. And what are the people back in Boston going to think of all this? (FANNY *stops and faces him quite simply and directly.*)

FANNY: Do you care what the people in Boston think? Back there you were merely the good-looking son of the famous Autocrat of the Breakfast Table. To them you were just some sort of literary ornament on the bench, more brilliant than sound. To them— (*This is all very honest, so honest* FANNY *turns away from* HOLMES *rather shyly—then finds she still has in her hand the perfumed letter addressed to the Judge.*)

HOLMES: Hold on. Are you for Boston or against it?

FANNY (*suddenly all steel again*): Oh, I'm not particular. (*Turns around to face him.*) Pick any side you want and I'll take the opposite.

HOLMES (*patting her playfully on the arm*): Woman, what's got into you today? Isn't that another new dress?

FANNY: Yes, milord. Do you like it?

HOLMES: Hmmm. Devilishly pretty. But not half so pretty as the woman wearing it.

FANNY: Oh, thank you, milord.

HOLMES (*with a grin*): Or so devilish either!

FANNY: You're a horrid old man and I hope Mr. Roosevelt beats you with the biggest stick he has. (FANNY *starts to march out, with head up. Then she remembers the letter in her hand. She comes back to him.*) Oh, I almost forgot. This came for you in the afternoon mail. It was marked personal—so I thought you *might* like to open it yourself! (FANNY *gives the Judge the letter and starts out again.* HOLMES *moves over near window to open and read letter.* FANNY *holds her position at door and watches the Judge as he scans the letter with increasing pleasure: it's a voice from the past and it intrigues him. He gives his mustache a twist while he reads the letter and shifts his position with a nice swagger. He is oblivious of the fact that* FANNY *has not left the room.*)

FANNY: Well, Wendell—who is she? (HOLMES *does not seem to hear her at first.*) Is she pretty?

HOLMES (*softly*): Yes. She's pretty—very pretty. (*Suddenly* HOLMES *looks up and realizes it's* FANNY *he's talking to—not himself.*) Eh? What's that? Oh now, don't misunderstand me. It's nothing—nothing at all. (HOLMES *moves over toward* FANNY.) For just a moment I was back at Antietam . . . on the road to Hagerstown with a bullet in my neck . . . and no one to care for me until the Kennedys took me in . . . and a girl named Ellen Jones nursed me back to health. . . . I never saw her again but she's in town now and . . .

FANNY (*briskly*): Well, let's have her out to dinner by all means.

HOLMES (*embarrassed*): Yes, that would be very nice but . . . (*gives her letter*) she wants to know if I'll have dinner with her at the Shoreham some night.

FANNY: The Shoreham?

HOLMES: That's where she's stopping. Of course it's all a little silly. I don't want to go at all but—

FANNY (*looking up from letter*): Don't be absurd, Wendell. Of course you want to go!

HOLMES: You don't think I should though—do you?

FANNY: My dear, what possible difference could it make to me? It's only that—

HOLMES: Only what?

FANNY: Some people do change, you know . . . in forty-two years . . . even if you don't.

HOLMES (*spontaneously*): Oh, not Ellen Jones. She was the prettiest thing that ever came out of Philadelphia. She— (*Then catching himself.*) I mean—well, it can't be forty-two years, Fanny. It can't be. Why, it was only yesterday. I can still hear the pound of cannon in the hills . . . I can still smell the powder burning. I can—

FANNY: Can you still smell the perfume she used? Or has she changed the brand by now, perhaps? (*This brings the Judge to with a start—but there's a rather pleasant gleam in his eye.*)

HOLMES: Fanny—you're not jealous—not at this late date?

FANNY: What do you mean by "this late date"? Was there a time when it would have been quite in order for me to be jealous of Miss Jones?

HOLMES: Now, Fanny—

FANNY: I always knew that half the girls in Boston had lost their hearts to you . . . but I had never given a thought to Philadelphia.

HOLMES: Woman, I'll have you know that in a democracy a man can still look at a pretty woman without violating either his marriage vows on the one hand or the Constitution of the United States on the other.

FANNY: Don't you talk about the Constitution to me, Mr. Holmes. Save that for Mr. Roosevelt. If you want to spend an evening mooning over the dear old days with an elderly hussy from Philadelphia—

HOLMES: She's not a hussy.

FANNY (*rushing on*): Why, you go right ahead. I have no objections. Only don't bring the Constitution into it. Take her some nice flowers—buy her a good wine and a wonderful dinner. But leave the Constitution home. You won't need it! (FANNY *is starting out, just as the door opens and the* HOUSEKEEPER *comes in.*)

HOUSEKEEPER: I beg your pardon, sir. Mr. Owen Wister to see Mrs. Holmes.

HOLMES (*delighted*): What? Wister here?—well, show him up —show him up right away.

FANNY (*quickly*): My dear, if I heard Mary correctly— (HOUSEKEEPER *goes out, leaving the door open behind her*)—it's on me that Owen is calling—not you.

HOLMES: Eh? Well, we'll see about that— (OWEN WISTER *comes in and moves forward gaily to greet* FANNY *and* HOLMES. *He's all of forty-four now and* The Virginian *is two years behind him. Success sits well on him. He's what the Judge would call a real swell but he's also pretty much what the Judge might have liked in a son; dash—fire— character—and a nice sense of humor.*)

WISTER (*to* FANNY): You will forgive me for breaking in on you like this— (*He kisses her hand, then draws back for a good look at her.*) Cara mia—I don't understand it. Each year you're just a little more enchanting. It isn't fair, you know. The rest of us grow older and older and you keep getting younger and younger.

HOLMES (*with a nice growl*): Enough of this, Whiskers—my boy. You could say the same things about me . . . if you tried hard enough.

WISTER (*turning gaily to* HOLMES): Oh, I was going to get around to you sooner or later, young fellow.

HOLMES (*imitating southern drawl*): I must remind you, sir, that the lady you are calling on is my wife . . . and while I am not of a jealous disposition . . .

FANNY (*sweetly*): You may leave us now, Wendell.

HOLMES: Very well, my love. (*Then to* WISTER.) But I warn you, sir—

WISTER (*laughing*): Sit down, both of you. I am a bearer of strange tidings, I shall have to have a few moments with you.

FANNY (*taking a chair*): Well, you do make it all sound most mysterious.

HOLMES (*also sitting down*): What's on your mind? (WISTER *looks* HOLMES *over carefully. Obviously he expects an explosion or two.*)

WISTER: I'm really here this afternoon as . . . as an unofficial ambassador.

HOLMES (*drily*): Hmmm. Well, we're honored, Your Excellency. Proceed—

WISTER: An ambassador—from President Roosevelt.

HOLMES (*starting to rise from chair*): Well, you can tell him for me—

FANNY: Wendell, be still.

HOLMES (*subsiding*): Very well. But not for long.

FANNY: Go on, Owen.

WISTER: It's really very simple. As far as I can gather, the President would like to refuse the Judge admission to the White House at any and all times—

HOLMES (*to* FANNY): May I say something now?

WISTER: But, as regards Mrs. Holmes—I am permitted to express the hope—oh, most unofficially, you understand— that at dinner this evening Mrs. Holmes will do the President the great honor of sitting at his right.

HOLMES (*flabbergasted*): Well, I'll be damned!

FANNY (*rising quickly*): Mr. Roosevelt is most kind, Mr. Ambassador. But it will not be possible for Mrs. Holmes to accept—because Mrs. Holmes isn't going to the White House dinner tonight.

HOLMES: Eh? What's that?

WISTER: But, my dear, you don't understand. No one can decline an invitation from the White House. It just isn't done.

FANNY: Oh, isn't it? Well, we'll see about that.

HOLMES (*explosively*): Damn it, Fanny—what's this all about anyway? Of course we're going. I don't give two straws for Teddy Roosevelt but wild horses wouldn't keep me away from the White House tonight. I'm going to look him straight in the eye and—

FANNY: Very well, Mr. Holmes. Look him in the eye if you want to—but you can look alone. (*Then more softly.*) Good heavens, Wendell. Where's your Yankee pride? Did you leave it behind you in Boston? Sit to the right of him, will I?— (*Turns to* WISTER.) You can tell the President for me, Mr. Ambassador, that he could carve a better dinner companion out of a banana! (FANNY *start to go out—pauses at door with a nice smile for* WISTER.) But you can tell that nice Mr. Wister that the Holmeses would be deeply honored if he would stay for tea. (FANNY *goes out, leaving an admiring* WISTER *and a baffled* HOLMES *behind her.*)

HOLMES (*softly*): You know, my boy—I'm married to a wonderful woman. She has made life poetry for me—(*then fingering perfumed letter and putting it away*)—but there are times when I know I can never be equal to her. Right now I'm not sure whether it's I or Mr. Roosevelt she is punishing.

WISTER: But what am I going to tell the President?

HOLMES (*with enjoyment*): My boy, I haven't the least idea! But enough of this fellow, Roosevelt— (HOLMES *waves* WISTER *toward a chair.*) Sit down and let me have a good look at you. Bloomin' swell, that's what you've turned out to be. *The Virginian* is a good book. Who would have thought a Harvard man could write so well!

WISTER (*smiling*): Thanks, Judge. How do you like Washington?

HOLMES (*expansively*): Not bad, Whiskers—not bad. Of course the New Willard isn't the Parker House—and I miss those three-alarm fires that you and I and Fanny used to race to in Boston. (*Moves over to windows.*) But Boston was looking backwards . . . and Washington is looking ahead. Of course the town is full of Congressmen and Senators . . . but every now and then you find a fellow whose mind begins to wriggle with the first sparks of thought. . . . Ah, yes—the place has something, especially on a day like this. (HOLMES *is looking out the windows at the fading spring sunshine.* WISTER *leans forward eagerly in his chair.*)

WISTER: I say, Judge, isn't there any way you and T. R. could bury the hatchet?

HOLMES (*turning back to* WISTER *amiably*): You mean he realizes that he's talked like a fool—and this is his way of saying he's sorry?

WISTER: T. R.? Good Lord no—he'd never admit a mistake. But he's a wonderful person, once you get to know him. And I do know him. I've hunted with him, fished with him, camped with him, and I tell you, Judge—

HOLMES (*sitting down*): All right, Whiskers. All right. If he's a great man to you, why he's a great man to you. I guess there's room enough for us both in the country.

WISTER: But what's it all about—what's the real trouble deep down underneath?

HOLMES (*looking up owlishly*): Who wants to know—you or the President?

WISTER: Right now, I do.

HOLMES: Well, my boy, mostly it's just that we're two different men doing two different jobs. I'm even willing to admit that my job is a little simpler than his—because, well, you see, my problems began to straighten out quite a lot when I woke up one fine day and decided that I was *not* God Almighty!

WISTER: Now you're joking.

HOLMES: Oh, no, my boy. Never more serious in my life. The magic moment is the moment when you decide that there are other people in the universe, and that it isn't your high destiny to be the one and only boss of the cosmos. Well, once I found out that I wasn't God Almighty, things shook themselves down quite a bit. But you take your friend Theodore Roosevelt now—he hasn't discovered yet that he's *not* God Almighty and that complicates matters for him.

The Magnificent Yankee

(HOUSEKEEPER *comes on left, with a tray full of tea things, which she puts down on a little table near the fireplace.*)

HOUSEKEEPER (*to* HOLMES): Excuse me, sir. Mrs. Holmes said you would like to have tea in here.

HOLMES: Thank you, Mary.

WISTER: But you can't get away from one thing, Judge. The people all love Roosevelt.

HOLMES (*drily*): Yes—but as one of the boys over in the Senate said the other day, what the folks really like about T. R. is that—he doesn't care a damn for the law.

WISTER: Well, I'll leave it to Mary. Mary, what do you think of Mr. Roosevelt? (HOUSEKEEPER *looks over to* HOLMES, *a little puzzled.*)

HOLMES (*with a chuckle*): It's all right, Mary. Nothing you say here will be held against you.

HOUSEKEEPER (*to* WISTER): Well, sir—as Mr. Dooley says, I guess he is a great hand for getting things done. (HOUSE-KEEPER *nods brightly and goes out.*)

WISTER (*to* HOLMES): There, you see?

HOLMES: Yes, he gets things done all right. Only trouble is he doesn't care how. Oh, I'll admit some of them are steps in the right direction. That square deal he's always talking about . . . some of it's pretty good stuff. But he ought to remember once in a while that this is the United States of America . . . not the United States of Theodore Roosevelt.

WISTER: Come, Judge. He's not that swell-headed.

HOLMES: Oh, no? I met a fellow the other day who read the proofs on the President's book about the Spanish War. Tells me they made T. R. cut out the line which read—"The bravest man I ever knew followed me up San Juan Hill"—!

WISTER: All right. Maybe T. R. is a bit obstinate—but I suppose he couldn't help hoping that you *might* see things his way when the Northern Securities case came up for decision. After all, you were his first appointee to the Court.

HOLMES: Of course. When he named me to the bench, he thought I was a labor judge because I happened to go labor's way in some cases back in Massachusetts. (*Then challengingly*.) But he's all wrong. A good judge isn't any-body's judge in particular. And most of all, he isn't some-thing that a President carries around in his vest pocket.

WISTER: I'm sorry, Judge. You're either with T. R. or against him.

HOLMES (*with something of a bark*): That wasn't what it said in the statute the day I took my oath of office. (*Then more warmly.*) Ah, look here, Whiskers—I know it was a hard case but hard cases make bad law. If the President wants to crack down on the big railroad mergers, let him go ahead and crack. But damn it to hell, let him get something stronger than the Sherman Antitrust Act. (HOLMES *slouches down in chair.*) It won't wash—not with me any-way. Why, it's ridiculous. Think of saying in a law that it's all right for railroads to compete—so long as none of them wins the competition. It doesn't make sense.

WISTER (*a little angry*): Maybe it doesn't. But right now the President can't be particular. Time is running short—and any stick to beat a dog is a good stick.

HOLMES (*with a snort*): Of course. That's what every strong man thinks when he starts to swing the big stick for the sheer joy of swinging it. (*Gets up and strides over to win-dows at right.*) Follow me—or get out of my way.

WISTER (*rising*): Very well, sir. If that's the way you feel about it, I guess there isn't anything anybody can do to bring you and the President together.

HOLMES: Hold on, you fire eater—this isn't going to make any difference as between you and me, is it?

WISTER: I don't know, sir. That all depends on you. (WISTER *starts out. He steps back in surprise as* FANNY *comes in, radiant in a beautiful new white evening dress.*) Why, cara mia—

HOLMES (*admiringly*): Well, I'll be damned. (*There's no doubt about it:* FANNY *is enchanting. She turns around archly, so that the men can admire the gown from every angle.*)

FANNY: Do you think Mr. Roosevelt will like it? (*Even at*

The Magnificent Yankee

sixty-two, FANNY *doesn't look a day over forty—and the evening dress of the Gibson-Girl period sets her off perfectly. Her waist is as slim as a girl's: the bare shoulders are a thing of grace and beauty—but above all there is the fire which is so completely captivating. Little wonder that T. R. wanted her to sit next to him at dinner. She had become one of the most charming women in Washington.*)

HOLMES: But, my dear, what made you change your mind?

FANNY (*blithely*): That's hard to say. Maybe it was the dress—(*Wheeling down to tea table at fireplace.*) Or maybe it was poor dear Mr. Roosevelt. After all, men are so easily misunderstood—(*to* HOLMES)—aren't they, darling?

HOLMES (*with a grin*): I give up, woman. If Teddy Roosevelt wants you to sit next to him, it serves him right. You are the devil of devils—and lovely to boot. Just tell me what you want to do with my life . . . it's yours to command.

FANNY (*purring*): Why, darling—how sweet of you. (*From offstage comes the sound of a fire alarm: the galloping of horses and the clanging of bells.*)

WISTER: Would it be permissible for an innocent bystander to ask just what this is all about?

FANNY: Why, Mr. Ambassador, it's just life—that's what it is. Some of us suddenly acquire a great passion for dining with Mr. Roosevelt . . . others for dining with old flames from Philadelphia. But it's a free country, thank God, and—

HOLMES: Damn it, woman—I've had enough. Why, being married to you is like being married to a— (HOLMES *looks up keenly. Bells stronger over scene now. To* WISTER.) I say—that sounds like a big one. (*Rushes over to window, followed by* WISTER. *They look out for a second, as the fire engine goes by.*) Come on, boy—let's go. (*The two men start out together.* FANNY *rushes after them.*)

FANNY: Oh, no, you don't. If you can still go racing to fires, so can I—

WISTER: But what about your new dress?

HOLMES: And what about the man you're wearing it for tonight—that man in the White House?

FANNY (*picking up the skirt of her dress*): What's the man in the White House compared to a fire— Come on. (FANNY *runs out quickly, followed by* WISTER *and* HOLMES. *The sound of bells continues faintly over scene.*)

ACT II

SCENE 1

SCENE: *The library of Justice Holmes on an evening in March, 1911.*

The room has not changed much. There are new drapes at the windows. The books are now two-thirds of the way to the ceiling.

There is a mellow glow upon the room; from a lamp on the Judge's desk; from the lamp behind the sofa down left and from a cheerful coal fire in the fireplace.

In contrast to the rapid climax of the first act, there is a leisurely, restful quality to this scene—at least for the first few minutes!

HOLMES *is dozing on the sofa while* FANNY, *at his side, is reading to him.*

FANNY: And when the wind in the tree-tops roared,
　　　The soldier asked from the deep dark grave;
　　　　　"Did the banner flutter then?"
　　　　　"Not so, my hero," the wind replied,
　　　　　"The fight is done, but the banner won,
　　　　　Thy comrades of old have borne it hence,
　　　　　　Have borne it in triumph hence."
(FANNY *looks up at* HOLMES.) Wendell, you're not listening.
HOLMES: Not listening? It takes me back fifty years. . . .
　　　Then he heareth the lovers laughing pass,
　　　　And the soldier asks once more:

"Are these not the voices of them that love,
That love—and remember me?"

"Not so, my hero," the lovers say,
"We are those that remember not;
For the spring has come and the earth has smiled,
And the dead must be forgot!"

Then the soldier spake from the deep dark grave
"I am content."

(HOLMES *gets up and moves over to fireplace at left. He is more than a little restless—yet it is a reflective kind of uneasiness.*) I wonder if that will sound the same in another fifty years . . . ah, the trouble is no book is worth reading twenty-five years after it has been written . . . the things that struck sparks for you as a boy have a way of fizzling out by the time you're—(*then wryly*)—you know, I begin to suspect that I must be quite an old man.

FANNY (*picking up embroidery*): Humph! You've been saying you were an old man ever since you were forty.

HOLMES: Odd too . . . the words you used to like . . . they're still the same words but they just don't say the same things any more. (FANNY *looks at him shrewdly, then smiles. Neither of them look a day older than when we saw them last but there is something about the Judge tonight that is a little different—a little diffident almost. A clock offstage strikes the half hour and HOLMES looks up briskly.*)

HOLMES: Didn't that scamp of a secretary say he'd be back by eight-thirty?

FANNY: Now—now—he'll be along. Wendell, what *is* the matter with you tonight?

HOLMES: Eh? Oh, nothing—nothing that a little Rabelais or Dante wouldn't fix.

FANNY: So that's it. Well, I'm not sure I approve of Dante—and as for Rabelais!—you'd be better off with Shakespeare.

HOLMES (*standing with back to fireplace*): No—not tonight. Oh, not that Shakespeare's so bad, mind you. Every so often he will come up with something that really catches your heart . . . "In Belmont lives a lady fair . . ." but Dante, ah, there's a man can sing you to paradise at least once in every twenty lines. Aye, and to hell too.

FANNY (*biting off a thread*): You're a fine one to talk about heaven and hell. You don't believe in either.

HOLMES (*slyly*): No—only when I read Dante! Ah, but you ought to give Rabelais a chance, Fanny. What temperament, what gusto. Everything on the hum—like culture in Chicago.

FANNY: It's no use, Wendell. I won't read Rabelais and I won't read any of those nasty French novels for you either.

HOLMES: What a thing is woman! (*Then with a flourish.*) You know, if I didn't have to be such a respectable old codger, I'd enjoy going out on a riproaring, old-fashioned, glorified toot.

FANNY (*sweetly*): Well, why don't you? Maybe you could get a few of the brethren to join you!

HOLMES: Enough, woman. When I set out to cut a caper, it will not be with men in gowns.

FANNY: Who is she, Wendell?

HOLMES: If only it were a she!

FANNY: You're being mighty secretive about it. What is it?

HOLMES: It's a speech, my love.

FANNY: But you don't make speeches. What's it about?

HOLMES: I'm not sure what it's about. That's just the trouble.

FANNY: I mean—well, whom is it for?

HOLMES (*drily*): It's for a lot of college boys. Going to get together in June and paint the town red. Somebody thought they ought to be held down a little and since my hair seems to be a bit greyer than that of most of the duffers around—

FANNY: The very idea—why, they ought to know better.

HOLMES: That's what I told them. But the Class of 1861 was a pretty obstinate bunch, even when it was in Harvard and—

FANNY: Wendell—your own class and you didn't tell me—you *are* a beast.

HOLMES (*kissing her hand lightly*): Beauty and the beast—a

pretty picture—but I can't make a speech about it. (HOLMES *moves toward fireplace.*) What am I going to tell them, Fanny? What can I tell them? Fifty years we've been out of Harvard now—and fifty years ought to add up to something, but do they—and if so, how much? I could put all I know about life on one small piece of white paper but on the other side I'd have to write "not proved." (FANNY *looks at him shrewdly. She's impressed by what he says but she's not going to let him moon around too much.*)

FANNY: Oh, no, you don't, Wendell. It's right pretty talk but it doesn't take me in a bit. When you're in a tight spot, I notice you always begin to twist the tail of the cosmos a bit. And do you know why? Well, I'll tell you.

HOLMES: Now—now—Fanny. Leave me something.

FANNY: You cover up pretty well, old man. But I'm on to you now. The trouble with you is you pretend to be a fire eating cynic. But deep down inside, you're a shameless, unmitigated believer. Of course, you're not too sure just what it is you believe in—

HOLMES: Woman—I protest.

FANNY (*rushing on*): But whatever it is, you're awfully scared somebody may find out about it some day. So you retire behind those beautiful white whiskers of yours and mutter "ah me, ah me, what is life." Why don't you come out in the open just once and let us all in on the secret? Why— (*There is a discreet knock on the door.* HOLMES, *with some relief, looks up eagerly.*)

HOLMES: Yes. Come in. (*The door opens and another new* SECRETARY *comes in. He's very much like the others who have preceded him—a shade handsomer perhaps but about the same age, twenty-four or twenty-five. He is wearing the smartest linen duster of the period and he is quite uneasy. In his hand is a very dashing motor cap, with goggles attached.*)

SECRETARY: I'm awfully sorry I'm late, sir. But—

HOLMES (*eagerly*): Well, Northrop—we won't go into that now. But as long as you're here, let's get to work.

SECRETARY (*not taking coat off*): You understand, I didn't *intend* to be late, sir. It was just that—

HOLMES (*moving over to his desk*): All right—all right, Northrop. Forget it.

SECRETARY: I thought I had allowed myself plenty of time, sir. But we went for a drive as far as Mt. Vernon—and the machine broke down—and—

HOLMES: Forget it, Northrop, Forget it— (*Then to* FANNY.) Now, my dear, if you will excuse us? Take off your coat, Northrop, and stay a while. We have a big evening ahead of us.

SECRETARY: I'm sorry, sir. I can't stay. In fact, I'll have to resign. You see, sir—

HOLMES: Resign? Why, that's ridiculous. You can't resign.

SECRETARY: Just the same, I have to, sir. The fact is I—I'm going to be married!

HOLMES (*with something of a bark*): Married? That's preposterous. Why, you promised you wouldn't. You—

SECRETARY: I realize that, sir. But you know how these things are.

HOLMES: I know nothing of the sort. Why, Northrop, this is amazing. This is unprecedented. This is—

FANNY (*moving in*): Nonsense, Wendell. Secretaries are getting married every day.

HOLMES: Not my secretaries.

FANNY (*to* SECRETARY): May I offer my congratulations Mr. Northrop, to you—and the lucky girl?

SECRETARY (*overcome*): Why—why—thank you—thank you very much, Mrs. Holmes. Thank you very much indeed.

HOLMES: Fanny—you keep out of this. Northrop, I want you to know—

FANNY: Hush, Wendell. (*To* SECRETARY.) I'm really very happy for you, Mr. Northrop. Is it permitted to ask—was this all a little sudden?

SECRETARY (*eagerly*): Well, it was—and it wasn't, ma'am.

We've been going together for nearly a year. And although I have asked her to marry me many times before—

HOLMES: Oh, you have, have you?

SECRETARY (*gulping*): Yes, sir. But she only laughed and put me off before. Only this time—

FANNY: What was different about this time, Mr. Northrop?

SECRETARY: Well, when the car broke down—there was nothing to do except to wait for the horses to come and tow us back into town . . . so I proposed again . . . and well, maybe it was because this time she had lots of time to think it over . . . well, she accepted me—(*then with mixed emotions*)—and now—now I'm the happiest man in the world . . . or would be, sir—if it weren't for the fact that I have to be leaving you.

FANNY: Nonsense. Who said anything about leaving us?

SECRETARY (*incredulous*): But, Mrs. Holmes—

HOLMES (*a little angry*): *Fanny*—you keep out of this—you—

FANNY (*to* HOLMES): Ah, I know, dear. A rule is a rule—but you only made up the rule for your secretaries. You can't possibly expect it to be binding on the girls they may be in love with. Besides, when a young man is in love with a young woman—why, he isn't any more responsible for what happens than a young soldier is when he meets a girl like . . . Ellen Jones. Sometimes things just happen. Sometimes—

HOLMES: Now just a minute. What has Ellen Jones to do with all this? I'll have you know—

FANNY: Darling, please. Why can't we forget the rule just for this once?

SECRETARY (*eagerly*): Mrs. Holmes—

FANNY: Why don't we really go on that spree you were talking about? Why don't we kick up our heels and give Mr. Northrop and his bride-to-be a real party?

HOLMES (*after a moment's hesitation*): All right, Northrop. I know when I'm licked. Consider your resignation refused.

SECRETARY (*starting to take off linen duster*): Why, Mr.

Justice—this is wonderful. I'll never forget it, I assure you, sir. I'll work as I've never worked before, sir. I'll—

HOLMES: There—there. Take it easy, Northrop. As a matter of fact, you might as well take the evening while you're about it. Get out of here as fast as you can but make sure you're on time in the morning.

SECRETARY (*beaming*): Mr. Justice—

HOLMES (*nicely*): Is she pretty, boy?

SECRETARY (*putting duster back on*): She's a peach, sir.

HOLMES: Hmmm. Well, then you might kiss her once for me. (*Then with one eye on* FANNY.) Or, better yet, bring her around some day—and I'll do the needful myself.

SECRETARY: Yes, sir. Anything you like, sir. I mean—well, good night, sir. (*Then to* FANNY.) Good night, Mrs. Holmes. It's nice to know that there are still people left in the world who . . . who know what it's like to be in love. (*With a nice impulsive gesture the* SECRETARY *kisses* FANNY's *hand and goes out quickly.* FANNY *stands watching him off, smiling softly.* HOLMES *eyes her sardonically.*)

HOLMES: Now as for you, my good woman—

FANNY (*hardly hearing him*): Did you notice his eyes, Wendell? Did you ever see anything so shining bright? (*Sitting in one of a pair of chairs.*) No wonder folks say some people carry their heart in their eyes. They do, you know—and sometimes it's just a little dazzling. You want to look closer and closer . . . and then suddenly you feel like a trespasser. You want to look away. You want—

HOLMES (*with a snort*): Very pretty. But let's face the facts, woman. (*Taking chair opposite her: a small table, with a bowl of flowers, stands between them.*) You tried to blackmail me just now!

FANNY: Really? I thought I got away with it rather well. Besides, milord, as I understand the law—it's only blackmail if there was anything black to back up the threat with. And surely there wasn't anything that wasn't pure white as between you and Ellen Jones—except that she *was* a

218

little fat when you finally caught up with her forty years later. Remember?

HOLMES: That's not so. She wasn't fat at all. Well, maybe she was a little plump but—

FANNY: Oh, Wendell—Wendell—what difference does it make? This boy is almost like a son—just like all the others.

HOLMES: That's neither here nor there. And if you ever say anything like that to any of them—I'll never forgive you.

FANNY: But what did he do that was so awful? Except put his girl above everything else in the world . . . including the great Mr. Holmes.

HOLMES: That's not the issue at all. The issue is—

FANNY (*softly*): But he's so young . . . and it's so wonderful to be young. Remember?

HOLMES (*grimly*): Woman—you're not fighting fair.

FANNY: Remember the day you came home from the Civil War . . . the night you went out to call on Emerson at Concord . . . you were on fire then too . . . just like this boy . . . life was a passionate and a profound thing, you said, or it was nothing . . . you said . . .

HOLMES (*getting up*): That wasn't the same at all . . . of course I said all that and I meant every word of it . . . but I had to work for one thing at a time . . . remember? First, the law—and then the girl I loved. But these young whippersnappers . . . they think they can have their cake and eat it too . . . they don't know what it's like to plunge deep down into a real piece of work . . . and trust to your own unshaken will . . . but, by heaven, they'd better learn . . . any man who wants to do a little original work in this life has got to reconcile himself to a certain amount of loneliness . . . any man . . .

FANNY (*quickly*): Fiddlesticks, so has any woman . . . who waits for any man like that. I ought to know. I did my share of waiting, while you charted those unknown seas. But I can't say I liked it.

HOLMES (*amazed and a little concerned*): Fanny—

FANNY: Oh, I'm not complaining, mind you. It worked out all right for you and me. But I'm not so sure that a lonely heart is the best heart to serve the law with . . . especially when you're young. After all, we're not running a monastery here. They don't *have* to be celibate, do they? Why isn't it all right just once to—oh, stop being such an eternal Yankee, Mr. Holmes. Do a little thinking with your heart instead of your head. This isn't the common law we're talking about. This is love—and I think it's wonderful. (FANNY *starts out. Before she is off, the door opens and* HOUSEKEEPER *steps in.*)

HOUSEKEEPER: I beg your pardon, sir—but Mr. Henry Adams is downstairs asking to see you.

HOLMES: What? At this hour of night? Oh, no—this is too much. Fanny—help me out of this like a good girl.

FANNY: But I'm not a good girl and I'm not at all sure I'd say the right thing. Just what is on Mr. Adams' mind, Mary?

HOUSEKEEPER: I can't make out exactly, ma'am. But he seems to be worried about something.

HOLMES: Oh, you can be sure it's President Taft. Each administration brings Adams new woes and, gad, how he enjoys them! Mary, my apologies to Mr. Adams. Tell him I'm sorry that I'm in conference . . . I can't be disturbed . . . but Mrs. Holmes will be down in just a few minutes. Tell him—

FANNY: Well, I like that—

HOLMES (*blithely*): I thought you would. All right, Mary. Start calming Mr. Adams. And as for you, my dear—(*to* FANNY)—suppose you help me out with this speech. (HOUSEKEEPER *goes out.* FANNY *moves back to chair.*)

FANNY: Oh, so I'm your secretary now, is that it?

HOLMES: Fanny, what am I going to tell my old classmates? What *can* I tell them? Listen, eh—while I gather a little wool?

FANNY: Very well. But don't forget—Mr. Adams is waiting downstairs. (*There's something electric in the air now and the mention of the word "Adams" sets off a spark in* HOLMES.)

HOLMES: Adams! Ah, don't you see, Fanny, the trouble was I was trying to add up the years the way Henry Adams would add them up. But life isn't doing a sum. It's painting a picture . . . and sometimes you have to have a little faith that the canvas will fill out as you go along. (HOLMES *moves away from* FANNY *with the easy air of a lawyer addressing a friendly jury.*) What difference does it make that I haven't reached all my objectives in my few years down here? No man ever can. We are lucky enough if we can give a sample of our best . . . and if in our hearts we can feel that it was nobly done. Well, at least I've made them see that the Constitution is a *living* thing . . . I've helped them see that the personal views of judges ought not to determine what is allowed and what is not allowed under the Constitution . . . it takes a lot of live and let live to put a republic together and keep it going . . . we ought to give the individual states as much leeway as we can when it comes to social experiments for the common good . . . we must not be afraid to trust the people to . . . (HOLMES *pauses and looks down at* FANNY *with a smile.*) Well, you were right, Fanny. I *am* a believer in spite of everything. I believe in my country. I believe in the people in it. I even believe in myself—and the universe I'm part of —though I'm damned if I know yet just what it is that holds us both together from one minute to the next. (*He starts on another turn about the room.*) Oh, I know—I don't have the evidence to back all this up. But life isn't a matter of how much evidence you have . . . because you never will have enough. It's a matter of how much faith you have . . . faith in a universe not measured by your fears. (*Then with a rising sense of excitement.*) Ah, there's the trick, Fanny, the real trick. Not to measure things by our fears but by our faith.

FANNY (*deeply moved but with a teasing sparkle that con-*

ceals her emotion): Now you are beginning to come out from behind those beautiful white whiskers!

HOLMES: Yes, and I feel naked somehow—naked but warm. (*Then snapping his fingers.*) You know, that's what's wrong with people like Henry Adams. They have no fire in the belly and where there's no fire, there's no hope. There's no—

FANNY: Now, Wendell, belly is *not* a nice word.

HOLMES: Well, I'll be damned. Here I go pouring out my very soul to you and all you can say is "belly is not a nice word."

FANNY: Well, it isn't . . . to some people.

HOLMES: Very well. If the word belly will shock the delicate sensibilities of the old boys at Harvard, we won't use it. But belly was what I said and belly, by heaven, is what I mean . . . it's the thing you crawl on when the bullets get too thick overhead . . . it's the thing you march on when everything else is gone . . . a belly, my good woman, is the place where a soldier's faith is born . . . a belly . . . (HOLMES *stops abruptly as* FANNY *breaks out into uncontrollable peals of laughter.*)

FANNY: I'm sorry, Wendell, really I am. (*Getting up.*) But I suddenly remembered poor Mr. Adams waiting downstairs . . . and I just got to thinking . . . (FANNY *goes off into laughter again and starts for the doorway.*)

FANNY (*pausing at doorway*): I'm sure Mr. Adams never thought of the word belly in his whole life . . . and if he did . . . if he did just once . . . I'm sure he wouldn't have the stomach for it! (FANNY *goes out, convulsed with laughter.* HOLMES, *puzzled and a little frustrated, looks after her—then gradually succumbs himself. He throws his head back and lets go with great roars of laughter.*)

ACT II

SCENE 2

SCENE: *The library of Justice Holmes on an afternoon in June, 1916.*

The windows are open—fresh flowers are in place. Summer is in the air.

HOLMES, *a little older now, but erect as ever, is working quickly at his desk, impatient to be up and out.*

There's a cheerful, decisive air about him as he scans some texts of his brother justices. He puts the last one down with a sigh of relief, looks across at his SECRETARY, *another young man from Harvard.*

HOLMES: Well, what do you think? Do you concur?

SECRETARY (*not at all humble*): Oh, it's well done, Mr. Justice—very well done. But—

HOLMES: But what?

SECRETARY: It's a very fine point, sir—but only one man in ten thousand will know what you're hitting at.

HOLMES (*wryly*): Young fellow, that's the man I'm writing for . . . that man in ten thousand. Now if you're ready—let's get out of here. Too nice a day to be bottled up with a lot of printer's ink. (HOUSEKEEPER *comes in with some folders, containing legal papers, just as* HOLMES *and* SECRETARY *are starting out. They stop like two culprits confronted by a policeman.*)

HOUSEKEEPER: A messenger from the Court just arrived with these, sir.

HOLMES (*with a sigh*): Very well, Mary. (HOLMES *thumbs through the papers quickly as* HOUSEKEEPER *goes out, then looks up at* SECRETARY.) You know, the double damned fertility of my brethren will kill me yet . . . time was when a Judge could sneak away on a nice afternoon and commune with nature . . . or whatever his luck turned up. But now—it's as I said to Bill James once . . . life is like an artichoke . . . you pull out a leaf, only the tip is edible . . . you pull out a day, only an hour or two is your own . . . for the things you really want to do . . . (*Then gaily, as he throws papers to* SECRETARY.) Well, son—you try your teeth on these. I'll see how things are coming on along the Potomac. (HOLMES *moves out, pauses at the door.*) Oh yes, if Mrs. Holmes wants to know where I am . . . tell her I've gone out to dig up a worm for her bird. . . . (HOLMES *goes out.* SECRETARY *picks up papers and starts to sort them. Doors open and* FANNY *comes in. At seventy-five she still doesn't look a day over sixty: she is slim, striking, and as indomitable as ever.*)

FANNY: Oh, Mr. Hamilton—

SECRETARY: Yes, Mrs. Holmes?

FANNY: Has the Judge ordered our reservations to New York and the North Shore yet?

SECRETARY: Not yet, Mrs. Holmes.

FANNY: Now isn't that just like a man?

SECRETARY: Well, of course we don't know yet . . . just when the Court will adjourn.

FANNY: No, but as soon as it does, he'll want to traipse off to Beverly Farms . . . just like that . . . Mr. Hamilton, if you were to make a guess, when would you say the Court might adjourn?

SECRETARY: I'm sure I don't know—but if the Senate keeps putting off a vote on the appointment of Mr. Brandeis, I suppose we could be here indefinitely.

FANNY: Well, I wouldn't wait too long about those reservations, Mr. Hamilton. Just to be on the safe side, suppose you ask what they have for a week from today.

SECRETARY: A week from today? Mrs. Holmes! Do you mean that the Brandeis appointment is coming up for a vote today?

FANNY: Why, Mr. Hamilton . . . did I say anything like that? (FANNY *starts out. The door opens and* HOLMES *comes in gaily, followed by* OWEN WISTER.)

HOLMES: Fanny—Fanny—look what I found on the doorstep!

WISTER (*moving to* FANNY): You remember me, madame. The bad penny—from the Philadelphia mint.

FANNY: Why, Owen—how nice.

HOLMES: Sit down, my boy, and let us "tell sad stories of the death of kings." How goes everything at Monte Carlo? What news of the girls on the Riviera, eh?

FANNY: Now, Wendell—behave yourself. (*Then to* WISTER.) You'll stay for tea, of course.

HOLMES: Of course he'll stay. But I wish you'd stop offering people tea all the time, Fanny. Bound to ruin their dinners.

FANNY: Nonsense. A good cup of tea . . . is even better than a good glass of wine. (FANNY *goes out left.*)

HOLMES (*To* WISTER, *as he sits on sofa*): Well, everybody to his taste. (*Then quoting a bit of* WISTER'S *own verse.*)
Said Aristotle unto Plato:
"Do have another sweet potato?"
Said Plato unto Aristotle;
"No thank you. I prefer the bottle."

WISTER: Shall I never live that down?

HOLMES: Never! . . . (*Then with a blithe wave to* SECRETARY.) Hamilton, meet Mr. Wister, etc. (SECRETARY *and* WISTER *shake hands.* HOLMES *takes chair.*) Whiskers, this is the twelfth secretary I've had since I began to camp out down here. Wasn't sure I was going to be too keen for the idea when I first started out—but it has its points. At least none of these bright boys from Harvard ever work with me long enough to catch on to me, eh Hamilton?

SECRETARY: I wouldn't be too sure about that, sir!

HOLMES: Oh, you wouldn't, eh? Well, run along, son—

SECRETARY: But what about all these certioraris that just came over, sir?

HOLMES (*blandly*): What do you mean—just came over? Why, the messenger never got here at all. Fact. Wasn't able to make delivery before morning. Understand? You'd better. Now get along out of here.

WISTER (*as* SECRETARY *goes out*): What are you going to do when they finally catch on to the fact that you're really rather fond of them?

HOLMES (*airily*): Simple. I'll just start to abuse them all over again. Well, boy—what brings you to Washington?

WISTER: Nothing. I'm just passing through. But I hardly hoped to find you still here . . . in the middle of June . . . and all this heat.

HOLMES (*evasively*): Oh, I'm as busy as a witch in a gale of wind. And I don't mind the heat. As June goes here, this is a pretty nice day.

WISTER: You know what I mean. Usually, you're champing at the bit to get away.

HOLMES (*suddenly quite frank*): I know—but big things are happening, boy—I don't want to miss any of the show.

WISTER (*tensely*): And what a show it's turning out to be . . . Judge, do you think we're going to be able to keep out of Kaiser Wilhelm's war?

HOLMES (*softly*): No, I don't think we can. Oh, I know—people say it isn't our fight—and maybe it isn't . . . yet. But I had a Commander-in-chief once who said a country couldn't endure half slave and half free. What's the difference between a country and a world?

WISTER: Maybe Hughes will have a war left on his doorstep, *if* he can beat Wilson. Think he can?

HOLMES: Hard to say. Both good men. But I was sorry to see Hughes resign from our bench. Now there's a man with a real sense of humor and a neat turn of mind.

WISTER: From all accounts, Hughes isn't the only one you're likely to lose. Is it true White may step down as Chief Justice?

HOLMES (*wryly*): My boy, you've been reading too many newspapers.

WISTER: Maybe. But people are already talking about who's

going to succeed him. Suppose Mr. Wilson *should* name Mr. Taft—

HOLMES: Whiskers, you ought to stick to stories about the great outdoors.

WISTER: I'm not saying Taft would be a bad choice, mind you. But it's bound to be a little confusing. First, you see a man on the bench, then he's heading for the White House —and next thing you know, you see a man in the White House and he's heading for the bench.

HOLMES (*with a chuckle*): They meet themselves coming and going . . . yes, we're quite the cradle for statesmen. But, if you ask me, I think they're better off with us. Nine times out of ten, the Court does something to a man. Now you take Taft. He wasn't a very good President but he'd make an efficient Chief Justice. Or take—

WISTER: No, I'll take a man named Holmes. When White resigns some day, why shouldn't the President name *you* to be Chief?

HOLMES (*uneasily*): Easy, Whiskers. I'm getting to be an old man—well, seventy-five anyway. (HOLMES *gets up and prowls about. We see fleetingly that the honor would mean much to him. He will always pretend that it did not matter but the truth is: it did. After all, he was a fine Chief Justice in Massachusetts and an excellent administrator, though in his Washington years he pretended not to be. In fact, he was a much better administrator than White and he admitted as much once in a letter to Pollock in England.*) And I'm only what we call a side judge . . . they never name a side judge to be Chief. It's much easier to designate someone who isn't already on the Court. (*Then breaking off abruptly.*) Besides, I'm fond of White . . . even if he was a Johnny Reb in his day . . . not bad fellows the Johnny Rebs . . . they had to be discouraged of course but they fought like gentlemen . . . they . . .

SECRETARY (*coming in*): I'm sorry, sir. But Mr. Adams is downstairs—Mr. Henry Adams—and he insists on seeing you, if it is at all possible.

WISTER (*with alacrity*): I'd better be going. I can look in on you tomorrow.

HOLMES: Oh, no you don't. If I have to listen to Henry Adams, I'm going to have company. (*To* SECRETARY.) What seems to be on his mind this time, Hamilton?

SECRETARY: I'm not sure, sir. But I think it's President Wilson!

HOLMES: Very well—have him come up. (SECRETARY *goes out.*) You know when I first came down here, it was T. R. that Adams was grousing about. Then it was Taft—and now it's Wilson. Well, I'll say this for him. He has no favorites.

WISTER (*lightly*): If he bothers you so much, why do you keep on seeing him?

HOLMES: I don't know. He's a fascinating kind of bird. He's like a hen that's always brooding and never hatching anything. Just stand by and maybe he won't stay very long. Maybe— (SECRETARY *opens door and shows in* ADAMS.)

SECRETARY: Mr. Adams—sir. (ADAMS *is wearing a darkish Palm Beach suit which is very neat but very faded. Alongside the spruce* WISTER, *who is very dapper in a light Palm Beach suit, and* HOLMES, *who is immaculate in a light tweed,* ADAMS *looks a shade on the wispy side. But he has a quaint dignity all his own.*)

ADAMS: Hello, Holmes. Very good of you to see me on such short notice. But this is urgent—really urgent. (SECRETARY *goes out up center.* HOLMES *greets* ADAMS *and presents him and* WISTER *to each other.*)

HOLMES: Hello, Adams. You remember Owen Wister, don't you?

ADAMS: Eh? Oh yes—of course. (*Vaguely.*) Harvard, weren't you?

WISTER: Now and then.

HOLMES: You can speak freely. I have no confidences from Wister.

ADAMS: Well, the fact is— (FANNY *opens door at left and comes in with* HOUSEKEEPER, *who is bringing tea and cakes.*)

The Magnificent Yankee

FANNY: Why, Mr. Adams—how nice to see you again. You will stay for tea, won't you?

ADAMS: Why, thank you—thank you very much. I—I'd be glad to.

FANNY: Good. I've made some special cookies—and somebody just has to eat them. (*With a look at* HOLMES.) Somebody who isn't afraid for his figure. (FANNY *pours tea and* HOUSEKEEPER *prepares to serve it.* WISTER *reaches for a cooky.*)

HOLMES: Touché, my dear. But Mr. Adams didn't come over to talk about my figure . . . or your cooking. (HOUSEKEEPER *moves across with tea for* ADAMS, *who takes one of two chairs at right.*)

WISTER: Hold on—if no one wants to talk about the cookies, I will. They're wonderful.

FANNY: Nice man—

HOLMES: Well, Adams—what's on your mind?

ADAMS: It's Mr. Wilson—that's what it is. I tell you— (HOUSE-KEEPER *gives him tea then returns to tea table.*) Oh, thank you—thank you very much. (*Then to* HOLMES.) I tell you, if the President keeps on dividing the country the way he has so far, there won't be any country left. (*Then abruptly.*) Everywhere you go, people are beginning to ask why doesn't he withdraw the nomination of Louis Brandeis? (HOLMES *moves over to windows.*)

HOLMES: Excuse me, Adams, that's none of my business and I would prefer not to discuss it. If I had known that was what you wanted to talk about, I would have declined to see you.

ADAMS: Please—don't misunderstand me, Holmes. Nobody asked me to come here . . . I realize that the Court could not possibly take a hand in this . . . one way or the other. (HOUSEKEEPER *moves across room again with tea for* HOLMES.)

WISTER (*to* ADAMS): But what's it all about? I thought nearly everybody liked Louis Brandeis.

FANNY (*sitting on sofa*): And why would it be so awful if the

Senate suddenly did decide to confirm him for the Court? (FANNY's *manner, in asking the question, implies more knowledge than she is willing to share with anyone for the moment.* WISTER, *amused and curious, sits down beside* FANNY *on the sofa.*)

ADAMS (*to* FANNY *and* WISTER): Please— I have the greatest admiration for Mr. Brandeis. He is a very able lawyer—and a very fine man. If the Senate would confirm him promptly —all well and good. But the Senate won't.

FANNY: But, Mr. Adams, if the President made a good choice, he should stand back of it, shouldn't he? Just what is it you're concerned about? (HOUSEKEEPER *goes out.*)

ADAMS: The country, ma'am, the country. It isn't good for the country to prolong a fight like this.

HOLMES (*moving in from windows*): On the contrary, Adams. With this kind of a fight, the longer it is prolonged, the better!

ADAMS: But can't you see what's going to happen? This may make for the worst split in the country since the Civil War. Jew will be lined up against non-Jew and—

HOLMES (*sitting in chair across from* ADAMS, *a small table between them*): Nonsense. This isn't a Jewish issue at all.

ADAMS: Of course it isn't. But people are beginning to *think* it is . . . and already it is being said that even the Court itself might not be too disappointed if—

HOLMES: Ridiculous. A few of the brethren may not be keen for Brandeis. But it's his ideas they are afraid of—not his religion. If Brandeis had never fought the utilities, if he had never taken the part of labor, if he hadn't been quite so *successful* at it, they would have called him a nice Jew— and accepted him. I tell you, Adams, the Jews have given a lot to this country and one of their prize contributions is Louis Brandeis. (*Reaching for his tea.*) If I were Wilson I'd hang on until hell freezes over—and then I'd skate on top of it. (*The door opens and* HOUSEKEEPER *comes in.*)

HOUSEKEEPER (*to* FANNY): Your pardon, ma'am—Mr. Brandeis has just arrived.

HOLMES: Eh? What's that?

HOUSEKEEPER: Shall I show him up? (FANNY *nods "yes" and* HOUSEKEEPER *starts out.*)

ADAMS (*getting up*): I think maybe I should be going.

HOLMES: Now just a moment, my dear. I'm always glad to see Brandeis, but—

FANNY (*brightly*): That's what I thought, darling—so I asked him to stop by for tea.

HOLMES: But I've been most scrupulous about not seeing Brandeis while the nomination is still before the Senate.

FANNY (*drily*): I know, dear—but today *is* a little different, isn't it? You see, the Administration is calling the appointment up this afternoon and if they call it up, that means they have the votes to put it over. It means—

WISTER: Mrs. Holmes, you're wonderful. How do you do it? Do you have a special secret service all your own?

FANNY: Yes, and a special messenger service all my own too. Just wait . . . and you may see things happen!

HOLMES (*to* FANNY): But if what you say is true, surely I would have heard of it?

FANNY: Darling, the justices of the Supreme Court are the last people in the world to hear anything about anything. And that's as it should be. You are sweet old darlings who live in a cloister . . . and try not to see too much of the wicked world outside. But Senators and the wives of Senators are something else again . . . especially the wives. (*The door opens and* HOUSEKEEPER *ushers in* BRANDEIS. HOLMES *moves up to greet him warmly.*)

HOUSEKEEPER: Mr. Brandeis—

HOLMES: Well, young feller—

FANNY: Is it too early to offer congratulations?

BRANDEIS: Please—it is not over yet. I think they are only voting on me now—(*then to* HOLMES)—and I am not at all sure of the proprieties at a moment like this.

HOLMES: To hell with the proprieties! (HOLMES *brings* BRANDEIS *forward to meet* ADAMS.) You remember Henry Adams?

BRANDEIS: Yes, indeed. How are you, Adams?

ADAMS (*flustered but wanting to say the right thing*): We need you here, Brandeis—need you badly!

HOLMES: And Owen Wister—

BRANDEIS (*shaking hands*): How are you, Wister.

WISTER: I'm very proud to be here, sir. When a Brandeis joins forces with a Holmes again, it's like old times in Boston. It's a great moment.

HOLMES: Well, it's a new firing line anyway, eh Brandeis?

BRANDEIS: Optimist! (*Then turning to* FANNY.) It was good of you to think of me today . . . of all days.

HOLMES: Look here, Fanny—this calls for something a little stronger than tea, doesn't it?

FANNY: Now, Wendell, a good cup of tea—

HOLMES: I know—a good cup of tea is better than a good cup of wine—if you can't find the cup of wine . . . but I can . . . I . . .

BRANDEIS: Please, my dear Holmes—considering that this isn't at all official yet, I think that tea will be quite adequate.

HOLMES: Very well. But between you and me, Brandeis, that's the trouble with tea. It *is* adequate—adequate, but nothing more. Now, if I had been planning this little party— (HOUSEKEEPER *enters from left and moves over to* FANNY.)

HOUSEKEEPER: A letter for Mr. Brandeis . . . a Senate messenger just delivered it.

FANNY (*to* WISTER): There, you see—

HOLMES: Well, I'll be damned— (HOUSEKEEPER *gives the letter to* BRANDEIS *and he looks to* FANNY. HOUSEKEEPER *moves on out.*)

BRANDEIS: May I—

FANNY: Of course—

HOLMES: I give up, my dear. I don't know how you do it and I won't ask. I'll only say—

BRANDEIS (*he has the envelope open but pauses before reading contents*): Odd, isn't it? . . . you wait six months for a certain moment . . . and when it comes, you think maybe you could wait a little longer . . . you think . . . (*Breaking off abruptly,* BRANDEIS *proceeds to read the note very slowly, with no show of emotion.*)

HOLMES (*breaking a silence of several seconds*): Brandeis— will you end this suspense and tell us what the hell that damned thing says? (BRANDEIS *smiles a wry kind of smile and hands the message to* FANNY. *Then he moves to* HOLMES.)

BRANDEIS: It's all right. They've confirmed my appointment. Only twenty-two votes against me!

HOLMES (*clapping him on the shoulder and shaking his hand*): Welcome, brother—welcome to the hall of disagreement!

ADAMS: Hear—hear!

HOLMES: My friends, I give you Mr. Justice Brandeis—a Daniel come to judgment. Come along, Daniel—I know a better way to celebrate than this. (HOLMES *starts out with* BRANDEIS.)

WISTER (*with alacrity*): I'm with you. (*He starts out after* HOLMES *and* BRANDEIS.)

ADAMS (*getting up quickly*): And I too! (*But* HENRY ADAMS *is an* ADAMS. *He moves only a foot or two, when he remembers the eternal amenities. He returns to* FANNY *and the tea table.*) Forgive me, I almost forgot—there's nothing quite like a good cup of tea, is there? (FANNY *laughs.* ADAMS *looks off wistfully toward the others, then sits down across from* FANNY *and picks up his tea cup.*)

ACT II

SCENE 3

SCENE: *The library of Justice Holmes on a Sunday evening in March, 1921, two days before his eightieth birthday.*

HOLMES, *immaculate in full evening attire, is standing before a bull's-eye mirror, at the fireplace, trying to give his white tie the right debonair angle.*

FANNY *comes in. She is as charming at eighty as she was at sixty. She is wearing an appropriate dressing gown of the period. Her hair has been done especially for the occasion and there is an air of suppressed excitement about her.*

FANNY: Well, darling—are you ready?

HOLMES (*his back to her*): Of course, I'm ready. But the man who invented bull's-eye mirrors should be fried in hell.

FANNY (*going to him*): Here, let me help you.

HOLMES (*turning around*): You're a fine one to talk. You aren't ready yet yourself.

FANNY: Oh, yes I am. I only have to change into my dress . . . it's a brand new one . . . I got it just for tonight and I expect you to be properly dazzled.

HOLMES: Woman, what's this all about anyway? We've been dining out at pothouses on Sunday evening for a good many years . . . without all this fuss and feathers. (FANNY *eyes him as one having a secret, which she will not share. She pats his tie and stands back to admire him.*)

FANNY: Because, my love—you're eighty years young.

HOLMES: Not till Tuesday, I'm not. (*Then reciting a verse he made up for his eightieth birthday.*)
And now that I've grown to be eighty—
(rhyme with "mighty")
I still sit in the seats of the mighty—

FANNY (*finishing the jingle*):
My pretty young wife
Is the joy of my life—

HOLMES: But Gad—how that woman is flighty!

FANNY: Who wouldn't be flighty married to you for fifty years, old man? But I'm going to show you off just the same . . . before someone else thinks of it!

HOLMES: Humph. Lot of foolishness, if you ask me.

FANNY: You're not fooling me, old man. You love to step out in your best bib and tucker, and you know it.

HOLMES: Woman, you are a dangerous—and beautiful creature.

FANNY: Humph. That's what you say to every pretty woman you meet.

HOLMES: True . . . but with the rest of 'em, I never mean it.

FANNY: Thank you, my love . . . I've really begun to believe that, I think. (FANNY, *who usually conceals her emotions, starts to move toward him tenderly. He teases her by drawing back.*)

HOLMES: Just a moment, young woman—

FANNY: Yes, milord?

HOLMES: I don't want to take you out under any false pretenses, you understand?

FANNY: Naturally, milord.

HOLMES: I just want you to know I don't feel eighty.

FANNY: Well, I should hope not, milord. I should certainly hope not! (FANNY *goes out gaily.* HOLMES *chuckles, pauses to take flower from small table. He then moves over to sofa. As he sits down a* SECRETARY (*vintage '21*) *comes in.* SECRETARY *is wearing full evening dress, dark overcoat and white muffler. He is properly dapper and his manner suggests that he has merely stopped by on routine detail. Actually, for the purposes of the play, he is an advance guard from* SECRETARIES *who are already gathered.*)

SECRETARY: Excuse me, Mr. Justice—

HOLMES: Hello, Mapes. What brings you back at this hour?

SECRETARY: Oh, I was just passing by—and I suddenly remembered these papers. I should have stopped over with them this afternoon. (*Moves over to desk at right and leaves thick envelope.*)

HOLMES: That's all right, boy. Everything in order?

SECRETARY: Yes, sir. There's only one thing if you don't mind my saying so.

HOLMES (*tolerantly*): Well, what is it?

SECRETARY: Your income tax seems a little high, sir. But no matter how I figured it, sir—it comes out just about the same.

HOLMES: Forget it, my boy. What difference does it make if

the government does get a few more dollars from me? I don't mind paying taxes—it's the way I buy civilization.

SECRETARY: Very well, sir. But, if you don't mind my saying so, civilization is getting a little expensive. Well, good night, sir. (*He starts out.*)

HOLMES: Hold on—where you going, all togged out like this? Some woman got you in tow too?

SECRETARY: Oh, no, sir. I'm just on my way to a little party with some of the boys.

HOLMES: Lucky dog—how I wish I were going along with you!

SECRETARY: Come along, sir.

HOLMES: I don't dare! Get on with you, you tempter.

SECRETARY (*smiling*): Yes, sir. (SECRETARY *is starting out as* HOUSEKEEPER *comes in.*)

HOUSEKEEPER: Mr. Justice Brandeis, sir. (BRANDEIS *comes in quickly, with a small etching under his arm.*)

BRANDEIS: Hello, Mapes. (*Then to* HOLMES, *as* SECRETARY *and* HOUSEKEEPER *move out.*) I hope I don't intrude. I'll stay only a minute.

HOLMES (*amiably*): What's the matter? Don't you like to be seen with me when I'm a bloomin' swell?

BRANDEIS: I know you're out to dinner with your wife, but I came across this today . . . and I thought you might like to have it for your birthday. (HOLMES *is pleased as punch but a little diffident too as he takes the etching.*)

HOLMES: Aren't you all rushing the season a bit? I'm not eighty for another two days, you know.

BRANDEIS: Yes, I know—but when you find something you like, you can't wait two whole days to share it with somebody . . . well, what do you think?

HOLMES (*examining etching*): Hmmm . . . why, why this is a Zorn! It's superb. Brandeis, what do you know about Zorn?

BRANDEIS: Nothing. But I knew you did. Not too modern?

HOLMES: Zorn? No, he has the ultimate thrust . . . you'll laugh at me, but when I was a boy I used to etch a little.

I didn't have that extra something—(*then briskly*)—but Zorn now, ah, he has the final wiggle which is pure genius!

BRANDEIS: Well, I'm delighted that you like it. I must run along—and, oh, yes, many happy returns of the day. (HOLMES *gets up and stops* BRANDEIS *with a question.*)

HOLMES: Hold on, I didn't thank you, did I?

BRANDEIS: Does one have to thank a friend for thinking of him?

HOLMES (*with a nice growl*): You know what I mean . . . I used to think there was no one . . . except Pollock in England . . . or Canon Sheehan in Ireland . . . who really knew or cared what I was driving for. But it's been a little different with you in there beside me.

BRANDEIS: It's been different for me too. You know—(*with some eagerness*)—sometimes I begin to believe that our dissenting opinions may yet change the mind of the public —and the courts too.

HOLMES (*with a nice detachment—at sharp contrast with the crusading spirit of* BRANDEIS): I wonder! We dissented pretty vigorously in *Hammer versus Dagenhart* and where did it get us? If a judge happens to like the idea of child labor, he can still go on making his personal prejudice the law of the land.

BRANDEIS: But it won't always be that way, mark my words. Some day *our* dissent will be the law of the land. Smile, if you want to, Holmes—but the world is getting better. And the judges along with it!

HOLMES (*teasing him and enjoying it*): Really, Sir Lancelot? What about those free-speech cases? The brethren went clear against us on most of them.

BRANDEIS: I know—I know. But give time a chance, Holmes.

HOLMES (*drily*): Give time a chance? I'd like to, my boy—I really would! But somehow I can't get that Abrams case out of my mind . . . think of it . . . twenty years in prison for men . . . who printed a few pamphlets and shouted "Workers of the World Awake" . . . I suppose you'd like to tell me that our dissent there will be the law of the land some day too?

BRANDEIS (*ardently*): Why not? People *can* change, can't they? You've said so yourself. You've said that change is the law of life—and the life of the law. You've said— (HOLMES *smiles and puts both hands on the shoulders of* BRANDEIS.)

HOLMES: All right, you fire eater, all right—I don't like being a dissenter any more than you do but if that's the way to make people think—let's keep on kicking—kicking like a pair of army mules! (BRANDEIS, *realizing now that* HOLMES *has been ragging him deliberately, smiles and starts out.*)

BRANDEIS: I see—you were just twisting the tail of the cosmos again, eh? Or was it the tail of a man named Brandeis? (*With a blithe wave,* BRANDEIS *goes out. Chuckling,* HOLMES *moves center. He hums softly to himself, picks up the Zorn, moves over to fireplace where he examines the etching with a pleased air.* FANNY, *a charming and radiant figure in evening dress, moves in. She looks off toward the stairs, then comes down quietly to* HOLMES. *He doesn't know she has come in, until she speaks.*)

FANNY: Ready, my dear?

HOLMES (*turning to her*): Good heavens, woman—how did you get in here without my hearing you?

FANNY: Oh, it's nothing—just a little trick I've been saving up for your birthday. All the New England witches knew how to do it. You just sail right through a wall . . . and there you are!

HOLMES (*admiring her dress*): You are a witch—one of the loveliest that ever was.

FANNY (*demurely*): Thank you, sir. Do I please you, sir?

HOLMES: You have me tied up in knots. Come on, let's get out of here—before I make a fool of myself with a witch— and in my own home too! (HOLMES *starts out gaily with* FANNY, *as we hear the faint hum of male voices from offstage. Some twenty male voices are starting to chant "Happy Birthday to You."*) Wait a minute—am I hearing things—

or is that someone singing? (*Through the doorway, one by one, come the twenty* SECRETARIES *who have served* HOLMES *in the last twenty years. Some are in dinner jackets, some in tails. They arrange themselves at left, as they wind up "Happy Birthday to You."* HOLMES, *a little diffident, a little pleased, looks from them to* FANNY.)

HOLMES: Well, I'll be damned—the chain gang! (*One by one, the* SECRETARIES *move over to shake* HOLMES' *hand. "Happy Birthday, sir" is the greeting from each* SECRETARY *to* HOLMES. *A simple "son" is the greeting from* HOLMES *to each* SECRETARY. *The circle of* SECRETARIES *moves around the sofa and back to a position on a diagonal from the center door to a point at the righthand side of the stage. As the last* SECRETARY *steps up to shake* HOLMES' *hand, the word "son" can just barely be heard.* HOLMES *looks up at the expectant faces of the* SECRETARIES, *then turns to* FANNY *who is standing beside him.*)

HOLMES: Fanny, you're to blame for this.

FANNY: Pshaw—is that all you can say on an occasion like this? (SECRETARIES *laugh.* HOLMES *looks up at them with a wry grin.*)

HOLMES: Well—all right. But if I don't come up to expectations, remember you asked for it. . . . (*Softly.*) When I was a boy, I was a lot better at this sort of thing . . . I had to be whether I liked it or not . . . my father liked to have witty people about him . . . especially at the breakfast table . . . so if I said anything good, the Governor . . . made sure I got an extra helping of marmalade. . . . I have not been able to face the damned stuff ever since. . . . (*The group laughs.* HOLMES *moves on more firmly.*) But if ever a man wanted to earn that bit of marmalade, I do tonight. You've been pretty good boys—some of you have turned out to be pretty important pumpkins. I couldn't be prouder of you if you were my own sons—and yet you are in a way—sons-at-law, I guess you'd call it. (*There's a small ripple of laughter. But* FANNY *shakes her head in disapproval of the pun.*) Sorry. Even the Governor never inflicted a worse pun than that. Well, I wish I had something special to pass on to you boys at a time like this. I will say this, though—I always had the idea that, when I got to be fourscore, I could wrap up my life in a scroll, tie a pink ribbon around it, put it away in a drawer, and go around doing the things I always wanted to do. But I'm just beginning to see once more that the good fight is never over . . . when you have taken one trench, there's always a new firing line just beyond . . . and that's as it should be . . . but don't ask me why . . . all I know is a man must go on charting his course by stars he has never seen . . . keep searching with the divining rod for springs he may never reach . . . because . . . because . . . well, enough of this preaching. Fanny, how are we going to cheer these boys now that Mr. Volstead's moral tornado has become the law of the land?

FANNY (*over laughter of* SECRETARIES): It's all arranged. The champagne is cooling downstairs. Oh, it's all very legal— we've had it for years.

HOLMES (*over more laughter of* SECRETARIES): Very well, gentlemen. In that case we shall drink to the United States of America . . . and a new firing line.

SECRETARY (*one of the younger ones*): And to the Supreme Court of the United States—and its next Chief Justice, Oliver Wendell Holmes. (*There are cries of "hear"—"hear" —from some of the* SECRETARIES, *quiet remonstrances from others.* HOLMES *doesn't flicker a muscle but there's a tense moment. He sees that some of the boys might have liked the idea.*)

HOLMES (*gruffly*): Sorry to disappoint you, boys. White *is* retiring soon . . . but the President wants a conservative and I think Taft will be the man. . . . I'm too old for that kind of goings on . . . and besides I never did understand ambition for high office. . . . (*Softly, almost to himself.*) Oh, it's nothing to be despised, if it comes your way . . . but the real challenge of life is to touch the superlative completely on your own . . . no outsider can give you that . . . (*then with a warm smile for the boys*) . . . the judgment of friends of course is a help at times . . . it gives you confidence and hope . . . (*then briskly*) . . . but don't you youngsters hope for the wrong thing . . . don't you . . . Fanny, do we get anything to go with that champagne or do we just forage in the neighborhood for our dinner?

FANNY: Silly . . . we have a wonderful dinner all ready downstairs . . . and a wonderful cake too . . . with eighty-one candles . . .

HOLMES: Eh? What's the extra one for?

FANNY: That, my dear, is for you to grow on. Go along, children—I'm hungry and you're thirsty! (SECRETARIES *laugh and start to go out. As they go, one of them starts humming "Gaudeamus Igitur." Others begin to pick it up, and as they move out into the hall and down the stairs, they are all singing it.* FANNY *moves out after the* SECRETARIES, *stops in the doorway and looks back at* HOLMES. *For the moment he is lost in his own thoughts.*)

FANNY (*moving down to him*): Wendell—

HOLMES (*looking up*): Eh? Oh, coming, my dear—coming.

FANNY: Wendell—it doesn't really matter, does it, about the Chief Justiceship?

HOLMES: No. Not really.

FANNY: Sure?

HOLMES: Of course. It's only—

FANNY: Yes?

HOLMES: For a moment—just for a moment, mind you—I had the idea that it might have mattered to some of the boys. (*From downstairs we still hear the* SECRETARIES, *lifting their voices in pleasant abandon with "Gaudeamus Igitur."*) I caught something in their eyes . . . they might have liked it, you know . . . why, damn it, I felt just like a father who's let his sons down somehow . . . and they're not my sons . . . they're . . . they're just a lot of fresh young scamps from Harvard . . . listen to them now . . . drinking my liquor and singing about how good it is to rejoice when you are young . . . they don't know, Fanny . . . the real trick is to rejoice when you're eighty . . . the real trick . . . Fanny, what the devil am I talking about anyway?

FANNY (*softly*): I'm sure I don't know, Wendell—and if I did, I wouldn't tell you. (FANNY *takes his arm and they start out together. As they reach the doorway,* FANNY *touches her head to his shoulder ever so lightly. From offstage the voices singing "Gaudeamus Igitur" come up softly.*)

ACT III

SCENE 1

SCENE: *The library of Justice Holmes on an afternoon in late January, 1929. The room looks very much the same, except that now the books at back reach clear up to the ceiling.*

HOLMES *is slouched down in a chair at his desk, as the curtain goes up. And here, for the first time, we have the picture of* HOLMES *most familiar to the man in the street. The hair and mustaches are pure white and there is a brooding, searching look about the eyes.*

SECRETARY (*Harvard Law '28*), *working on the opposite side of the desk, looks up pleasantly.*

SECRETARY: I think we're all caught up now, sir.

HOLMES (*coming out of a daydream*): Eh? Oh, very well, Rogers. (*Turning to work on the desk.*) You can run along.

SECRETARY (*getting up*): Thank you, sir. Thank you very much. But wouldn't you like to come too?

HOLMES: Come? Come where?

SECRETARY (*with a nice jauntiness*): I've just bought a new car—and I thought you might like to help me try it out.

HOLMES: Thanks, boy. But my racing days are behind me. Another time, maybe.

SECRETARY (*disappointed*): Very well, sir—but it's a wonderful day—and there's no denying it certainly feels like spring.

HOLMES: Feels like spring? My boy, I'm surprised at you. Where's your sense of evidence? Surely you're not taken in by a little sun in January. Why, a day like this doesn't mean a thing. It's a cheat and a fraud . . . a snare and a delusion. You mark my word—there's a frost behind this touch of spring somewhere. There's— (*Suddenly the Judge stops showing off. He looks up at his* SECRETARY *with a rueful grin.*) Will you forgive me if I tell you to get the hell out of here and be quick about it?

SECRETARY (*nicely*): Of course, sir. Right away, sir. (SECRETARY *goes out.* HOLMES *returns to his papers but finds it difficult to continue. He gets up restlessly, looks at his watch, moves across to the sofa. As* HOLMES *moves across the room, the shoulders seem to sag for the first time. There is just a bit of bending at the knees. At eighty-eight he is still a gallant and a dominating figure but now he has the look of a man who is fighting an enemy who cannot be defeated. His wife has been in poor health for three years and, while she has not yet had the final accident which will hasten her end, he is beginning to face the parting of the ways. The door opens and* HOUSEKEEPER *enters, followed quickly by* BRANDEIS, *who is now seventy-two.*)

HOUSEKEEPER: Mr. Justice Brandeis— (HOLMES *turns around with a determined effort to keep up a gay front.*)

HOLMES: Hello, young feller.

BRANDEIS: I hardly expected to find you home. (HOUSEKEEPER *goes out.*) On a day like this I thought you'd be out on the towpath with Rogers.

HOLMES (*lightly*): So did Rogers. Only he wanted to make it a ride instead of a walk—and I wouldn't have it. (*Waves* BRANDEIS *to a chair.*) I tell you, Brandeis, I'm not so old that I have to be carried around in a motorized perambulator. I— (*Quite abruptly* HOLMES *abandons his pretense and slumps down in a chair beside the sofa.*) Sorry. No use trying to fool you. I *am* feeling a little old today . . . and I don't like it. . . . I don't like it the least damned bit!

BRANDEIS: How is your wife today? (HOLMES *is not quite*

ready to admit that the prolonged poor health of FANNY *is causing him increasing concern.*)

HOLMES: Oh, she's getting better all the time. Just won't admit the possibility of a Yankee being an invalid.

BRANDEIS: Well, what seems to be the trouble then?

HOLMES (*with a grin*): Maybe I'm just spoiling for a good fight. If I am, that's easily remedied. I think they're going to lick us on this Rosika Schwimmer decision.

BRANDEIS: Oh, I don't know about that. It won't come to a final vote for some time yet and who knows—in the meanwhile—

HOLMES (*fondly*): Brandeis, you are a poor benighted optimist. But then I guess all crusaders are . . . or they wouldn't be crusaders.

BRANDEIS: Well, let's see now—there's McReynolds—he'll vote with us.

HOLMES: Yes, I think he will—though I'll be damned if I know why.

BRANDEIS: And then there's—there's—well, there's always you and I.

HOLMES: Humph. How do you know I'll stick with you all the way?

BRANDEIS (*spiritedly*): You know, Holmes—if I did not esteem you as much as I do, I would get mad at you a lot more often than I do. You are so—so eternally impartial about everything. Why, you—you doubt your own position even while you are advancing it.

HOLMES (*amiably*): Sometimes to doubt a little . . . is to advance a little.

BRANDEIS: But if you believe a certain thing is right . . . you have to fight for it just as hard as anyone else . . . even if you are a judge.

HOLMES: Well, that's one way of looking at it. . . .

BRANDEIS: Very well—are you with me or against me on this?

HOLMES (*getting up and moving left*): Why, I'm with you, of course.

BRANDEIS: Well, then, what is all the argument about?

HOLMES: Who said there was an argument?

BRANDEIS: I give up. I should know better. Only the next time, permit me to be the impartial one, for a change, eh? And you be the crusader. You ought to try it just once, you know.

HOLMES (*softly*): Maybe I should. By heaven, I'd like to win one of these big fights just once . . . and this is a big fight. This isn't just a matter of denying citizenship to a sincere woman pacifist. It's a matter of denying to ourselves just what that citizenship means . . . freedom of opinion doesn't mean merely freedom for the ideas we happen to like . . . it means just as much freedom for the ideas we happen to despise. For either this country of ours is a country where each man's right to his own point of view is respected and protected by every other man or—or— (HOLMES *stops and seems unable to go on. He passes his hand across his forehead wearily.*) I'm sorry, Brandeis. My heart's with you but I can't seem to make my mind behave. I'm worried . . . I'm worried about Fanny.

BRANDEIS: Surely, there is no special cause for alarm.

HOLMES: I know. She's no worse than she was . . . but she's no better either . . . and it's been all of three years now. . . . I might as well face it . . . everything comes to an end sometime . . . even the Holmeses.

BRANDEIS: You're just tired. You've had a hard day. You'll feel better tomorrow.

HOLMES: The trouble is it's not the kind of fight I have a liking for . . . to storm across an open field, with the shells and bullets whistling about you, is one thing . . . there's a desperate joy of battle there . . . and in the fury of the fighting there's no time for the doubts and uncertainties that sometimes assail you later . . . but this . . . this quiet waiting for an enemy to whom you must bow in the end . . . it baffles me. . . . I think for myself I could face the unknown without a quiver . . . but to stand by and watch it strike down the woman you have been married to for fifty-seven years . . . it breaks you up in little pieces.

BRANDEIS: But none of us is eternal. . . .

HOLMES: I know . . . I know . . . but people in love like to think they are . . . oh, it's a good joke on me in a way . . . all my life I have shouted that I didn't believe in heaven and I didn't believe in hell . . . and I had a lot of fun doing the shouting . . . felt pretty smart about it too. . . . I was so all-fired legal about it . . . "not proved" I shouted at the universe and the universe echoed back "not proved" . . . or so I thought . . . but now . . . maybe I wouldn't be so finicky about the proof if anybody thought he *could* prove it. . . .

BRANDEIS (*amazed*): My dear Holmes—

HOLMES (*wryly*): Steady, Brandeis. I'll deny I ever said these things tomorrow . . . or the next day . . . so not a word to Fanny . . . ah, the trouble is there are moments when a man has a hankering for immortality . . . and this is one of them. (*Then with a flash of fire.*) By Jupiter, I don't want things to wind up on me forever . . . oh, I know, I've bragged that life came out of nothing and would in time dissolve into nothing . . . but those are mere words . . . and I've always urged people to think things instead of words . . . well, I am thinking things now for just one split second . . . and I wish . . . I wish to heaven I had one of those souls Dante is always talking about. I wish— (*The door at left opens and* FANNY *comes in quietly. At eighty-eight she is still an indomitable spirit—but there is an almost transparent air about her now. She has the look of one who has suffered much but been very quiet about it. She is accompanied for the moment by the* HOUSEKEEPER.)

FANNY (*brightly*): Good heavens, Wendell—what are you shouting about. (HOLMES *and* BRANDEIS *get up quickly and move to her.*)

HOLMES: My dear—

FANNY: I could hear you clear upstairs— (*Then to* BRANDEIS.) Hello, Judge.

HOLMES: You know you shouldn't have come down.

FANNY: Mercy, Wendell—what's the matter with you today?

I'm not a china doll. (*To* HOUSEKEEPER, *who has made her comfortable on the sofa.*) Thank you, Mary. I think I have everything I want. (*Then to* BRANDEIS.) Judge, it's always good to see you. How's your wife? (HOUSEKEEPER *goes out.* HOLMES *and* BRANDEIS *hover about* FANNY.)

BRANDEIS: Oh, she is fine—very fine. How are you?

FANNY: Well, for an old lady who never has quite got used to the idea of an electric elevator, I'm doing as well as can be expected.

HOLMES: Nonsense. She insists she put it in for me—but the truth is it's become her toy. I never get a chance to play with it!

FANNY (*picking up sewing*): Well, gentlemen, don't let me interrupt . . . from upstairs it sounded like a most interesting argument. Pray, do go on—

HOLMES: Eh? What's that?

FANNY: Now, Wendell, don't look at me with that innocent stare. It may impress your brethren but I've lived with you too long to be taken in by it any more.

HOLMES (*lamely*): Well, the truth is, my dear—

BRANDEIS (*to the rescue*): We were discussing the Rosika Schwimmer case.

HOLMES: Yes . . . weren't getting very far, were we? Maybe —maybe we need a woman's angle. (*Then to* FANNY.) My dear, do you mind pretending that you are one of the brethren for a moment or two? Brandeis, let me get you a good cigar. (HOLMES *starts out.*)

FANNY (*quizzically*): But Justice Brandeis doesn't smoke.

HOLMES (*gaily*): Did I ask whether he did or not?

FANNY: On that basis, you might just as well bring one for me too!

HOLMES (*with a grin*): With pleasure, my dear. (HOLMES *goes out gaily.* FANNY *watches him off then turns to* BRANDEIS.)

FANNY: You know, I'm worried about that man.

BRANDEIS (*with a start*): You are?

FANNY (*teasingly*): Yes. He's smoking altogether too many cigars!

BRANDEIS (*relieved*): Oh, I wouldn't worry about an extra cigar or two. (*Sits down beside* FANNY).

FANNY (*quite simply*): It isn't just the cigars. If I tell you something, promise you won't say a word to the Judge?

BRANDEIS: Of course—

FANNY: Sometimes lately I have the feeling . . . I haven't very much more time.

BRANDEIS: Nonsense. You are just imagining things. Why, just look at you—you're looking wonderful today.

FANNY: Thank you. I do feel well today . . . but the end of the road is in sight just the same . . . it's bound to be when you've just turned eighty-eight.

BRANDEIS: You don't leave me very much to say.

FANNY: There isn't very much to say. . . . I don't mind going when I have to . . . but I could wish he were the first to go . . . he'll be so lonely without me . . . and women are so much better at waiting than men . . . especially when you're not too sure just what it is you're waiting for . . .

BRANDEIS (*gently*): Please—it isn't good to think too soon about things like that . . .

FANNY: I know . . . life is for the living . . . and death is for the dying . . . but we Yankees were always ones for putting our houses in order . . . before times.

BRANDEIS: Is there anything I can do?

FANNY: No. But I often wonder . . . tell me, Judge, do you think there *is* anything that survives after everything is over . . . here?

BRANDEIS: My dear, who can say for sure—but I do believe this: nothing good is ever lost. It renews itself constantly. As the prophets of old used to say, the memory of virtue is immortal. The—

FANNY (*with a wry smile*): Thank you, Judge, but the memory of virtue isn't enough. Oh, I don't mean to be greedy but if there is anything that survives, I want something more than a memory. I want—the trouble is I don't know

what I want . . . I've had everything a woman could want,
I guess . . . and it rather spoils you . . . even for a thing
called heaven. It— (HOLMES *comes in gaily. He has two
cigars in one hand and a small nosegay in the other, held
behind his back. He moves to fireplace and addresses*
FANNY *and* BRANDEIS.)

HOLMES (*blithely*): Well, milords, have you reached a decision?

BRANDEIS (*blankly*): Decision?

HOLMES (*pocketing cigars*): Hmmm. No work—no cigar.
(*Then to* FANNY.) And as for you, my dear—

FANNY: It's no use, old man. You can't bribe me to do your
work for you . . . not even with a Havana Perfecto!

HOLMES (*bringing forth flowers*): How about violets?

FANNY: Wendell . . . violets in January?

HOLMES: Of course they're only hothouse stuff, ma'am . . .
but I understand they bespeak a loving heart.

FANNY: Silly—

BRANDEIS (*getting up*): Well, I must be going. My wife has
tickets for a concert tonight and—

HOLMES: Careful, my boy. First thing you know, you'll be
knee deep in culture.

BRANDEIS: Why don't you come along?

HOLMES: No, thanks. I paid ten dollars once to hear Chalia-
pin sing . . . and if you ask me, I don't think it was worth
the price . . . not that he didn't sing nice and loud, mind
you, but—

FANNY (*softly—to* BRANDEIS): Good-by. You will come again
soon, won't you?

BRANDEIS: Why, of course—of course. (HOLMES *looks up
sharply: is this an overtone he's missing? He dismisses it
as accidental. He moves over to show* BRANDEIS *out.*)

HOLMES: Take care of yourself, young fellow.

BRANDEIS: I'll try, sir—I'll try. (HOLMES *watches* BRANDEIS
off, then comes back to FANNY, *who is staring off into
space.*)

HOLMES: You know, there's something wonderful about

Louis Brandeis. Every time he leaves me, I say to myself, "There goes a good man."

FANNY (*admiring the flowers*): I know— (HOLMES *moves over and sits down beside* FANNY. *For a moment neither says anything. Then, with an air of determination,* FANNY *puts flowers aside and turns to* HOLMES.)

FANNY: Wendell—

HOLMES: Yes? (*For a moment it looks as if* FANNY *is going to tell* HOLMES *something of what she told* BRANDEIS. *But she veers off quickly.*)

FANNY: Is—is the Rosika Schwimmer decision so difficult?

HOLMES: Eh? No—of course not. It's just that—oh, I'm a little stale, I guess. The right words don't seem to come. (*We see that* FANNY *is only talking to make conversation but we also see that* HOLMES *soon fires up, stimulated as usual by* FANNY's *interest.*)

FANNY: What seems to be the trouble?

HOLMES: Oh, the real trouble is I don't agree with the dear lady's pacifist ideas at all.

FANNY: But whether you agree with them or not has nothing to do with whether she will make a good citizen, has it?

HOLMES: Of course not. That's exactly what the case is about. But the fact that I don't have much personal enthusiasm for the lady's slant on things is likely to make for a pretty flat opinion . . . when I come to defend her point of view.

FANNY: Just what's wrong with her point of view?

HOLMES (*in his old stride again*): Now isn't that just like a woman? The trouble with Rosika Schwimmer is . . . *she* thinks like a woman. She thinks the impending destiny of mankind is to unite in peaceful leagues and alliances. She—

FANNY: Would that be so bad?

HOLMES (*rushing on*): And as a consequence she will not promise to bear arms for her country in time of trouble. Well, considering the fact that Rosika Schwimmer is well past fifty now, I don't think the promise would mean much one way or the other.

FANNY: I suppose it's odd of me, Wendell, but everything you say about her sounds most attractive.

HOLMES: Now isn't *that* just like a woman? Look, Fanny—I know what war is. When you're at it, it's a messy and a dirty business . . . as well as being an organized bore. But out of it sometimes comes heroism . . . and a faith in heroism. For you can't fight for a thing, without believing in it. . . . Call it a soldier's faith if you like but there it is. Now I'm not saying it's the only kind of faith there is, but—

FANNY (*with deep intensity*): No, after all, there's the faith that takes the Sermon on the Mount as gospel truth.

HOLMES: Eh? What's that?

FANNY: And I suppose we have never held it against the Quakers that they seemed to take the Sermon on the Mount a little more seriously than some of us do . . . or can. . . .

HOLMES (*with excitement*): Fanny, my dear—that's it. That's it—I have it now—the twist I need to give it. Old girl, you're worth two of me any day. I don't know what I'd do without you, I— (*Suddenly the full force of his casual line hits them both. They eye each other searchingly. For a flashing second they read each other's hearts—then promptly pretend they haven't.*)

FANNY (*softly*): The trouble is—you've never tried.

HOLMES (*trying to generalize lightly*): Shucks, woman—it's as the minister said the day we were married . . . remember?

FANNY: Yes, I remember . . . it was the biggest church in Boston . . . (*for a moment they suggest the eagerness of their youth: they are not two old people . . . they are two people who are young . . . eternally young*) . . . it had to be if it was to hold all your old girls.

HOLMES: That for all my old girls . . . when he read that part about two people becoming one . . . well, he was right, you know . . . two people did become one . . . only trouble was . . . (*with mock gruffness*) . . . *you* were the one.

HOUSEKEEPER (*coming in*): I'm sorry to bother you, sir—but Mr. Adams is downstairs to see you.

HOLMES (*with a start*): Adams? . . . I thought *he* was dead!

HOUSEKEEPER (*smiling*): Mr. Charles Francis Adams, sir. The Secretary of the Navy.

HOLMES: Oh . . . what did I tell you, Fanny—there's always an Adams somewhere, especially in Washington. You can't get away from them. All right, Mary, tell him I'll be right down. (HOUSEKEEPER *goes out.*)

FANNY: Now, darling—do be nice to him. He's quite different from his uncle—and besides, you don't have to be jealous of the Adamses any more.

HOLMES: Oh, I don't—don't I?

FANNY: No, you have twenty-seven boys all your own now . . . remember?

HOLMES: By Jove, that's right . . . why, by now they outnumber all the Adamses put together . . . and they'll be around a long time after . . . (HOLMES *was about to say* "after you and I are gone" *but he corrects himself quickly*) . . . after the people who hound Rosika Schwimmer are gone and forgotten. (*Getting up.*) Humph, almost forgot about Adams. (*Moves out, then speaks up with a deliberate effort to be cheerful.*) Cheer up, Fanny, if a man has enough secretaries, the good fight is never lost . . . there's always somebody left to carry the battle to the enemy . . . another day. . . . (*With a blithe wave of the hand,* HOLMES *goes out and shuts the door behind him.* FANNY *picks up the violets that* HOLMES *gave her.*)

FANNY (*softly*): Another day . . . (FANNY *lifts the Judge's flowers to her lips.*)

ACT III

SCENE 2

SCENE: *The library of Justice Holmes on an afternoon in March, 1933.*

The room is very much the same, except for one or two touches. We miss the flowers which were so characteristic of FANNY, *and by the window at right is a small radio on a table, an innovation that* FANNY *would never have approved.*

The day outside is cold and brisk: in the fireplace, there is a pleasant glow.

At curtain HOUSEKEEPER *is listening to the radio.*

VOICE OF COMMENTATOR: The crowds are cheering, flags are waving, and all up and down Pennsylvania Avenue thousands of people are shouting themselves hoarse . . . and so, ladies and gentlemen, Franklin Delano Roosevelt has just become the thirty-second President of these United States. The band is playing "Hail to the Chief" and in a few moments the President's party will leave the Capitol for— (HOUSEKEEPER *shuts off the radio and turns around, just as* WISTER *appears in doorway. He is nearly seventy-five now but he still has the jauntiness that* HOLMES *always loved.*)

WISTER: Hello, Mary—

HOUSEKEEPER: Why, Mr. Wister, where did you come from?

WISTER: P-s-s-sh. I'm just a ghost—down from Philadelphia for the day. Where's the Judge? Did he go over to the inauguration?

HOUSEKEEPER: Oh, no, sir. I think he went out to . . . to the cemetery at Arlington . . . he goes there nearly every day, sir.

WISTER: Oh . . . I see. Well, in that event I had better drop by later.

HOUSEKEEPER: Please, sir . . . I'm sure he'll be back quite soon . . . and he'll be quite mad with me if he should miss you.

WISTER (*lightly*): Very well, Mary. I wouldn't have him mad with you for anything in the world.

HOUSEKEEPER: Oh, thank you—sir.

WISTER: Tell me, Mary—how is the Judge these days?

HOUSEKEEPER: Oh, he's wonderful, sir . . . wonderful. But—

WISTER: Yes?

HOUSEKEEPER (*simply*): I don't think he's ever been quite the same since Mrs. Holmes died, sir. It isn't anything you can put your finger on exactly. It's just—well it's as if someone had taken away the light from inside a lamp. But he never lets on, sir—he never lets on. (HOUSEKEEPER *starts out but* WISTER *stops her with a question.*)

WISTER: Just one thing more, Mary. I shouldn't be asking you this, but I wouldn't dare ask him. What does he do with himself now that he has resigned from the Court? Does time hang heavy on his hands or—

HOUSEKEEPER: Oh, no, sir. He's quite busy and quite happy, sir . . . after a fashion. If you ask me, I don't think he needed to resign at all, sir. I'm sure no one wanted him to.

WISTER: Then why did he?

HOUSEKEEPER: I suppose he was a little tired. . . . I suppose anyone gets a little tired once they pass ninety . . . but, most of all, I think he wanted to stop while he was still as good as ever he was . . . and sometimes I think . . .

WISTER: Yes, Mary?

HOUSEKEEPER (*softly*): Sometimes I think . . . he just wanted time to face . . . the end of things. Anybody else would rather things just caught up with them at the end . . . quite suddenly . . . without time for facing anything . . .

but not the Judge. He has to look everything square in the eye . . . including the very devil himself. (*Offstage we hear the voice of* HOLMES *as he comes in with his* SECRETARY.)

HOLMES' VOICE (*offstage*): German pessimism, my boy—nothing but German pessimism.

HOUSEKEEPER (*to* WISTER): There, aren't you glad you waited?

WISTER: I certainly am, Mary. (HOUSEKEEPER *moves out, as the figure of the Judge appears in the doorway. Here, for a moment, we have one of the most familiar of all the portraits: the striped trousers, the dark topcoat, the white muffler, and the black homburg hat, set at a discreet angle.*)

HOLMES (*as* SECRETARY *helps him off with his overcoat*): Of course this man Spengler has a head on him—a swelled head—but the beast has ideas. But what's he mean—*Decline of the West?* (HOLMES *starts to move on into the room. He has not yet caught sight of* WISTER *and there's a little sag to the shoulders, a shade more bend at the knees. But he's a smartly turned-out figure in his frock coat and striped trousers. Even at ninety-one he has a certain elegance all his own.*) The only thing that's declining in the West is Mr. Spengler himself—and if you ask me—(*then catching sight of* WISTER *but not recognizing him for an instant*)—ah, how do you do? (*Then, in a flash, the recognition is established.* HOLMES *brightens and straightens up with a quickened pulse.*)

HOLMES: Whiskers!

WISTER (*moving toward him to shake his hand*): Hello, Judge.

HOLMES: Well, I'll be damned!

WISTER: I wouldn't count on it somehow!

HOLMES (*with a chuckle*): Always the optimist, eh? Well, that's what comes from living in Philadelphia. My boy—(*Introducing* WISTER *and* SECRETARY.) You remember Jackson, don't you?

SECRETARY (*shaking hands with* WISTER): I'm honored to meet you again, Mr. Wister.

WISTER: Of course. We met back in—back—

SECRETARY: I think it was 1912, sir.

WISTER: You'll have to forgive me, Jackson. But there have been *quite* a few of you and—

HOLMES (*sitting in chair near sofa*): You don't know the half of it. There not only *were*—there still *are*. They keep coming back all the time . . . turning up all over the place . . . taking turns, by gad, watching over the old man, just to make sure he doesn't cut a few capers in the wrong places, eh Jackson?

JACKSON: Oh, I assure you, sir—

HOLMES: Now—now—run along and tell Mary— (*Then to* WISTER.) Stay for lunch?

WISTER: No. But I'll take a rain check for dinner.

HOLMES: Fine. (*Then to* SECRETARY.) Tell Mary to forget about lunch but to spread herself for dinner. And, oh, yes, I'd take a little sherry and a cracker right now, if she urged me to. So would Mr. Wister.

SECRETARY (*going out*): Right away, sir. (HOLMES *turns to* WISTER, *as* SECRETARY *goes out. The Judge is keeping up a pretty good front but it isn't easy going.* WISTER *is an old friend and old friends have a way of seeing deep at times.*)

HOLMES: You know, except that they're beginning to treat me as some kind of foxy grandpa—they're not bad boys at all . . . and if they keep at it, by gad, they'll make a real educated feller out of me before I kick off. (*Lifts up a book with mock impressiveness.*) Thucydides!

WISTER (*sitting in chair*): Now don't tell me you read that stuff in the original.

HOLMES (*with a sly grin*): Only the purple passages!

WISTER: Going pretty heavy on the classics, aren't you?

HOLMES: Oh, we're practically surrounded by culture. (*Then in a whisper.*) It's all I can do to squeeze in a good detective story or a spicy French novel any more. (*Then more briskly.*) I'll have you know we even have a radio now . . . one of the boys brought it down . . . nothing but long-hair music . . . especially Brahms. (*Then with a chuckle.*) You know, Fanny would never stand for a radio, Brahms or no Brahms. Fanny— (*The casual mention of* FANNY'S *name brings* HOLMES *up short. It's hard to go on.*)

WISTER: Would you rather I go?

HOLMES: No—no—of course not. Please don't.

WISTER: But if you'd rather be alone?

HOLMES: That's just it. I am alone now . . . and somehow I can't quite get used to it. I try to carry on as best I can but—

WISTER: Perhaps you try too much . . .

HOLMES: No. A man has to keep on trying . . . no matter how alone he may be . . . no matter how little time he may have left . . . it's as I said on the radio . . . the day I was ninety . . . (HOLMES *leans back in chair and speaks with more confidence.*) The riders in a race don't stop short when they reach the goal. There's a little finishing canter . . . just before the end . . . there's time to hear the kind voice of friends and to say to one's self . . . "the work is done" . . . but just as you say that, the answer comes back "the race is over but the work is never done while the power to work remains" . . . and so the canter that brings you to a pause need not be the end. It cannot be while you still live. For to live is to function. To live— (*This is* HOLMES' *basic creed and as he recites it, the fires burn in him brightly. He raises his head proudly . . . eagerly. But the moment is quickly broken. The* HOUSEKEEPER *comes in with sherry and biscuits.*)

HOUSEKEEPER: Your sherry, sir.

HOLMES (*to* WISTER): You see? To live is to function—to reach for a bottle of sherry when you can . . . and to leave your mind alone. Put it down on the table there, Mary.

HOUSEKEEPER: They telephoned again, sir—about sitting for another portrait.

HOLMES: Oh, *no*, Mary. I've done enough posing to last me a lifetime. . . . (*Getting to his feet.*) Tell them . . . tell them I've run out of poses. (HOUSEKEEPER *goes out.* HOLMES *moves over to* WISTER *and pours him a glass of sherry, then one for himself.*)

HOLMES: Now what about you? What brings you to Washington . . . today of all days?

WISTER (*drily*): How could I stay away . . . another Roosevelt being inaugurated.

HOLMES (*giving him sherry*): You know, you're getting old too . . . positively ancient . . . must be nearly all of seventy-five, eh?

WISTER: Just about . . .

HOLMES: Infant! You know what I think every time I see a pretty girl?

WISTER: No—what?

HOLMES (*lifting his glass*): Oh—to be eighty again! (HOLMES *takes a sip of the sherry, straightens up a bit and moves toward chair with just the faintest suggestion of a swagger.*)

WISTER (*chuckling*): We've had some good times together . . . remember our first big argument about T. R.?

HOLMES (*in chair*): Will I ever forget it? That was the day Fanny set out to charm the President.

WISTER: And took time out for a three-alarm fire along the way.

HOLMES: She charmed him all right . . . but I was never quite sure the old boy ever forgave me.

WISTER (*getting up*): Judge, you'll laugh at me for saying so—but I'm just as worried about this Roosevelt as you were about the other one.

HOLMES: Eh? You're joking.

WISTER: Never more serious in my life.

HOLMES: Oh, come now, Whiskers. For a second you sounded just like Henry Adams.

WISTER: I can't help how I sound. I'm worried. All kinds of things are in the wind now. (*Getting up and moving around.*) Do you know the newest—they say that the Presi-

258

dent is going to declare a bank holiday before the day is over.

HOLMES: About time, isn't it? Only way to save the banks.

WISTER: And after that—

HOLMES: Oh, I don't know, Whiskers. If I were still on the Court, maybe I wouldn't agree with Cousin Franklin any more than I did with Cousin Theodore. But I do know this —no one President ever wrecked this country yet and no one President ever will.

WISTER (*stiffly*): Very well—if that's the way you feel about it—

HOLMES: Hold on, you fire eater. This is 1933—not 1902. And I, heaven help me, am defending a Roosevelt while you're attacking one. Come on, Whiskers—where's—where's —your sense of humor? (HOLMES' *voice fades a bit, he stares off into space, his head drops a little, he raises one hand to his forehead: he is a man who, without warning, seems to lose focus for an instant.*)

WISTER: Sorry, Judge. I guess I lost my sense of humor (*breaks off, as he realizes* HOLMES *is not listening, then continues half-heartedly: he is all concern for the Judge now*) the day—the day—this new Roosevelt was elected to office.

HOLMES (*coming to*): Eh? Sorry, Whiskers—I didn't quite catch all of that . . . but then I'm living a little behind a cloud these days . . . a little behind a cloud . . . (*Then more briskly.*) But I can still pull my brains together, my boy, if I have to, and call a man a— (*From door another* SECRETARY *comes in. This one is of more recent vintage than the preceding one and there is a definite Gaelic lilt to his talk.*)

SECRETARY: I have the day's mail sorted, sir, but I— (*Then seeing* WISTER.) Oh, I'm sorry, Judge. I didn't know you were in conference.

WISTER (*getting up*): It's all right. I was just going.

HOLMES (*to* WISTER): See here—you're not mad, are you?

WISTER (*with a nice grin*): No, I'm not mad.

HOLMES (getting up): Then stop back for dinner . . . it won't be the most wonderful menu in the world . . . just a bit of lonely chicken and a dab of homemade ice cream . . . (then brightly) . . . but we might dig up a good bottle of fizz . . . say about seven?

WISTER: I'll be here . . . (then taking in the SECRETARY) . . . oh, who's this?

HOLMES: You remember him . . . Halloran . . . (sinking back into chair) . . . another one of the nursing corps . . . afternoon trick.

SECRETARY (with spirit): If I may be allowed to say so, sir—it's quite the other way around. The truth is it's the Judge who's looking out for us.

HOLMES: Nonsense. Nothing of the sort.

WISTER: Well, be sure you take good care of each other, anyway. (To HOLMES.) See you at seven. (WISTER goes out. HOLMES eyes SECRETARY with mock severity, as the young man moves over to desk at right.)

HOLMES: Humph. Getting to be quite a rebel, aren't you? (SECRETARY, not at all disturbed, arranges letters on desk for the Judge's signature.)

SECRETARY: That may be, sir.

HOLMES: Almost insubordinate, wouldn't you say?

SECRETARY: Quite possibly, sir.

HOLMES: Hmmm. The Irish in you, of course.

SECRETARY: Undoubtedly, sir.

HOLMES (getting up): Humph. Well, whatever it is—don't lose it, boy. Not many people left any more with real fire in the belly . . . including me. (Moving to desk.) Must be getting old, I guess . . . got into the damnedest argument with Wister just now . . . and I can't seem to remember what the hell it was all about . . . well, what have we here? (HOLMES sits down at his desk and looks over the letters that the SECRETARY has brought.)

SECRETARY: Just a few letters for you to sign. I answered

them the way I thought you might like to have them go
out.

HOLMES (*reaching for pen*): Hmmm. Even starting to steal
the old man's style, eh?

SECRETARY: I did my best, sir.

HOLMES (*starting to sign*): You're all right, boy.

SECRETARY: I didn't know what you'd want to do with this
one . . . it's just another request to serve on a committee
but—

HOLMES (*busy signing letters*): Sorry. You know my rule.
I've kept off committees for ninety years and I don't intend to wind up on a committee now.

SECRETARY: Still, this is a little different, sir—and you did
ask me to hold it out for a while.

HOLMES (*looking up vaguely*): Eh? I did—what for—what's
it about?

SECRETARY: It's a committee from a school in New York—a
committee to help refugee scholars who have had to leave
Germany on account of Hitler.

HOLMES (*quickly*): Hitler? Eh—of course—of course. I remember now. Humph. That madman is breaking all the
rules. . . . (*Signs a letter briskly.*) I guess it's all right for
me to break one. Tell them I accept, boy—and send them a
check too. (*Then pushing pen aside.*) I don't understand
what's going on in Germany . . . I don't understand it and
I don't like it . . . lot of things I don't understand any
more . . . lot of things you don't see so clearly . . . when
you're living behind a cloud . . . when . . . (*he gets up
and moves forward*) . . . last night I drove out to Spotsyl-
vania . . . to the Bloody Angle where we fought when I
was twenty-one . . . I got out of the car and walked along
the ridge just as night was coming in . . . and once more
I heard the spat of bullets on the trees . . . I heard . . .
(*The old man has literally drifted off into a daydream
and suddenly becomes aware of it. He looks over at SECRE-
TARY a little embarrassed.*) Oh, it's nothing—just daydreaming again. I guess even the strongest clock has to unwind

once in a while. (HOLMES *slouches down on sofa, obviously preparing for a nap.*)

SECRETARY: Would you like me to read to you, sir?

HOLMES (*slyly*): Fine. That ought to put me to sleep without any trouble at all.

SECRETARY (*with a grin*): I'll do my best, sir.

HOLMES: Oh, yes . . . one thing more . . . you'll find a copy of my will in the desk over there . . . make a note on it that the original is with John Palfrey . . . up in Boston. (SECRETARY *sits down at desk at right to make the notation on the will. When he gets the will out, he pauses—and looks over at the Judge.*)

SECRETARY: I say, sir—are you feeling all right?

HOLMES: When you get to be my age, boy, you'll understand that death isn't the same to an old man . . . as it is to a young one . . . to die a little sooner now would be to miss the little bits of pleasure . . . not the point of being . . . (HOLMES *starts to doze a bit.* SECRETARY *scribbles the notation on the will folder—then looks down speculatively at the package.*)

HOLMES (*opening one eye*): If you're wondering what I've done with all my ill-gotten gains, I'll be glad to tell you.

SECRETARY: Sorry, sir. (*Putting will away.*) I was curious but it's none of my business. Please forgive me.

HOLMES: Oh, it's no secret . . . but I don't go around telling people . . . they might think I was a little touched in the head. . . .

SECRETARY (*moving over to sofa*): What would you like me to read, sir?

HOLMES (*drowsily . . . almost as if dictating the will again*): To my nephew the portrait of my great-grandfather by Copley . . . to the Library of Congress my library and works of art . . . to the Harvard Law School and Boston Museum $25,000 each . . . to my servants gifts of cash . . . and the rest to the United States of America . . .

SECRETARY (*softly*): Mr. Justice! You do believe in the government, don't you?

HOLMES: It isn't much, boy . . . a quarter million maybe . . . it would have gone to my wife . . . if she had lived. . . .

SECRETARY: I understand, sir. (HOLMES *eyes the* SECRETARY *with tart affection: he has no intention of baring his heart to even so genial a lad as this one.*)

HOLMES: Oh, you do, do you? . . . well, suppose you read to me now . . . read me about Roland and the Saracens . . . the part where they left him for dead, and fled before the horns of Charlemagne's returning host. . . . (SECRETARY *picks up well-thumbed book from the table behind the sofa, then sits down beside the Judge.*)

SECRETARY (*reading*): "Roland came back to consciousness on feeling a Saracen marauder tugging at his sword Durendal. With a blow of his ivory horn he killed the pagan, then feeling death near, he prepared for it. . . ." (*The Judge begins to drop off to sleep. The head nods, the hands relax.* SECRETARY *throws him a quick look, goes on with reading.*) "His first thought was for Durendal, his sword, which he could not leave to infidels . . . three times he struck with all his force against the rock; each time the sword rebounded without breaking. . . ." (SECRETARY *looks over at* HOLMES *again; the Judge is almost asleep now.*) "The third time—" (*The* SECRETARY *gets up, tiptoes softly to the left, brings a blanket and drapes it carefully about the Judge. Suddenly the door opens and the* HOUSEKEEPER *comes in. She is highly excited and completely unnerved.*)

HOUSEKEEPER: Oh, Mr. Justice—Mr. Justice—you'll have to do something right away—right away— (*The Judge stirs and looks up slowly.*)

SECRETARY: Mary— Whatever's the matter? You know the Judge can't be disturbed now. It's time for his nap—

HOUSEKEEPER: Nap, is it? Well, he better pick another time for it! Do you know who's downstairs at this very minute— (*Then to* HOLMES.) It's President Roosevelt—that's who it is and he's driven over to see you, sir!

HOLMES (*throwing blanket aside*): Teddy Roosevelt in my house? What's he want *now?*

HOUSEKEEPER: Oh, no, sir. It's not Theodore Roosevelt—it's Franklin Roosevelt—and they're taking the elevator down for him now.

HOLMES (*getting up slowly, with a pleased smile*): Well, show him in—show him in!

SECRETARY (*as* HOUSEKEEPER *goes out*): I can't make it out —the President here—what can he possibly want, sir?

HOLMES: I don't know, my boy. I was born a Republican and he was born a Democrat. But he's my Commander-in-chief, by heaven, and we'll receive him accordingly.

SECRETARY: But there's no precedent for a thing like this . . . the White House never does the calling . . . it's the other way around . . . and besides, he's only been in office an hour.

HOLMES: Now, my boy, don't you worry . . . this is the last canter . . . and I'm going to enjoy it. . . . (*Then briskly waving* SECRETARY *to the right.*) Now, let me see—you stand over there—and I'll stand over here— (HOLMES *takes a position at left, then decides to change the order of things.*) No, you'd better go out and meet him at the elevator—hurry. (SECRETARY *dashes out, stops at the doorway.*)

SECRETARY: But, Mr. Justice, what will you say to the President? What *can* you say to him on a day like this?

HOLMES: My boy, when you bring my Commander-in-chief in here, I'll tell him what any good soldier could tell him on a day like this. I'll merely say—"Young fellow, you're in the middle of a war . . . *fight* like hell!" (SECRETARY *exits quickly into hall.* HOLMES, *his figure a little bent and bowed, moves over from left to center. This is the last canter and he looks forward to it with the eagerness of an old soldier. As he reaches center, he turns and looks toward hall—his back now to the audience. From offstage we pick up the voice of the* SECRETARY.)

SECRETARY'S VOICE (*offstage*): Mr. President—Mr. Holmes is waiting. (*Quietly, the figure of the Judge begins to straighten. The heels come together, the shoulders go back, the hands touch the seam of the trousers with careful precision. And, as the curtain comes down slowly, a soldier with a soldier's faith is at attention, ready to salute his commander-in-chief.*)

Production Notes

This anthology is designed for your reading pleasure. In most instances a performance fee is required from any group desiring to produce a play. Usually the organization that handles such performance rights also publishes individual production copies of the plays. Any group interested in additional information concerning performance fees or production copies of the plays in this anthology should apply to the following companies:

Golden Boy	Harold Freedman
	c/o Brandt & Brandt
High Tor	Dramatic Department
	101 Park Avenue
	New York 17, N.Y.
The Magnificent Yankee	Samuel French, Inc.
	25 West 45th Street
	New York 36, N.Y.